THE

# LIVERPOOL
# FOOTBALL

## MISCELLANY

As soon as I started to compile and write this book I knew straight away that I wanted to dedicate it to three very special people.

Firstly, I would like to dedicate my book to the greatest Liverpool fan I have ever known and that man is George Lundy Jnr from the Short Strand in Belfast.

Secondly, I wish to dedicate my book to my publisher, Martin Corteel. Martin, thank you for placing your faith in me in all the books we have worked on together.

Finally, to Andy Philip, many thanks for all your input, for proofreading my work and for just being at the other end of an email when I needed advice.

Yours in Sport,
John White

This edition published in 2006

Copyright © Carlton Books Limited 2006

Carlton Books Limited
20 Mortimer Street
London W1T 3JW

A CIP catalogue record for this book is available from the British Library

ISBN 13: 978-184442-159-6
ISBN 10: 1-84442-159-7

Editor: Martin Corteel
Project art editor: Darren Jordan
Production: Lisa French

Printed in Great Britain

THE

# LIVERPOOL
# FOOTBALL

## MISCELLANY

JOHN WHITE

WITH A FOREWORD BY PHIL THOMPSON

**CARLTON**
BOOKS

## ❖ LIST OF ABBREVIATIONS ❖

| | | |
|---|---|---|
| EC | = | European Cup |
| ECWC | = | European Cup-winners Cup |
| FA | = | The Football Association |
| FC | = | Fairs Cup *also* Football Club |
| FIFA | = | Federation of International Football Federations |
| FWA | = | Football Writers' Association |
| H (h)/A (a)/N (n) | = | Home/Away/Neutral |
| P/W/D/L/F/A | = | Played/Won/Drawn/Lost/(Goals) For/Against |
| PFA | = | Professional Footballers' Association |
| QPR | = | Queens Park Rangers |
| UCL | = | UEFA Champions League |
| UEFA | = | Union of European Football Associations |
| WBA | = | West Bromwich Albion |

## ❖ FOREWORD ❖

Many of the proudest and most memorable moments of my life have been in football grounds around the world. There is something very special about representing a club as famous and globally recognized as Liverpool Football Club. Playing for Liverpool enabled me to travel around the world and meet fans in far-off places whose love the club is as strong as mine.

I was very fortunate to be able to follow Liverpool just as they were rising to the top of the tree in English football in the 1960s and I can remember standing on the Kop watching my heroes. But when, one day after my 17th birthday, I joined the club as a player, I didn't think it could get any better than that. I was wrong because I was lucky enough to make a career as a footballer and, even better, a Liverpool player. I was good enough to represent my country and also to be named captain, but to lead out the club I love in the final of European Cup and, after 120 minutes, to lift the trophy ... it doesn't get any better than that. I have also had the chance, albeit through unfortunate circumstances, to be the club's acting manager for almost half a season, so I have seen this great club from three very different angles: supporter, player and manager.

When John White invited me to write this foreword, I was delighted because Liverpool Football Club has been a part of my life for more years than I can remember. John's book is all about England's most successful club, both at home and abroad. No other British club can match the Reds' 18 League championships, five European Cups, seven League Cups, seven FA Cups and three UEFA Cups. But this book is about more than those glorious days; it is about everything to do with Liverpool FC, the present-day heroes, long-forgotten legends, successes, failures, humorous incidents, moments of tragedy, club records, highs and lows. Turning the pages reminded me of players and incidents that I had almost forgotten.

I wish John every success with his book. It is a superb record of Liverpool Football Club and I warmly recommend it to every Reds fan.

**Phil Thompson**
*May 2006*

## ❖ ACKNOWLEDGEMENTS ❖

First of all, my sincere thanks to Phil Thompson for his kind words in the foreword. Secondly, a very special thanks goes to Andy Philip at www.liverweb.org.uk for kindly allowing me to use material from his excellent website to include in my book and for taking the time to proofread my work and thereby help keep the entries as accurate as they possibly can be. Andy was also a great help compiling the Liverpool Fantasy XIs.

I would also like to thank Chris at http://liverpool.rivals.net for kindly allowing me to use material from his excellent website to include in my book and for taking the time to proofread my work and thereby also help keep the entries as accurate as they possibly can be.

Finally, my thanks must go to my wife, Janice, for all her unwavering support and help throughout the compilation of this book. And to my two sons, Marc and Paul, thanks boys for all your help. I really appreciate it.

## ❖ INTRODUCTION ❖

Welcome to this miscellaneous collection of facts, figures, trivia, quotes and notes, all about Britain's most successful football club, Liverpool FC. The nuggets of information here are in random order because the joy of a miscellany is that every page offers a different surprise.

There are many books that cover the history of Liverpool, some have been written from a statistical standpoint, others are autobiographies, biographies and even hagiographies. This book contains a little bit of everything: league tables from the 18 seasons when Liverpool were crowned champions of England, line-ups from the glory nights in Europe, biographies of superstars who graced the Anfield turf and tantalizing facts about the club, players, staff and ground. Each one has been carefully researched with the aim of giving fans a greater insight into Liverpool Football Club.

Liverpool FC is known throughout the world and its success stands as a benchmark to all clubs who aspire to follow in the footsteps of the trail they have blazed both at home and abroad. With 18 League titles, 15 domestic cup successes and eight more Europe trophies, ignoring victories in the European Super Cup, Charity/Community Shield, no English club can come close to matching Liverpool's record. Almost from the moment Bill Shankly walked into Anfield in 1959, Liverpool has gone onwards and upwards.

In researching Liverpool FC, and its great history, I found thousands of items that could have been included, so I had to be ruthless in weeding out those that didn't quite match what I wanted. Championship teams and tables were a must, as were the line-ups in all the European finals and many of the domestic cups too. Biographies of Anfield legends – on the pitch and in the dugout – as well as tales of other significant Reds had to be here; so did stories on great matches and events, quotes and other insights.

This is not necessarily a book to be read in one sitting; indeed, the format is ideal for dipping in and out of when you feel the need to brush up on or expand your knowledge of the club. I doubt that even the most devoted and dedicated Reds' fan will be able to go through this book and say at the end of it, "I learned nothing I didn't already know about Liverpool." If you get as much fun and pleasure from reading this book as I got from compiling it, then everything I have written about will have been worthwhile.

**John White**
*May 2006*

## ❖ LIVERPOOL ENGLAND XI (PRE-1979) ❖

**1**
Ray
*CLEMENCE*

**2**
Phil
*NEAL*

**4**
Tommy
*SMITH*

**5**
Larry
*LLOYD*

**3**
Alec
*LINDSAY*

**8**
Ray
*KENNEDY*

**6**
Emlyn
*HUGHES*
*(captain)*

**11**
Ian
*CALLAGHAN*

**7**
Kevin
*KEEGAN*

**9**
Roger
*HUNT*

**10**
David
*JOHNSON*

*Substitutes*
Sam *HARDY* • Chris *LAWLER* • Laurie *HUGHES*
Terry *McDERMOTT* • Alan *A'COURT*
*Player-Manager*
Kevin *KEEGAN*

### *Did You Know That?*

After leaving Anfield, Larry Lloyd joined Nottingham Forest, where he won one League Championship, one League Cup and two European Cup winners medals with Brian Clough's side.

## ❖ WHAT THE REDS SAID (1) ❖

"Shankly gave the players and the city their pride and passion back. If you didn't have the pride and the passion, then you didn't play for Shankly and you didn't play for Liverpool."
*Actor and fan **Ricky Tomlinson***

## ❖ REDS MATCH TOFFEES ❖

Before Liverpool won the FA Cup in 2006 after a penalty shoot-out at the Millennium Stadium, the last team to win the trophy after trailing by two goals was Everton in 1966. They trailed Sheffield Wednesday 2–0 before winning 3–2 at Wembley,

## ❖ NEVER TOO YOUNG … NOR TOO OLD ❖

The youngest player to score a first-team goal for Liverpool was Michael Owen, who netted against Wimbledon on 6 May 1997, aged 17 years and 144 days. At the other end of the seniority spectrum, Billy Liddell became the club's oldest goalscorer when he struck against Stoke City on 5 March 1960, aged 38 years and 55 days.

## ❖ THE TROPHY CABINET ❖

**League Division One champions** *(record 18 occasions)*
1901, 1906, 1922, 1923, 1947, 1964, 1966, 1973, 1976, 1977, 1979, 1980, 1982, 1983, 1984, 1986, 1988, 1990

**League Division Two champions** *(4 occasions)*
1894, 1896, 1905, 1962

**FA Cup winners** *(7 occasions)*
1965, 1974, 1986, 1989, 1992, 2001, 2006

**League Cup winners** *(record 7 occasions)*
1981, 1982, 1983, 1984, 1995, 2001, 2003

**FA Charity Shield winners** *(9 occasions)*
1966, 1974, 1976, 1979, 1980, 1982, 1988, 1989, 2001
Joint winners: 1964, 1965, 1977, 1986, 1990

**European Cup/Champions League winners** *(5 occasions)*
1977, 1978, 1981, 1984, 2005

**UEFA Cup winners** *(3 occasions)*
1973, 1976, 2001

**European Super Cup winners** *(3 occasions)*
1977, 2001, 2005

**Screen Sport Super Cup winners** *(1 occasion)*
1986

**Carlsberg Trophy winners** *(3 occasions)*
1998, 1999, 2000

**Manager of the Year Awards** *(11 occasions)*

## ❖ GOING UP, GOING UP, GOING UP (1) ❖

In 1893–94 Liverpool won their first ever League title, the Second Division Championship, just two years after they were formed. And at the end of the season, which was their inaugural campaign in the Football League, they beat Newton Heath (later to become Manchester United) in a promotion/relegation play-off game to clinch promotion to the first division. The pillar of Liverpool's success was their home form – they won all 14 games at Anfield for a maximum 28 points. Their away form was also pretty impressive – Liverpool won eight games and drew six. Thus the Reds were unbeaten all season, scoring 77 goals and conceding just 18. Liverpool's nearest challengers, Small Heath, were eight points behind in second place, and the Reds' two wins over them were significant victories in the race for the title.

### *Football League Division 2*
1893–94

|  | P | W | D | L | F | A | W | D | L | F | A | Pts |
|---|---|---|---|---|---|---|---|---|---|---|---|---|
| 1. Liverpool | 28 | 14 | 0 | 0 | 46 | 6 | 8 | 6 | 0 | 31 | 12 | 50 |
| 2. Small Heath* | 28 | 12 | 0 | 2 | 68 | 19 | 9 | 0 | 5 | 35 | 25 | 42 |
| 3. Notts County | 28 | 12 | 1 | 1 | 55 | 14 | 6 | 2 | 6 | 15 | 17 | 39 |
| 4. Newcastle United | 28 | 12 | 1 | 1 | 44 | 10 | 3 | 5 | 6 | 22 | 29 | 36 |
| 5. Grimsby Town | 28 | 11 | 1 | 2 | 47 | 16 | 4 | 1 | 9 | 24 | 42 | 32 |
| 6. Burton United | 28 | 9 | 1 | 4 | 52 | 26 | 5 | 2 | 7 | 27 | 35 | 31 |
| 7. Burslem Port Vale** | 28 | 10 | 2 | 2 | 43 | 20 | 3 | 2 | 9 | 23 | 44 | 30 |
| 8. Lincoln City | 28 | 5 | 4 | 5 | 31 | 22 | 6 | 2 | 6 | 28 | 36 | 28 |
| 9. Woolwich Arsenal*** | 28 | 9 | 1 | 4 | 33 | 19 | 3 | 3 | 8 | 19 | 36 | 28 |
| 10. Walsall | 28 | 8 | 1 | 5 | 36 | 23 | 2 | 2 | 10 | 15 | 38 | 23 |
| 11. Middlesbro' Ironopolis | 28 | 7 | 4 | 3 | 27 | 20 | 1 | 0 | 13 | 10 | 52 | 20 |
| 12. Crewe Alexandra | 28 | 3 | 7 | 4 | 22 | 22 | 3 | 0 | 11 | 20 | 51 | 19 |
| 13. Ardwick**** | 28 | 6 | 1 | 7 | 32 | 20 | 2 | 1 | 11 | 15 | 51 | 18 |
| 14. Rotherham Town | 28 | 5 | 1 | 8 | 28 | 42 | 1 | 2 | 11 | 16 | 49 | 15 |
| 15. Northwich Victoria | 28 | 3 | 3 | 8 | 17 | 34 | 0 | 0 | 14 | 13 | 64 | 9 |

*\* became Birmingham FC in 1905 and Birmingham City in 1945; \*\* later became Port Vale; \*\*\* became Arsenal in 1914; \*\*\*\* became Manchester City in 1894*

### *TEST MATCH (PROMOTION/RELEGATION PLAY-OFF)*
Liverpool    2–0    Newton Heath

On 28 April 1894, Liverpool beat Newton Heath 2–0 at Anfield to earn the right to play in the First Division in 1894–95.

### ❖ EXPENSIVE COMINGS AND GOINGS ❖

The record amount paid for a player by Liverpool was the £14 million with which they parted for Djibril Cisse when he transferred from Auxerre in July 2004. The record fee going the other way was for Robbie Fowler, for whom Leeds United paid £12.5 million in November 2001.

### ❖ TOP MARKSMEN ❖

The legendary Roger Hunt holds the career record for most League goals for Liverpool with 245, including a record 41 in a season in 1961–62. The club's top marksman overall, however, is Ian Rush, with 346 first-team goals, including record career tallies of 39 goals in the FA Cup and 48 in the League Cup.

### ❖ RED DRAGON ❖

Ian Rush[†] holds the record for gaining the most international caps while a Liverpool player, with 67 for Wales (Kenny Dalglish's 102 Scottish caps were gained with Celtic and Liverpool). Rush is also the club's record international goalscorer, having struck 26 times for his country while at Liverpool.

### ❖ LONG-TIME SERVANT ❖

Liverpool's longest-serving player was goalkeeper Elisha Scott, who was with the club for 21 years and 52 days, from 1913 to 1934.

### ❖ HAT-TRICK SPECIALISTS ❖

Gordon Hodgson holds the club record for the most hat-tricks in a career with 17, while Roger Hunt's tally of five hat-tricks in 1961–62 remains the highest for Liverpool in a season.

### ❖ LIVERPOOL SNUB FA CHARITY SHIELD ❖

Liverpool declined the invitation of the Football Association to participate in the 1973 FA Charity Shield, even though they had just been crowned League champions.

[†] *Ian Rush scored 28 goals for Wales overall in a total of 73 appearances, making him his country's all-time top goalscorer.*

## ❖ JOHN BARNES MBE ❖

John Barnes was born on 7 November 1963 in Kingston, Jamaica. As a footballer, Barnes was simply exceptional. He made his first-team debut for Watford in 1981, scoring 13 league goals in his first season to help the club win promotion to the first division. On 28 May 1983 Barnes made his international debut, aged just 19, coming on as a substitute for his Watford team-mate Luther Blissett against Northern Ireland at Windsor Park in Belfast. The following year Barnes scored his first international goal, and what a goal it was as he wriggled his way through the entire Brazil defence before coolly slotting the ball into the net at the Maracana Stadium in Rio de Janeiro. Barnes travelled with England to the 1986 World Cup Finals in Mexico and helped his country reach the quarter-finals before Maradona and his "Hand of God" goal put them out of the tournament.

When Ian Rush left Liverpool for Juventus in 1987, Kenny Dalglish signed Barnes for the Reds from Watford in a deal worth £900,000. On 15 August 1987 Barnes made his Liverpool debut in a 2–1 (Aldridge, Nicol) away win over Arsenal. His first Liverpool goal came on 12 September that year in a 2–0 home win over Oxford United, John Aldridge netting the other. He was a tremendously gifted left-sided player who possessed agility, speed and suppleness. Barnes claimed that he possessed all three attributes thanks to his Caribbean childhood.

Barnes won the League Championship with Liverpool in his first season at the club, scoring 17 goals, and was crowned both the Professional Football Association's Player of the Year and the Football Writers' Association Player of the Year in 1988. In 1990 he picked up his second FWA award and also helped England reach the semi-finals of the World Cup in Italy. John scored 11 international goals in 79 England appearances, his last cap being won against Colombia in 1996. With Liverpool he won two First Division Championships (1988, 1990), two FA Cups (1989, 1992) and the League Cup (1995). Barnes left Liverpool in 1997 and had spells at Newcastle United and Charlton Athletic as a player before joining Kenny Dalglish's coaching team at Celtic in 1999. Barnes's foray into coaching ended the following February, however, and John now works in the football media.

## ❖ HUNT OFF TO A FLYER ❖

Roger Hunt scored on his England debut in the 3–1 win over Austria at Wembley on 4 April 1962.

## ❖ THE YOUNG AND THE OLD ❖

The youngest player to turn out for Liverpool was Max Thompson, who made his sole appearance against Tottenham Hotspur on 8 May 1974, aged 17 years and 129 days. Liverpool's oldest debutant was Ned Doig, who played against Burton United on 1 September 1904, aged 37 years and 307 days. Doig went on to become the oldest player to appear for the club when he took the field against Newcastle United on 11 April 1908 at the age of 41 years and 165 days.

## ❖ LIVERPOOL TESTIMONIALS ❖

| Date | Player/Manager | Opposition |
|---|---|---|
| 21 April 1960 | Billy Liddell | International XI |
| 30 April 1973 | Ian St John | Chelsea |
| 13 May 1974 | Ron Yeats | Celtic |
| 29 April 1975 | Bill Shankly | Don Revie XI |
| 27 May 1977 | Tommy Smith[†] | Bobby Charlton XI |
| 19 September 1977 | Ian Callaghan | Lancashire XI |
| 27 March 1979 | Emlyn Hughes | B. Moenchengladbach |
| 14 May 1980 | Ray Clemence | Anderlecht |
| 11 May 1981 | Steve Heighway | Everton |
| 12 August 1985 | Phil Neal | Everton |
| 1 March 1988 | Sammy Lee | Osasuna |
| 14 August 1990 | Kenny Dalglish | Real Sociedad |
| 10 October 1992 | Bruce Grobbelaar | Everton |
| 9 August 1993 | Ronnie Whelan | Newcastle United |
| 6 December 1994 | Ian Rush | Celtic |
| 9 August 1996 | Jan Molby | PSV Eindhoven |

## ❖ SCOUSE WIT ❖

At the 1977 European Cup final, fans unfurled a banner that read "Joey Ate The Frogs Legs, Made The Swiss Roll, Now He's Munching Gladbach". Liverpool beat St Etienne (France) in the quarter-finals, FC Zurich (Switzerland) in the semi-finals and Borussia Moenchengladbach in Rome. The banner is now displayed in the club museum at Anfield.

In 2005, during a radio phone-in debating the merits of a new stadium to host Liverpool and Everton home games, an Evertonian said, "I wouldn't share a Twix with a Red, let alone a stadium."

[†]*Tommy Smith's testimonial against a Bobby Charlton XI ended in a 9–9 draw, in which Ray Clemence scored twice for Liverpool.*

## ❖ SOCCER SCHOOL ❖

During the school summer holidays, boys can take part in a series of one- or three-day coaching courses with Liverpool Academy's experts. The Soccer School includes coaching from academy staff in all areas of the game, and students receive a certificate of attendance.

## ❖ THE ACADEMY ❖

In 2000 Liverpool took the decision to fund and build a multimillion-pound football academy in order to continue nurturing and developing their own young talent. Situated at Kirkby under the expert guidance of academy director and Liverpool legend Steve Heighway, the academy is a world-class facility designed to give every young boy on the club's books the best possible chance of emulating past products of the Liverpool youth system, such as Michael Owen, Steven Gerrard, Robbie Fowler, Steve McManaman and Jamie Carragher.

## ❖ KOP THAI ❖

On 10 May 2004 Prime Minister Thaksin Shinawatra of Thailand announced that he had struck a deal to buy a significant stake in Liverpool for £75 million. "Lots of our products need a brand and Liverpool is one that we can use on the world market. It's an established club with a lot of popularity in Asia," said Thaksin. The deal failed to materialize.

## ❖ LIVERPOOL CONFIRM USA INTEREST ❖

On 9 November 2005 Liverpool chief executive Rick Parry confirmed he had visited the United States for a meeting with the Kraft family as it emerged there had been interest in the club from potential purchasers in the Middle East. Parry had been a guest of the tycoon Robert Kraft and the Kraft family, owners of the New England Patriots NFL team. Parry spoke after claims that he had gone to discuss a major investment in Liverpool to salvage the club's stadium plans. Initially the proposed new Stanley Park stadium had been expected to cost £80 million but with the likely cost having risen to £150 million, it was believed the board were unable to finance the plans without external investment. It was suggested that Parry had been in Boston to discuss the possibility of the Kraft family buying the naming rights to the new ground.

## ❖ GOING UP, GOING UP, GOING UP (2) ❖

After one season in the top flight, Liverpool were relegated back to Division Two at the end of the 1894–95 season following their 1–0 defeat to Bury in a promotion/relegation play-off game. However, the Reds made an immediate return to Division One by clinching their second Division Two championship in three years in 1895–96. As had been the case in their 1893–94 campaign, the Reds' home form was the key to their success – they won 14 of their 15 games at Anfield and drew the remaining fixture. Liverpool scored an amazing 65 League goals at Anfield at an average of 4.3 per game. On the last day of the season Liverpool travelled to Manchester City with both teams sitting on 45 points. City needed to win since Liverpool had the superior goal average, but the game ended 1–1 (Allan) and Liverpool went on to clinch promotion to Division One via success in the end-of-season Test Matches.

### Football League Division 2
### 1895–96

|  | P | W | D | L | F | A | W | D | L | F | A | Pts |
|---|---|---|---|---|---|---|---|---|---|---|---|---|
| 1. Liverpool | 30 | 14 | 1 | 0 | 65 | 11 | 8 | 1 | 6 | 41 | 21 | 46 |
| 2. Manchester City | 30 | 12 | 3 | 0 | 37 | 9 | 9 | 1 | 5 | 26 | 29 | 46 |
| 3. Grimsby Town | 30 | 14 | 1 | 0 | 51 | 9 | 6 | 1 | 8 | 31 | 29 | 42 |
| 4. Burton Wanderers | 30 | 12 | 1 | 2 | 43 | 15 | 7 | 3 | 5 | 26 | 25 | 42 |
| 5. Newcastle United | 30 | 14 | 0 | 1 | 57 | 14 | 2 | 2 | 11 | 16 | 36 | 34 |
| 6. Newton Heath | 30 | 12 | 2 | 1 | 48 | 15 | 3 | 1 | 11 | 18 | 42 | 33 |
| 7. Woolwich Arsenal* | 30 | 11 | 1 | 3 | 43 | 11 | 3 | 3 | 9 | 16 | 31 | 32 |
| 8. Leicester City | 30 | 10 | 0 | 5 | 40 | 16 | 4 | 4 | 7 | 17 | 28 | 32 |
| 9. Darwen | 30 | 9 | 4 | 2 | 55 | 22 | 3 | 2 | 10 | 17 | 45 | 30 |
| 10. Notts County | 30 | 8 | 1 | 6 | 41 | 22 | 4 | 1 | 10 | 16 | 32 | 26 |
| 11. Burton United | 30 | 7 | 2 | 6 | 24 | 26 | 3 | 2 | 10 | 15 | 43 | 24 |
| 12. Loughborough | 30 | 7 | 3 | 5 | 32 | 25 | 2 | 2 | 11 | 8 | 42 | 23 |
| 13. Lincoln City | 30 | 7 | 1 | 7 | 36 | 24 | 2 | 3 | 10 | 17 | 51 | 22 |
| 14. Burslem Port Vale | 30 | 6 | 4 | 5 | 25 | 24 | 1 | 0 | 14 | 18 | 54 | 18 |
| 15. Rotherham Town | 30 | 7 | 2 | 6 | 27 | 26 | 0 | 1 | 14 | 7 | 71 | 17 |
| 16. Crewe Alexandra | 30 | 5 | 2 | 8 | 22 | 28 | 0 | 1 | 14 | 8 | 67 | 13 |

### TEST MATCHES (PROMOTION/RELEGATION PLAY-OFFS)

| | | |
|---|---|---|
| Liverpool | 4–0 | Small Heath |
| Small Heath | 0–0 | Liverpool |
| Liverpool | 2–0 | West Bromwich Albion |
| West Bromwich Albion | 2–0 | Liverpool |

## ❖ WE ARE THE CHAMPIONS (1) ❖

Liverpool won the first of their 18 First Division Championships in 1900–01. Sunderland pressed Liverpool hard all season and beat the Reds 2–1 (Wilson) at Anfield on 29 September 1900 in the fifth game of the League campaign. On 16 February 1901 Liverpool lost 1–0 away to Bolton Wanderers in a game that was originally scheduled for 2 February 1901, but was rearranged following the death of Queen Victoria on 22 January. In their next game Liverpool faced Sunderland at Roker Park in a game that was to mark the turning point of the season. Liverpool won 1–0 (Cox) on 23 February, then went on to win eight and draw three of their remaining eleven League games to clinch their maiden First Division Championship by two points from the Rokerites.

### *Football League Division 1*
### 1900–01

| | P | W | D | L | F | A | W | D | L | F | A | Pts |
|---|---|---|---|---|---|---|---|---|---|---|---|---|
| 1. **Liverpool** | 34 | 12 | 2 | 3 | 36 | 13 | 7 | 5 | 5 | 23 | 22 | 45 |
| 2. Sunderland | 34 | 12 | 3 | 2 | 43 | 11 | 3 | 10 | 4 | 14 | 15 | 43 |
| 3. Notts County | 34 | 13 | 2 | 2 | 39 | 18 | 5 | 2 | 10 | 15 | 28 | 40 |
| 4. Nottingham Forest | 34 | 10 | 4 | 3 | 32 | 14 | 6 | 3 | 8 | 21 | 22 | 39 |
| 5. Bury | 34 | 11 | 3 | 3 | 31 | 10 | 5 | 4 | 8 | 22 | 27 | 39 |
| 6. Newcastle United | 34 | 10 | 5 | 2 | 27 | 13 | 4 | 5 | 8 | 15 | 24 | 38 |
| 7. Everton | 34 | 10 | 4 | 3 | 37 | 17 | 6 | 1 | 10 | 18 | 25 | 37 |
| 8. Sheffield Wednesday | 34 | 13 | 2 | 2 | 38 | 16 | 0 | 8 | 9 | 14 | 26 | 36 |
| 9. Blackburn Rovers | 34 | 9 | 4 | 4 | 24 | 18 | 3 | 5 | 9 | 15 | 29 | 33 |
| 10. Bolton Wanderers | 34 | 10 | 5 | 2 | 21 | 12 | 3 | 2 | 12 | 18 | 43 | 33 |
| 11. Manchester City | 34 | 12 | 3 | 2 | 32 | 16 | 1 | 3 | 13 | 16 | 42 | 32 |
| 12. Derby County | 34 | 10 | 4 | 3 | 43 | 18 | 2 | 3 | 12 | 12 | 24 | 31 |
| 13. Wolverhampton W. | 34 | 6 | 10 | 1 | 21 | 15 | 3 | 3 | 11 | 18 | 40 | 31 |
| 14. Sheffield United | 34 | 8 | 4 | 5 | 22 | 23 | 4 | 3 | 10 | 13 | 29 | 31 |
| 15. Aston Villa | 34 | 8 | 5 | 4 | 32 | 18 | 2 | 5 | 10 | 13 | 33 | 30 |
| 16. Stoke City | 34 | 8 | 3 | 6 | 23 | 15 | 3 | 2 | 12 | 23 | 42 | 27 |
| 17. Preston North End | 34 | 6 | 4 | 7 | 29 | 30 | 3 | 3 | 11 | 20 | 45 | 25 |
| 18. West Bromwich Albion | 34 | 4 | 4 | 9 | 21 | 27 | 3 | 4 | 10 | 14 | 35 | 22 |

## ❖ WORLD CHAMPIONS ❖

England's 1966 World Cup winning squad included three Liverpool players:

Gerry Byrne ❖ Ian Callaghan ❖ Roger Hunt

## ❖ WHAT THE REDS SAID (2) ❖

"There are two great teams in Liverpool: Liverpool and Liverpool Reserves."
**Bill Shankly**

## ❖ THE CLUB BADGE ❖

The club badge is dominated by the Liver Bird, an imaginary cross between a cormorant and an eagle. When King John granted Liverpool its city status, an impression of the Liver Bird was incorporated into the wax that sealed the city's charter. Situated above the Liver Bird are the words "You'll Never Walk Alone", the title of the famous Liverpool anthem, contained within the iron curlicues of the Shankly Gates. At the foot of the crest "EST. 1892" signifies the year of the club's formation. Finally, the flame was incorporated following the Hillsborough Disaster in 1989 in lasting memory of the 96 Liverpool supporters who died in the tragedy.

## ❖ YOUNGEST ENGLAND SCORER ❖

On 27 May 1998 Michael Owen became the then youngest player to score an international goal for England when he found the net in the 1–0 win over Morocco in Casablanca. He was 18 years, 147 days old. He held the record until Everton's Wayne Rooney (17 years, 317 days) scored against Macedonia in Skopje on 6 September 2003.

## ❖ LIVERPOOL'S TWELFTH MAN ❖

The following table lists the first ten own goals scored for Liverpool by an opposing player in an FA Premier League game:

| Date | Player (Team) | Venue | Score |
|------|---------------|-------|-------|
| 16.10.93 | Andy Barlow (Oldham Ath) | Anfield | 2–1 (w) |
| 6.11.93 | Alvin Martin (West Ham Utd) | Anfield | 2–0 (w) |
| 28.12.93 | John Scales (Wimbledon) | Anfield | 1–1 (d) |
| 5.2.94 | Ian Culverhouse (Norwich City) | Carrow Rd | 2–2 (d) |
| 19.3.94 | Craig Burley (Chelsea) | Anfield | 2–1 (w) |
| 1.10.94 | Des Walker (Sheffield Weds) | Anfield | 4–1 (w) |
| 28.12.94 | Terry Phelan (Man City) | Anfield | 2–0 (w) |
| 14.3.95 | David Burrows (Coventry City) | Anfield | 2–3 (l) |
| 19.3.95 | Steve Bruce (Man Utd) | Anfield | 2–0 (w) |
| 1.1.96 | Colin Cooper (Notts Forest) | Anfield | 4–2 (w) |

## ❖ BILLY LIDDELL ❖

William "Billy" Liddell was born on 10 January 1922 in Townhill, Dunfermline, Scotland. It was while he was with the Lochgelly Violet club, aged 16 and having turned down a chance to join Hamilton Academicals, that Liddell was persuaded by Liverpool manager George Kay to move south of the border and sign for the Reds. Kay paid Lochgelly Violet £200 for Liddell, who signed for Liverpool as a professional in 1939. However, the start of his career for the Reds was delayed by World War II, during which Liddell served with the RAF in both Britain and Canada. On 5 January 1946, however, the day duly arrived and Liddell made his first-team debut against Chester in the third round of the FA Cup. The game ended 2–2 with Liddell netting a debut goal.

Liddell appeared 34 times for the Liverpool team that lifted the First Division Championship in 1946–47. That season he played alongside future Liverpool manager Bob Paisley, who once said of Liddell: "Billy was so strong, he was unbelievable. From beginning to end he would battle, challenge and show tenacity." It was this fighting spirit that endeared the little Scot to the hearts of the Liverpool fans. However, despite his superhuman performances for the Reds on the pitch, Liverpool inexplicably went downhill after their 1946–47 Championship success.

That First Division Championship winners' medal plus the FA Cup runners-up medal he picked up after the Reds' 1950 FA Cup final defeat to Arsenal seem scant reward for a career which spanned more than 20 years. His career took in over 40 consecutive FA Cup ties and a total of 534 appearances for the Reds in which he scored 228 goals, including one after only 18 seconds in a 3–1 away win over Bristol City at Ashton Gate on 20 September 1958. Liddell topped the Liverpool goalscoring charts for eight seasons. Billy also played 26 additional wartime games for the Reds, finding the back of the net a further 18 times.

Billy Liddell won 28 international caps for Scotland and also made eight "unofficial" international appearances for Scotland during the war. He and Stanley Matthews were the only players selected for the Great Britain representative side in both 1947 and 1955. Liddell's testimonial attracted 38,750 fans, which speaks volumes for the affection in which the Liverpool Scot was held. In August 1960, just a few months before his 40th birthday, Billy Liddell made his final appearance for Liverpool. Much of his career was played in the second division and it was somewhat ironic that the year after he retired Liverpool won the first division title (1961–62). Billy Liddell, nicknamed "The Flying Scot", had it all – the strength of an ox and the speed of a gazelle.

## ❖ GOALKEEPING CAPTAINS ❖

Ray Clemence is one of only four goalkeepers to have captained England at full international level since 1945, having skippered the team against Brazil at Wembley on 12 May 1981 (0–1). The others were Frank Swift, Peter Shilton and David Seaman.

## ❖ OWEN'S THREE ❖

Michael Owen was the last Liverpool player to record a hat-trick for England. He scored three times in England's 5–1 win over Germany in Munich on 1 September 2001. He scored his second hat-trick for England in their 3–2 win over Colombia in New Jersey, USA, on 31 May 2005, while at Real Madrid.

## ❖ TRIBUTE TO A LEGEND ❖

On 4 December 1997 Tom Murphy's bronze statue of Bill Shankly was unveiled at the club's new visitor centre in front of the Kop at Anfield. Standing over eight feet high, Murphy's creation shows Shankly in a familiar pose[†], accepting the plaudits of the Anfield crowd and wearing a fan's scarf around his neck. The statue was commissioned and financed by the club sponsors, Carlsberg, and unveiled by Ron Yeats in the presence of Bill's wife, Nessie. Past and present Liverpool players attended the ceremony, including Tommy Lawrence, Chris Lawler, Gerry Byrne, Willie Stevenson, Ian Callaghan, Roger Hunt, Ian St John and Peter Thompson, as well as Roy Evans, the club manager at the time.

## ❖ MELWOOD ❖

Melwood has been Liverpool's training ground since the club purchased the land in 1950 from Saint Francis Xavier College and is the place where all the club's greatest players learned their trade. Over recent years the complex in West Derby has undergone a multimillion-pound renovation. Former manager Gerard Houllier was the mastermind behind the most recent refurbishment.

---

[†]*The pose, which was specifically selected by Murphy, is from the day in May 1973 when Shankly and his players paraded the First Division Championship trophy in front of the Kop. A young fan threw his scarf onto the pitch in front of Shankly and a policeman kicked it away. Shanks looked at the constable and said, "It's only a scarf to you, but it's the boy's life." Shankly then picked the scarf up and tied it around his neck.*

## ❖ THE KOP'S LAST STAND ❖

"The Kop's Last Stand" was the name given to Liverpool's match programme for the visit of Norwich City to Anfield on 30 April 1994. It marked the last ever game in front of a standing Kop, and before the match a tearful Gerry Marsden performed the Liverpool anthem "You'll Never Walk Alone". However, many Liverpool fans among the crowd of 44,339 will want to forget the game itself, since Norwich City spoiled the party, winning 1–0, thanks to a goal from Jeremy Goss – in front of the Kop!

## ❖ NORWEGIANS PUT TO THE SWORD ❖

On 17 September 1974 Stromsgodset visited Anfield in the first round of the European Cup Winners' Cup. The Reds crushed the Norwegian amateur side 11–0, with everybody appearing on the scoresheet at least once bar Brian Hall and Ray Clemence in goal. It remains Liverpool's record victory. Stromsgodset went down just 1–0 in the second leg.

## ❖ STANDING ROOM ONLY ❖

The record attendance at Anfield is 61,905, set against Wolverhampton Wanderers in the fourth round of the FA Cup on 2 February 1952. Liverpool won the match 2–1 with goals from Cyril Done and Bob Paisley. The highest ever League attendance is 58,757, set on 27 December 1949, when the Reds drew 2–2 with Chelsea through two goals from Willie Fagan.

## ❖ BITTERSWEET GOODBYE ❖

Kevin Keegan's last appearance for Liverpool on British soil was the 2–1 (Case) FA Cup final defeat to Manchester United at Wembley on 21 May 1977. Nevertheless, four days later there was a happier ending to Keegan's final match for the club. Liverpool won the European Cup final in Rome 3–1 (McDermott, Smith, Neal) to claim their first European Cup victory.

## ❖ LIVERPOOL HELP OUT FAMILIES ❖

On 1 February 1983 Liverpool sent a team up to Blackpool to help raise funds for the families who lost loved ones in the Blackpool Sea Tragedy. The Reds won the game 6–2.

## ❖ GOING UP, GOING UP, GOING UP (3) ❖

In 1904–05, Liverpool won their third Division Two Championship in 11 years, an indication of the yo-yo period in between. Bolton Wanderers proved to be the Reds' biggest adversaries during the campaign, closely followed by Manchester United, who were known as Newton Heath up until 1902. Indeed, Liverpool only took a single point from the four available against Bolton while they managed two against United – a 4–0 (Cox, Raybould 3) win at Anfield in the penultimate game of the season. Liverpool won their last League game 3–0 (Parkinson, Robinson, Cox) against Burnley to clinch the Championship at Anfield by two points from Bolton Wanderers and five clear of United. From their 17 home League games, Liverpool notched up 14 wins and three draws, scoring 60 goals and conceding only 12.

### *Football League Division 2*
#### 1904–05

| | | P | W | D | L | F | A | W | D | L | F | A | Pts |
|---|---|---|---|---|---|---|---|---|---|---|---|---|---|
| 1. | Liverpool | 34 | 14 | 3 | 0 | 60 | 12 | 13 | 1 | 3 | 33 | 13 | 58 |
| 2. | Bolton Wanderers | 34 | 15 | 0 | 2 | 53 | 16 | 12 | 2 | 3 | 34 | 16 | 56 |
| 3. | Manchester United | 34 | 16 | 0 | 1 | 60 | 10 | 8 | 5 | 4 | 21 | 20 | 53 |
| 4. | Bristol City | 34 | 12 | 3 | 2 | 40 | 12 | 7 | 1 | 9 | 26 | 33 | 42 |
| 5. | Chesterfield | 34 | 9 | 6 | 2 | 26 | 11 | 5 | 5 | 7 | 18 | 24 | 39 |
| 6. | Gainsborough Trinity | 34 | 11 | 4 | 2 | 32 | 15 | 3 | 4 | 10 | 29 | 43 | 36 |
| 7. | Barnsley | 34 | 11 | 4 | 2 | 29 | 13 | 3 | 1 | 13 | 9 | 43 | 33 |
| 8. | Bradford City | 34 | 8 | 5 | 4 | 31 | 20 | 4 | 3 | 10 | 14 | 29 | 32 |
| 9. | Lincoln City | 34 | 9 | 4 | 4 | 31 | 16 | 3 | 3 | 11 | 11 | 25 | 31 |
| 10. | West Bromwich Albion | 34 | 8 | 2 | 7 | 29 | 20 | 5 | 2 | 10 | 28 | 28 | 30 |
| 11. | Burnley | 34 | 10 | 1 | 6 | 31 | 21 | 2 | 5 | 10 | 12 | 31 | 30 |
| 12. | Glossop North End | 34 | 7 | 5 | 5 | 23 | 14 | 3 | 5 | 9 | 14 | 32 | 30 |
| 13. | Grimsby Town | 34 | 9 | 3 | 5 | 22 | 14 | 2 | 5 | 10 | 11 | 32 | 30 |
| 14. | Leicester Fosse* | 34 | 8 | 3 | 6 | 30 | 25 | 3 | 4 | 10 | 10 | 30 | 29 |
| 15. | Blackpool | 34 | 8 | 5 | 4 | 26 | 15 | 1 | 5 | 11 | 10 | 33 | 28 |
| 16. | Burslem Port Vale | 34 | 7 | 4 | 6 | 28 | 25 | 3 | 3 | 11 | 19 | 47 | 27 |
| 17. | Burton United | 34 | 7 | 2 | 8 | 20 | 29 | 1 | 2 | 14 | 10 | 55 | 20 |
| 18. | Doncaster Rovers | 34 | 3 | 2 | 12 | 12 | 32 | 0 | 0 | 17 | 11 | 49 | 8 |

*\* Leicester Fosse ceased to exist in 1919 and Leicester City took over the club's fixtures*

## ❖ KING KENNY OF SCOTLAND ❖

Kenny Dalglish is joint top goalscorer for Scotland with 30 goals. He shares top spot with Denis Law.

# ❖ LIVERPOOL ENGLAND XI (1980–2006) ❖

**1**
David
*JAMES*

**2** | **6** | **5** | **3**
Rob | Phil | Mark | Alan
*JONES* | *THOMPSON* | *WRIGHT* | *KENNEDY*

**7** | **4** | **8**
Peter | Steven | Steve
*BEARDSLEY* | *GERRARD* | *McMANAMAN*

**9** | **10** | **11**
Robbie | Michael | John
*FOWLER* | *OWEN* | *BARNES*
| *(captain)* |

*Substitutes*
Chris *KIRKLAND* • Neil *RUDDOCK* • Danny *MURPHY*
Sammy *LEE* • Emile *HESKEY*
*Player-Manager*
Mark *WRIGHT*

***Did You Know That?***
The Reds paid Coventry City £6 million for Chris Kirkland in August 2001, and although he played for the England Under-21 team, he has yet to make his full international debut.

## ❖ SPANISH TV STAR ❖

Former Liverpool striker Michael Robinson[†] is one of Spain's most famous television stars. He writes, directs and presents *El Dia Despues* (*The Day After*), a programme about Spanish football.

## ❖ CAPTAINS OF TWO COLOURS ❖

Two players have captained Liverpool and Everton: Steve McMahon and Andrew Hannah.

---

*'Robinson also did the Spanish commentary at Anfield for the Reds' 1–0 (Garcia) win over Chelsea in the 2004–05 UEFA Champions League semi-final.*

## ❖ HUNT'S BIG APPLE SUCCESS ❖

Roger Hunt was the first Liverpool player to score a hat-trick for England. He netted four times in England's 10–0 win over the USA in New York on 27 May 1964.

## ❖ HALL OF FAME ❖

In 2002 Liverpool introduced its Hall of Fame, which was peopled by means of fans and ex-players making nominations to a panel of judges. The panel consisted of Ian Callaghan, Alan Hansen, Phil Thompson, Brian Hall and Rick Parry. The club wanted the panel to elect two players from each decade of the Liverpool's existence. Here are the players who have been inducted to date:

| Decade | Players |
|---|---|
| 1892–1900 | Harry Bradshaw, Matt McQueen |
| 1900–1910 | Alex Raisbeck, Jack Cox |
| 1910–1920 | Ephraim Longworth, Arthur Goddard |
| 1920–1930 | Elisha Scott, Donald McKinlay |
| 1930–1940 | Gordon Hodgson, Jimmy McDougall |
| 1940–1950 | Albert Stubbins, Jack Balmer |
| 1950–1960 | Billy Liddell, Alan A'Court |
| 1960–1970 | Ron Yeats, Roger Hunt |
| 1970–1980 | Ray Clemence, Ian Callaghan |
| 1980–1990 | Kenny Dalglish, Alan Hansen |
| 1990–2000 | John Barnes, Ian Rush |

## ❖ PLAYERS OF THE 20TH CENTURY ❖

Kevin Keegan was one of four England players who were named in the International Federation of Football History and Statistics Players of the 20th century list. The other three were Bobby Charlton, Stanley Matthews and Bobby Moore.

## ❖ A VERY RARE MATCH PROGRAMME ❖

Liverpool were due to face Newcastle United at Anfield on 31 August 1997, but the game was called off when the news broke that Princess Diana had been killed in a car crash in Paris. Although a match programme was produced for the game, it was never circulated and all except approximately ten of the programmes were destroyed by the printers.

## ❖ WE ARE THE CHAMPIONS (2) ❖

Following their Division Two success in 1904–05, Liverpool were crowned Division One champions in 1905–06 for the second time in the club's history. Preston North End pushed the Reds hard all season, but a 2–1 (Chorlton, Hewitt) win over their nearest rivals at Deepdale on 24 March 1906 edged the Reds' noses in front and they held on to win three, draw two and lose only one of their remaining six League games to clinch the Division One Championship title by four points. Liverpool's away form was erratic during the campaign – they won nine, drew two and lost eight of their games on the road, including a 1–3 (Robinson) reversal on the opening day of the season to Woolwich Arsenal but also a 5–1 (Hewitt 3, Carlin 2) win over Middlesbrough.

### Football League Division 1
#### 1905–06

|  | P | W | D | L | F | A | W | D | L | F | A | Pts |
|---|---|---|---|---|---|---|---|---|---|---|---|---|
| 1. Liverpool | 38 | 14 | 3 | 2 | 49 | 15 | 9 | 2 | 8 | 30 | 31 | 51 |
| 2. Preston North End | 38 | 12 | 5 | 2 | 36 | 15 | 5 | 8 | 6 | 18 | 24 | 47 |
| 3. Sheffield Wednesday | 38 | 12 | 5 | 2 | 40 | 20 | 6 | 3 | 10 | 23 | 32 | 44 |
| 4. Newcastle United | 38 | 12 | 4 | 3 | 49 | 23 | 6 | 3 | 10 | 25 | 25 | 43 |
| 5. Manchester City | 38 | 11 | 2 | 6 | 46 | 23 | 8 | 3 | 8 | 27 | 31 | 43 |
| 6. Bolton Wanderers | 38 | 13 | 1 | 5 | 51 | 22 | 4 | 6 | 9 | 30 | 45 | 41 |
| 7. Birmingham | 38 | 14 | 2 | 3 | 49 | 20 | 3 | 5 | 11 | 16 | 39 | 41 |
| 8. Aston Villa | 38 | 13 | 2 | 4 | 51 | 19 | 4 | 4 | 11 | 21 | 37 | 40 |
| 9. Blackburn Rovers | 38 | 10 | 5 | 4 | 34 | 18 | 6 | 3 | 10 | 20 | 34 | 40 |
| 10. Stoke City | 38 | 12 | 5 | 2 | 41 | 15 | 4 | 2 | 13 | 13 | 40 | 39 |
| 11. Everton | 38 | 12 | 1 | 6 | 44 | 30 | 3 | 6 | 10 | 26 | 36 | 37 |
| 12. Woolwich Arsenal | 38 | 12 | 4 | 3 | 43 | 21 | 3 | 3 | 13 | 19 | 43 | 37 |
| 13. Sheffield United | 38 | 10 | 4 | 5 | 33 | 23 | 5 | 2 | 12 | 24 | 39 | 36 |
| 14. Sunderland | 38 | 13 | 2 | 4 | 40 | 21 | 2 | 3 | 14 | 21 | 49 | 35 |
| 15. Derby County | 38 | 10 | 5 | 4 | 27 | 16 | 4 | 2 | 13 | 12 | 42 | 35 |
| 16. Notts County | 38 | 8 | 9 | 2 | 34 | 21 | 3 | 3 | 13 | 21 | 50 | 34 |
| 17. Bury | 38 | 8 | 5 | 6 | 30 | 26 | 3 | 5 | 11 | 27 | 48 | 32 |
| 18. Middlesbrough | 38 | 10 | 4 | 5 | 41 | 23 | 0 | 7 | 12 | 15 | 48 | 31 |
| 19. Nottingham Forest | 38 | 11 | 2 | 6 | 40 | 27 | 2 | 3 | 14 | 18 | 52 | 31 |
| 20. Wolverhampton W. | 38 | 7 | 5 | 7 | 38 | 28 | 1 | 2 | 16 | 20 | 71 | 23 |

## ❖ FA CUP DEBUT ❖

Liverpool made their debut in the FA Cup on 15 October 1892, beating Nantwich 4–0 away with goals from Miller (3) and Wylie.

## ❖ STEVIE G ❖

Steven Gerrard, a product of Liverpool's Youth Academy which he joined in 1989, made his Liverpool debut against Blackburn Rovers in November 1998. In 2001 he was named the PFA Young Player of the Year, during which year he started in all three of Liverpool's finals, scoring the second goal against Alaves in the UEFA Cup final. An established England international, he was one of three Liverpool players who scored against Germany in Munich in England's 5–1 win in September 2001, his first goal for his country. In 2003, Gerrard was appointed Liverpool captain, and he was an inspirational leader in the Reds' 2005 UEFA Champions League-winning campaign, scoring vital goals at every stage, including the first in the amazing fightback against AC Milan in Istanbul. Gerrard became the second-youngest skipper – after Marseille's Didier Deschamps in 1993 – to lift the Champions League. In 2005–06, he helped Liverpool win the FA Cup, scoring twice in the final against West Ham United. And, to cap another outstanding season, he was named PFA Player of the Year.

## ❖ IN THE BEGINNING ❖

Before the establishment of Liverpool Football Club, Anfield was home to Merseyside rivals Everton. Indeed, Anfield was the Everton headquarters when they won the 1891 First Division Championship. However, after a rent dispute in 1892, the Toffees moved to Goodison Park.

## ❖ MOST CAPPED UNDER-21 ❖

Up to the end of the 2004–05 season, Jamie Carragher had made the highest number of appearances for the England Under-21 side, with 27 to his name.

## ❖ COUNTRY OPPONENTS ❖

Liverpool have played several friendlies against national sides:

| Date | Opposition | Venue | Score |
|---|---|---|---|
| 2 October 1978 | Saudi Arabia | Jeddah | 1–1 |
| 28 May 1979 | Israel | Tel Aviv | 3–3 |
| 10 May 1983 | England XI | Anfield | 0–2 |
| 16 May 1983 | Israel | Tel Aviv | 3–4 |
| 10 June 1983 | Thailand | Bangkok | 3–0 |

## ❖ RAFAEL BENITEZ ❖

Rafael Benitez was a product of Real Madrid's famous Cantera, joining the club in 1974. He made gradual progress through Real Madrid's youth team ranks, playing for Castilla CF but never making it into the Real first team. In 1981 he moved to Tercera Division side AD Parla, in his first season helping them gain promotion to Segunda B. He continued to play for AD Parla up to 1985 before joining Linares CF in Segunda B. However, during the 1985–86 season a serious knee injury ended Rafael's playing career. In 1986 he joined the coaching staff at Estadio Santiago Bernabeu, gaining valuable experience in charge of Castilla B (1986–89), Real Madrid Youth B (1989–91) and Real Madrid Under-19s (1991–93), winning six trophies as a junior coach. In 1989, while he was on the coaching staff of Real Madrid, Benitez attained his coaching certificate, and the following summer he taught at a football camp at UC Davis, California.

From 1993 to 1995 Benitez coached Real Madrid B in Segunda A and for a short while was an assistant to Vicente Del Bosque. In 1995–96, Benitez was appointed manager of Real Valladolid but was sacked after the team won just two of the 23 games for which he was in charge. Then during the 1996–97 season Rafa took charge at CA Osasuna (Segunda A) but was sacked for the second time in his career after one win in nine games. In 1997 he joined CF Extremadura and led the Segunda A side to promotion. They finished second in the table behind CD Alaves after winning 23 of 42 games played in 1997–98. Regrettably CF Extremadura only survived one season in La Liga and at the end of the 1998–99 season were relegated after finishing in seventeenth position and losing a play-off to Villareal CF.

Benitez quit his job at CF Extremadura and took a year out coaching at various clubs across Europe, including Arsenal and Manchester United. He also worked as a commentator/analyst for El Mundo, Marca, Eurosport and local Madrid TV. In 2000 Benitez was offered and accepted the position of manager at CD Tenerife and guided the Segunda A side to a third-place finish in the table behind Sevilla FC and Real Betis and into La Liga. Benitez then replaced Hector Cuper at Valencia CF and won two La Liga titles with "Los Ches" (2002 and 2004) as well as the UEFA Cup (2004) before becoming the manager of Liverpool during the summer of 2004.

In 2005 he guided Liverpool to their fifth European Cup/ Champions League and to the European Super Cup. Despite interest from Real Madrid during the 2005–06 season, Benitez committed his future to Anfield, guiding the club to a third-place finish in Premier League and victory in the FA Cup.

## ❖ WHAT THE REDS SAID (3) ❖

"For those of you watching in black and white, Liverpool are the team with the ball."
*Liverpool fans tease Everton before the 1984 Milk Cup final*

## ❖ ENGLAND CAPTAINS ❖

The following Liverpool players have all captained England:

Ephraim Longworth ❖ Thomas Lucas ❖ Emlyn Hughes
Kevin Keegan ❖ Phil Thompson ❖ Ray Clemence ❖ Phil Neal
Peter Beardsley ❖ Paul Ince ❖ Michael Owen ❖ Steven Gerrard

## ❖ LIVERPOOL'S 100 CLUB ❖

The following players have all scored 100 or more goals for Liverpool:

| | | | |
|---|---|---|---|
| Ian Rush | 346 | Jack Parkinson | 128 |
| Roger Hunt | 286 | Samuel Raybould | 128 |
| Gordon Hodgson | 240 | Dick Forshaw | 124 |
| Billy Liddell | 229 | Ian St John | 118 |
| Robbie Fowler | 173 | Jack Balmer | 111 |
| Kenny Dalglish | 172 | John Barnes | 108 |
| Michael Owen | 158 | Kevin Keegan | 100 |
| Harry Chambers | 151 | *Up to the end of the 2005–06 season.* | |

## ❖ THREE GOALS DISALLOWED ❖

In the World Club Championship final, played at the International Stadium, Yokohama, Japan, on 18 December 2005, Liverpool lost 1–0 to the Copa Libertadores champions, Sao Paulo from Brazil. Amazingly Liverpool had three goals disallowed in the game.

## ❖ A POOR SUBSTITUTE ❖

When Liverpool were crowned First Division champions in 1964, they were presented with a papier mâché trophy because Everton, the reigning champions, refused to hand the real trophy over to their city neighbours. The Reds clinched the title at Anfield on 18 April 1964, with three games still to play. Liverpool's visitors that day were Arsenal, who were thumped 5–0 (St John, Thompson (2) and Hunt).

## ❖ HILLSBOROUGH MEMORIAL ❖

The Hillsborough Memorial is situated alongside Anfield's Shankly Gates and is a lasting tribute to the 96 fans who tragically lost their lives at the FA Cup semi-final at Sheffield Wednesday's Hillsborough Stadium on 15 April 1989. At the heart of the memorial burns the eternal flame, signifying that they will never be forgotten. Each year at 3.06 p.m. on 15 April, thousands of Liverpool fans all over the world stop what they are doing and remember the supporters who died in the disaster. Sheffield Wednesday Football Club erected a memorial at Hillsborough in 1999.

## ❖ THREE-DECADE EMLYN ❖

Emlyn Hughes's[†] international career spanned the 1960s, 1970s and 1980s, and he was the only player to be capped at full international level by England in all three decades:

| | | |
|---|---|---|
| 5 November 1969 | v Holland | England won 1–0 |
| 25 February 1970 | v Belgium | England won 3–1 |
| 26 March 1980 | v Spain | England won 2–0 |

## ❖ REDS PAY TRIBUTE TO BIG JOCK ❖

On 14 August 1978 Liverpool visited Glasgow Celtic for Jock Stein's testimonial match. Liverpool won 3–2 in front of a bumper crowd of 62,000. Kenny Dalglish, a former hero of Parkhead's famous "Jungle", scored twice against his old club; Alan Kennedy got Liverpool's other goal. Parkhead is also known as Celtic Park.

## ❖ KEEGAN MANAGES ENGLAND ❖

Kevin Keegan is the only Liverpool player who has gone on to manage England. He was appointed England manager in 1999 and took charge of his first game on 27 March, a 3–1 win over Poland at Wembley. On 7 October 2000, England lost a World Cup qualifying game 1–0 to Germany at Wembley. It was the last ever international beneath the famous Twin Towers, and Keegan resigned shortly after the game ended. England played 17 games under Keegan, winning seven, drawing seven and losing three, with 26 goals for and 15 against.

[†]*Emlyn Hughes was transferred from Liverpool to Wolverhampton Wanderers in 1979.*

## ❖ WE ARE THE CHAMPIONS (3) ❖

Thirty years after Liverpool were formed in 1892, they won their third Division One Championship title in 1921–22, their first title in a barren 16-year period. Tottenham Hotspur were the Reds' closest challengers in the race for the title, and Liverpool's early season success over their London rivals, a 1–0 (Beadles) away win on 22 October 1921 and a 1–1 (Lewis) draw at Anfield a week later, proved decisive come the end of the campaign. In the end Liverpool won the title by six points, having won 22, drawn 13 and lost 7 of their 42 League games. Liverpool had finished the previous two seasons' campaigns in fourth position in Division One.

### *Football League Division 1*
### 1921–22

| | P | W | D | L | F | A | W | D | L | F | A | Pts |
|---|---|---|---|---|---|---|---|---|---|---|---|---|
| 1. Liverpool | 42 | 15 | 4 | 2 | 43 | 15 | 7 | 9 | 5 | 20 | 21 | 57 |
| 2. Tottenham Hotspur | 42 | 15 | 3 | 3 | 43 | 17 | 6 | 6 | 9 | 22 | 22 | 51 |
| 3. Burnley | 42 | 16 | 3 | 2 | 49 | 18 | 6 | 2 | 13 | 23 | 36 | 49 |
| 4. Cardiff City | 42 | 13 | 2 | 6 | 40 | 26 | 6 | 8 | 7 | 21 | 27 | 48 |
| 5. Aston Villa | 42 | 16 | 3 | 2 | 50 | 19 | 6 | 0 | 15 | 24 | 36 | 47 |
| 6. Bolton Wanderers | 42 | 12 | 4 | 5 | 40 | 24 | 8 | 3 | 10 | 28 | 35 | 47 |
| 7. Newcastle United | 42 | 11 | 5 | 5 | 36 | 19 | 7 | 5 | 9 | 23 | 26 | 46 |
| 8. Middlesbrough | 42 | 12 | 6 | 3 | 46 | 19 | 4 | 8 | 9 | 33 | 50 | 46 |
| 9. Chelsea | 42 | 9 | 6 | 6 | 17 | 16 | 8 | 6 | 7 | 23 | 27 | 46 |
| 10. Manchester City | 42 | 13 | 7 | 1 | 44 | 21 | 5 | 2 | 14 | 21 | 49 | 45 |
| 11. Sheffield United | 42 | 11 | 3 | 7 | 32 | 17 | 4 | 7 | 10 | 27 | 37 | 40 |
| 12. Sunderland | 42 | 13 | 4 | 4 | 46 | 23 | 3 | 4 | 14 | 14 | 39 | 40 |
| 13. West Bromwich Albion | 42 | 8 | 6 | 7 | 26 | 23 | 7 | 4 | 10 | 25 | 40 | 40 |
| 14. Huddersfield Town | 42 | 12 | 3 | 6 | 33 | 14 | 3 | 6 | 12 | 20 | 40 | 39 |
| 15. Blackburn Rovers | 42 | 7 | 6 | 8 | 35 | 31 | 6 | 6 | 9 | 19 | 26 | 38 |
| 16. Preston North End | 42 | 12 | 7 | 2 | 33 | 20 | 1 | 5 | 15 | 9 | 45 | 38 |
| 17. Arsenal | 42 | 10 | 6 | 5 | 27 | 19 | 5 | 1 | 15 | 20 | 37 | 37 |
| 18. Birmingham City | 42 | 9 | 2 | 10 | 25 | 29 | 6 | 5 | 10 | 23 | 31 | 37 |
| 19. Oldham Athletic | 42 | 8 | 7 | 6 | 21 | 15 | 5 | 4 | 12 | 17 | 35 | 37 |
| 20. Everton | 42 | 10 | 7 | 4 | 42 | 22 | 2 | 5 | 14 | 15 | 33 | 36 |
| 21. Bradford City | 42 | 8 | 5 | 8 | 28 | 30 | 3 | 5 | 13 | 20 | 42 | 32 |
| 22. Manchester United | 42 | 7 | 7 | 7 | 25 | 26 | 1 | 5 | 15 | 16 | 47 | 28 |

## ❖ SHANKLY'S TWELFTH MAN ❖

Bill Shankly signed Geoff Strong in 1964 as his "twelfth man".

## ❖ WE ARE THE CHAMPIONS (4) ❖

In 1922–23 Liverpool took their second consecutive Division One Championship, their fourth overall, 17 years after they completed another League double by winning Division Two in 1904–05 followed by the Division One Championship in 1905–06. Just as they had been when Liverpool clinched their first Division One title in 1901, Sunderland were once again Liverpool's closest adversaries in the race for the Championship. Indeed, the Reds lost their second League game of the campaign 1–0 at Roker Park, but then one week later Liverpool hammered the Rokerites 5–1 (Forshaw, Chambers 2, Johnson, MacKinlay) at Anfield. In the end Liverpool won the title by six points, having won 26, drawn eight and lost eight of their 42 games during the campaign. Newcastle United were the only club to beat Liverpool at Anfield in 21 home League games, which included a 5–1 (Chambers 3, McNab, Bromilow) thumping of Everton.

### *Football League Division 1*
#### 1922–23

| | P | W | D | L | F | A | W | D | L | F | A | Pts |
|---|---|---|---|---|---|---|---|---|---|---|---|---|
| 1. **Liverpool** | 42 | 17 | 3 | 1 | 50 | 13 | 9 | 5 | 7 | 20 | 18 | 60 |
| 2. Sunderland | 42 | 15 | 5 | 1 | 50 | 25 | 7 | 5 | 9 | 22 | 29 | 54 |
| 3. Huddersfield Town | 42 | 14 | 2 | 5 | 35 | 15 | 7 | 9 | 5 | 25 | 17 | 53 |
| 4. Newcastle United | 42 | 13 | 6 | 2 | 31 | 11 | 5 | 6 | 10 | 14 | 26 | 48 |
| 5. Everton | 42 | 14 | 4 | 3 | 41 | 20 | 6 | 3 | 12 | 22 | 39 | 47 |
| 6. Aston Villa | 42 | 15 | 3 | 3 | 42 | 11 | 3 | 7 | 11 | 22 | 40 | 46 |
| 7. West Bromwich Albion | 42 | 12 | 7 | 2 | 38 | 10 | 5 | 4 | 12 | 20 | 39 | 45 |
| 8. Manchester City | 42 | 14 | 6 | 1 | 38 | 16 | 3 | 5 | 13 | 12 | 33 | 45 |
| 9. Cardiff City | 42 | 15 | 2 | 4 | 51 | 18 | 3 | 5 | 13 | 22 | 41 | 43 |
| 10. Sheffield United | 42 | 11 | 7 | 3 | 41 | 20 | 5 | 3 | 13 | 27 | 44 | 42 |
| 11. Arsenal | 42 | 13 | 4 | 4 | 38 | 16 | 3 | 6 | 12 | 23 | 46 | 42 |
| 12. Tottenham Hotspur | 42 | 11 | 3 | 7 | 34 | 22 | 6 | 4 | 11 | 16 | 28 | 41 |
| 13. Bolton Wanderers | 42 | 11 | 8 | 2 | 36 | 17 | 3 | 4 | 14 | 14 | 41 | 40 |
| 14. Blackburn Rovers | 42 | 12 | 7 | 2 | 32 | 19 | 2 | 5 | 14 | 15 | 43 | 40 |
| 15. Burnley | 42 | 12 | 3 | 6 | 39 | 24 | 4 | 3 | 14 | 19 | 35 | 38 |
| 16. Preston North End | 42 | 12 | 3 | 6 | 41 | 26 | 1 | 8 | 12 | 19 | 38 | 37 |
| 17. Birmingham | 42 | 10 | 4 | 7 | 25 | 19 | 3 | 7 | 11 | 16 | 38 | 37 |
| 18. Middlesbrough | 42 | 11 | 4 | 6 | 41 | 25 | 2 | 6 | 13 | 16 | 38 | 36 |
| 19. Chelsea | 42 | 5 | 13 | 3 | 29 | 20 | 4 | 5 | 12 | 16 | 33 | 36 |
| 20. Nottingham Forest | 42 | 12 | 2 | 7 | 25 | 23 | 1 | 6 | 14 | 16 | 47 | 34 |
| 21. Stoke City | 42 | 7 | 9 | 5 | 28 | 19 | 3 | 1 | 17 | 19 | 48 | 30 |
| 22. Oldham Athletic | 42 | 9 | 6 | 6 | 21 | 20 | 1 | 4 | 16 | 14 | 45 | 30 |

## ❖ MORE THAN HALF OF ENGLAND ❖

England have fielded six Liverpool players in an international on three separate occasions. The first was against Switzerland on 7 September 1977 at Wembley. England manager Ron Greenwood selected Ray Clemence, Phil Neal, Terry McDermott, Emlyn Hughes (*captain*), Ray Kennedy and Ian Callaghan. The game ended goalless.

## ❖ THREE-TIME CUP FINAL LOSER ❖

John Barnes was on the losing side in FA Cup finals with three different teams:

| | |
|---|---|
| 1984 | Watford lost 2–0 to Everton |
| 1988 | Liverpool lost 1–0 to Wimbledon |
| 1998 | Newcastle United lost 2–0 to Arsenal |

## ❖ UNITED, CITY, LIVERPOOL AND EVERTON ❖

Peter Beardsley is the only England international to have played for Manchester United, Manchester City, Liverpool and Everton[†].

## ❖ ELEVEN-YEAR WAIT BETWEEN CAPS ❖

Ian Callaghan made his international debut for England in the 2–0 win over France at Wembley on 20 July 1966. However, he did not win his second England cap until recalled by Ron Greenwood to play in the goalless draw against Switzerland on 7 September 1977, also at Wembley. The gap of 11 years and 49 days is a record between caps for an England player, excluding those whose careers were interrupted by either World War.

## ❖ 13-YEAR-OLD SIGNS FOR LIVERPOOL ❖

In January 1936 Liverpool were so impressed with the performances of a young Flintshire schoolboy named Ray Lambert that they signed him when he was only 13 years old. However, as a result of World War II it was ten years before Lambert made his debut for the Reds in an FA Cup tie against Chester City on 5 January 1946. He would go on to play 341 games for the Reds, plus 113 wartime matches.

*[†]John Gidman was released by Liverpool without playing for them and went on to play for Manchester United, Manchester City and Everton.*

## ❖ THE FIELDS OF ANFIELD ROAD ❖

*(to the tune of "The Fields of Athenry")*

Outside the Shankly Gates
I heard a Kopite calling:
Shankly they have taken you away
But you left a great eleven
Before you went to heaven
Now it's glory round the Fields of Anfield Road

*Chorus:*
All round the Fields of Anfield Road
Where once we watched the King Kenny play (and he could play)
Stevie Heighway on the wing
We had dreams and songs to sing
Of the glory round the Fields of Anfield Road

Outside the Paisley Gates
I heard a Kopite calling
Paisley they have taken you away
You led the great 11
Back in Rome in 77
And the redmen they are still playing the same way

All round the Fields of Anfield Road
Where once we watched the King Kenny play (and he could play)
Stevie Heighway on the wing
We had dreams and songs to sing
Of the glory round the Fields of Anfield Road

## ❖ WHEN STANLEY MET SHANKLY ❖

The Liverpool comedian Stan Boardman once told a story in which he said that when he was on the books at Liverpool for two years as a teenager, Bill Shankly told him he would be better off as a comedian than a footballer. Stan and a few of his mates travelled down to London to watch the Reds take on Arsenal in the 1971 FA Cup final at Wembley. When the lads got a puncture, they hitched a ride to Hendon where they knew the Liverpool team were staying. When Shanks approached them and found out what had happened he went away and came back with four Cup final tickets and offered the lads a lift in the team's back-up coach for the trip to London.

## ❖ REDS IN THE MUSEUM ❖

The National Football Museum is situated at Preston North End's Deepdale Stadium. It was opened on 1 December 2002 with induction open to football figures of any nationality who have made a significant contribution to the English game. The first 29 inductees comprised 22 players, six managers and one player from the women's game and were selected by a panel of 20 football experts from a short list of 96 nominees. Kenny Dalglish, Kevin Keegan, Bob Paisley and Bill Shankly were in that first group of inductees.

## ❖ FWA FOOTBALLER OF THE YEAR AWARD ❖

In 1947 Charles Buchan, the author and publisher of *Football Monthly* as well as one of the founding members of the Football Writers' Association (FWA), suggested that an award should be given "to the professional player who by precept and example is considered by a ballot of members to be the footballer of the year". Almost 60 years later, the Football Writers' Association Footballer of the Year Award is one of the most prestigious awards in the British game. Voted for annually by the FWA members, its first recipient was the legendary Sir Stanley Matthews. Eight Liverpool players have been honoured:

| Year | Player |
|---|---|
| 1990 | John Barnes |
| 1989 | Steve Nicol |
| 1988 | John Barnes |
| 1984 | Ian Rush |
| 1983 | Kenny Dalglish |
| 1980 | Terry McDermott |
| 1979 | Kenny Dalglish |
| 1977 | Emlyn Hughes |
| 1976 | Kevin Keegan |
| 1974 | Ian Callaghan |

## ❖ HILLSBOROUGH DISASTER APPEAL GAME ❖

This game took place against Celtic at Celtic Park, Glasgow, on 30 April 1989 in front of a crowd of 60,437. Liverpool won the game 4–0, with two goals from John Aldridge and one each from Kenny Dalglish and Ian Rush. It was the first match Liverpool played following the Hillsborough Disaster of 15 April 1989.

## ❖ WHAT THE REDS SAID (4) ❖

"Every time I come to this place [Anfield], I think, 'This is brilliant. I'm playing for Liverpool.'"
*Nick Barmby*

## ❖ PFA PLAYERS' PLAYER OF THE YEAR ❖

The Professional Football Association's Players' Player of the Year award was introduced in 1974. It goes to the player who in the opinion of his fellow professionals was the outstanding English League player of the season. Since its inception, only five Liverpool players have won it while they were at the club:

| Year | Player |
|------|--------|
| 2006 | Steven Gerrard |
| 1988 | John Barnes |
| 1984 | Ian Rush |
| 1983 | Kenny Dalglish |
| 1980 | Terry McDermott |

## ❖ FIRST GOAL ON *MATCH OF THE DAY* ❖

On 22 August 1964 Anfield was the first venue for BBC's *Match of the Day* programme. Liverpool beat Arsenal 3–2 and the first goal ever seen on the programme was scored by Roger Hunt. Gordon Wallace netted the other two for the Reds.

## ❖ ARE YOU AVI'N A LAUGH? ❖

An old story is often heard around Anfield on a match day about Avi Cohen, the Israeli international whom Bob Paisley signed in 1979. Avi was a huge Kenny Dalglish fan even before he arrived at the club, and on his first morning at Melwood he placed his training gear next to Kenny's. Avi then tapped his hero on the shoulder, and with a broad smile said: "You, me, the same." Dalglish smiled at the new arrival and carried on getting changed for the morning's training session. The very next morning Avi once again placed his training gear next to Kenny's, smiled at him and said: "You, me, the same." However, this time an irritated Dalglish looked at Avi and said in his broad Glaswegian accent: "What are ye talkin' aboot, Avi?" Avi looked straight at the Liverpool star and said "You, me, we the same. We both learn English." The rest of the boys in the training room could not control their laughter.

## ❖ WE ARE THE CHAMPIONS (5) ❖

Liverpool won their fifth Division One title in 1946–47 by a narrow one-point margin over the team that was set to dominate English football throughout the 1950s – Manchester United. In the fourth game of the season United thrashed Liverpool 5–0 at Maine Road, a ground United used for their home games for several years after Old Trafford was bombed during World War II. The crunch fixture came five games before the end of the season, when United visited Anfield for what was effectively a Championship decider. Liverpool won the game 1–0 thanks to a goal from Albert Stubbins. Liverpool's last four games were all away from home and they went on to win three of them and draw one to claim the title. Liverpool's success was helped by their Chairman, Willam McConnell, who had acted as an adviser to the Government during the war on nutrition. "Billy Mac" ensured the players ate the right foods prior to games.

### *Football League Division 1*
#### 1946–47

|  | P | W | D | L | F | A | W | D | L | F | A | Pts |
|---|---|---|---|---|---|---|---|---|---|---|---|---|
| 1. **Liverpool** | 42 | 13 | 3 | 5 | 42 | 24 | 12 | 4 | 5 | 42 | 28 | 57 |
| 2. Manchester United | 42 | 17 | 3 | 1 | 61 | 19 | 5 | 9 | 7 | 34 | 35 | 56 |
| 3. Wolverhampton W. | 42 | 15 | 1 | 5 | 66 | 31 | 10 | 5 | 6 | 32 | 25 | 56 |
| 4. Stoke City | 42 | 14 | 5 | 2 | 52 | 21 | 10 | 2 | 9 | 38 | 32 | 55 |
| 5. Blackpool | 42 | 14 | 1 | 6 | 38 | 32 | 8 | 5 | 8 | 33 | 38 | 50 |
| 6. Sheffield United | 42 | 12 | 4 | 5 | 51 | 32 | 9 | 3 | 9 | 38 | 43 | 49 |
| 7. Preston North End | 42 | 10 | 7 | 4 | 45 | 27 | 8 | 4 | 9 | 31 | 47 | 47 |
| 8. Aston Villa | 42 | 9 | 6 | 6 | 39 | 24 | 9 | 3 | 9 | 28 | 29 | 45 |
| 9. Sunderland | 42 | 11 | 3 | 7 | 33 | 27 | 7 | 5 | 9 | 32 | 39 | 44 |
| 10. Everton | 42 | 13 | 5 | 3 | 40 | 24 | 4 | 4 | 13 | 22 | 43 | 43 |
| 11. Middlesbrough | 42 | 11 | 3 | 7 | 46 | 32 | 6 | 5 | 10 | 27 | 36 | 42 |
| 12. Portsmouth | 42 | 11 | 3 | 7 | 42 | 27 | 5 | 6 | 10 | 24 | 33 | 41 |
| 13. Arsenal | 42 | 9 | 5 | 7 | 43 | 33 | 7 | 4 | 10 | 29 | 37 | 41 |
| 14. Derby County | 42 | 13 | 2 | 6 | 44 | 28 | 5 | 3 | 13 | 29 | 51 | 41 |
| 15. Chelsea | 42 | 9 | 3 | 9 | 33 | 39 | 7 | 4 | 10 | 36 | 45 | 39 |
| 16. Grimsby Town | 42 | 9 | 6 | 6 | 37 | 35 | 4 | 6 | 11 | 24 | 47 | 38 |
| 17. Blackburn Rovers | 42 | 6 | 5 | 10 | 23 | 27 | 8 | 3 | 10 | 22 | 26 | 36 |
| 18. Bolton Wanderers | 42 | 8 | 5 | 8 | 30 | 28 | 5 | 3 | 13 | 27 | 41 | 34 |
| 19. Charlton Athletic | 42 | 6 | 6 | 9 | 34 | 32 | 5 | 6 | 10 | 23 | 39 | 34 |
| 20. Huddersfield Town | 42 | 11 | 4 | 6 | 34 | 24 | 2 | 3 | 16 | 19 | 55 | 33 |
| 21. Brentford | 42 | 5 | 5 | 11 | 19 | 35 | 4 | 2 | 15 | 26 | 53 | 25 |
| 22. Leeds United | 42 | 6 | 5 | 10 | 30 | 30 | 0 | 1 | 20 | 15 | 60 | 18 |

# ❖ LIVERPOOL SCOTTISH XI ❖

**1**
Thomas
*YOUNGER*

**2**
Matt
*BUSBY*

**4**
Alan
*HANSEN*

**5**
Ron
*YEATS*
*(captain)*

**3**
Steve
*NICOL*

**6**
Graeme
*SOUNESS*

**7**
Kenny
*DALGLISH*

**8**
John
*WARK*

**9**
Don
*McKINLAY*

**10**
Malcolm
*McVEAN*

**11**
Billy
*LIDDELL*

*Substitutes*
Bert *SLATER* • Gary *GILLESPIE* • Gary *McALLISTER*
Jimmy *McDOUGALL* • Ian *ST JOHN*
*Player-Manager*
Matt *BUSBY*

### *Did You Know That?*

Thomas Younger won two Scottish Championship winners' medals with Hibernian. During a game against Derby County in October 1957, Younger left the pitch injured and later returned to the field of play as a centre-forward.

## ❖ THE GREAT DANE ❖

Joe Fagan brought Jan Molby to Anfield from Ajax Amsterdam in August 1984 for £200,000. Molby was one of many exciting up-and-coming players at Ajax, who included Marco van Basten, Frank Rijkaard and Jesper Olsen. Molby was a colossus in the heart of the Reds' midfield during his 12 years with the club. Although he was not the quickest of players, and sometimes struggled with his weight, his passing ability was second to none at the time. He made 291 appearances for the Reds, scoring 60 times, and won two First Division Championship winners' medals and two FA Cup winners' medals. In February 1996 Molby was appointed the player-manager of Swansea City.

## ❖ ENGLAND'S SPRINGBOK AMATEUR ❖

Gordon Hodgson was signed by the Reds in 1925 after he was spotted playing in South Africa. He was a prolific scorer, holding the club's goalscoring records until Roger Hunt arrived at the club. In 1930–31 he scored 36 goals, and in total he scored 240 goals in 378 games. He won three caps for England Amateurs at inside-right against Northern Ireland, Wales and Scotland in 1930 and 1931 while playing for Liverpool. He had already played for South Africa's amateur national team. Gordon Hodgson died in 1951.

## ❖ WORLD CLUB CHAMPIONSHIP ❖

Liverpool have played in three World Club Championship finals and lost them all:

| Date | Opposition (Country) | Venue | Result |
|---|---|---|---|
| 13.12.1981 | Flamengo (Brazil) | Tokyo | 0–3 |
| 9.12.1984 | Independiente (Argentina) | Tokyo | 0–1 |
| 18.12.2005 | Sao Paulo (Brazil) | Yokohama | 0–1 |

## ❖ SOME FAMOUS LIVERPOOL FANS ❖

| | |
|---|---|
| Curtly Ambrose | cricketer |
| Johnny Ball | TV personality |
| Sue Barker | TV presenter |
| Ian Broudie | musician (*Lightning Seeds*) |
| Cilla Black | TV personality |
| Stan Boardman | comedian |
| Mel C | pop singer |
| Craig Charles | comedian and actor |
| Elvis Costello | musician |
| Chris de Burgh | musician |
| Kelly Dalglish | TV presenter |
| Dr Dre | rap artist |
| Kirsty Gallagher | TV presenter |
| Ian McCulloch | musician (*Echo and the Bunnymen*) |
| Mike Myers | actor |
| John Peel | former DJ and radio presenter |
| Peter Sissons | TV news presenter |
| Jimmy Tarbuck | comedian |
| Ricky Tomlinson | actor |

## ❖ GOING UP, GOING UP, GOING UP (4) ❖

After Liverpool had spent eight seasons in the wilderness of the Second Division, Bill Shankly led the club to Division Two Championship success in 1961–62. The Reds' fourth Division Two title proved to be the catalyst for a period of success for the club. After taking charge in December 1959, Shankly guided Liverpool to third place in Division Two in seasons 1959–60 and 1960–61 and built them into a side that could score freely and defend doggedly. Of their 21 home League games in 1961–62, the Reds won 18 and drew three, scoring 68 times at Anfield at an average of more than three goals per game. The Reds' nearest challengers, Leyton Orient, finished a distant eight points behind Liverpool, although they did draw both games against them. Ever since the Reds' promotion to the First Division in 1962, they have remained in the top flight. More impressively, in those 44 seasons, they have never finished below eighth place.

### Football League Division 2
#### 1961–62

|  | P | W | D | L | F | A | W | D | L | F | A | Pts |
|---|---|---|---|---|---|---|---|---|---|---|---|---|
| 1. **Liverpool** | 42 | 18 | 3 | 0 | 68 | 19 | 9 | 5 | 7 | 31 | 24 | 62 |
| 2. Leyton Orient | 42 | 11 | 5 | 5 | 34 | 17 | 11 | 5 | 5 | 35 | 23 | 54 |
| 3. Sunderland | 42 | 17 | 3 | 1 | 60 | 16 | 5 | 6 | 10 | 25 | 34 | 53 |
| 4. Scunthorpe United | 42 | 14 | 4 | 3 | 52 | 26 | 7 | 3 | 11 | 34 | 45 | 49 |
| 5. Plymouth Argyle | 42 | 12 | 4 | 5 | 45 | 30 | 7 | 4 | 10 | 30 | 45 | 46 |
| 6. Southampton | 42 | 13 | 3 | 5 | 53 | 28 | 5 | 6 | 10 | 24 | 34 | 45 |
| 7. Huddersfield Town | 42 | 11 | 5 | 5 | 39 | 22 | 5 | 7 | 9 | 28 | 37 | 44 |
| 8. Stoke City | 42 | 13 | 4 | 4 | 34 | 17 | 4 | 4 | 13 | 21 | 40 | 42 |
| 9. Rotherham United | 42 | 9 | 6 | 6 | 36 | 30 | 7 | 3 | 11 | 34 | 46 | 41 |
| 10. Preston North End | 42 | 11 | 4 | 6 | 34 | 23 | 4 | 6 | 11 | 21 | 34 | 40 |
| 11. Newcastle United | 42 | 10 | 5 | 6 | 40 | 27 | 5 | 4 | 12 | 24 | 31 | 39 |
| 12. Middlesbrough | 42 | 11 | 3 | 7 | 45 | 29 | 5 | 4 | 12 | 31 | 43 | 39 |
| 13. Luton Town | 42 | 12 | 1 | 8 | 44 | 37 | 5 | 4 | 12 | 25 | 34 | 39 |
| 14. Walsall | 42 | 11 | 7 | 3 | 42 | 23 | 3 | 4 | 14 | 28 | 52 | 39 |
| 15. Charlton Athletic | 42 | 10 | 5 | 6 | 38 | 30 | 5 | 4 | 12 | 31 | 45 | 39 |
| 16. Derby County | 42 | 10 | 7 | 4 | 42 | 27 | 4 | 4 | 13 | 26 | 48 | 39 |
| 17. Norwich City | 42 | 10 | 6 | 5 | 36 | 28 | 4 | 5 | 12 | 25 | 42 | 39 |
| 18. Bury | 42 | 9 | 4 | 8 | 32 | 36 | 8 | 1 | 12 | 20 | 40 | 39 |
| 19. Leeds United | 42 | 9 | 6 | 6 | 24 | 19 | 3 | 6 | 12 | 26 | 42 | 36 |
| 20. Swansea Town | 42 | 10 | 5 | 6 | 38 | 30 | 2 | 7 | 12 | 23 | 53 | 36 |
| 21. Bristol Rovers | 42 | 11 | 3 | 7 | 36 | 31 | 2 | 4 | 15 | 17 | 50 | 33 |
| 22. Brighton & Hove A. | 42 | 7 | 7 | 7 | 24 | 32 | 3 | 4 | 14 | 18 | 54 | 31 |

## ❖ AN EARLY PIONEER ❖

Joe McQue was a member of the original "Team of the Macs" and won the Second Division Championship with the Reds in both 1893–94 and in 1895–96. He played a total of 142 games for Liverpool, scoring 12 goals, after signing from Celtic during the summer of 1892. McQue played in Liverpool's first ever game, against Rotherham Town on 1 September 1892, and also played in Liverpool's first ever league game, the 8–0 Lancashire League thrashing of Higher Walton at Anfield on 3 September 1892, a game in which he scored twice, along with Smith (2), Cameron (2), McBride and McVean. He also played in and scored in Liverpool's first ever Football League game, the 2–0 away win over Middlesbrough Ironopolis on 2 September 1893. Malcolm McVean scored the Reds' other goal that day.

## ❖ EUROPEAN REGULARS ❖

Liverpool is one of only 15 clubs to date that have played 20 or more consecutive seasons in major European competition (European Cup/Champions League, European Cup Winners' Cup, UEFA Cup)[†]:

| No. of Seasons | Club | Period |
|---|---|---|
| 48 | Barcelona | 1957–58 to 2005–06 |
| 42 | Anderlecht | 1964–65 to 2005–06 |
| 41 | Benfica | 1960–61 to 2000–01 |
| 32 | FC Porto | 1974–75 to 2005–06 |
| | PSV Eindhoven | 1974–75 to 2005–06 |
| 29 | Sporting Lisbon | 1977–78 to 2005–06 |
| 28 | Juventus | 1963–64 to 1990–91 |
| 25 | Glasgow Rangers | 1981–82 to 2005–06 |
| 24 | Ajax Amsterdam | 1966–67 to 1989–90 |
| | Crvena Zvezda Belgrade | 1968–69 to 1991–92 |
| | Spartak Moscow | 1980–81 to 2003–04 |
| 23 | Sparta Prague | 1983–84 to 2005–06 |
| 22 | Real Madrid | 1955–56 to 1976–77 |
| 21 | **Liverpool** | **1964–65 to 1984–85** |
| 20 | Austria Vienna | 1976–77 to 1995–96 |

[†]*Liverpool were banned, along with all English teams, from European competition from 1985–86 to 1990–91 as a result of the Heysel Stadium Disaster in 1985; in 1989 Ajax Amsterdam were banned from European competition for two years as a result of crowd trouble; Crvena Zvezda Belgrade were banned from European competition in 1992–93 as a result of a United Nations boycott.*

### ❖ KENNY DALGLISH MBE ❖

Kenneth "Kenny" Mathieson Dalglish was born on 4 March 1951 in Dalmarnock, Glasgow, and is one of the greatest players to have worn the shirt of Liverpool Football Club. He arrived at Anfield from Celtic on 10 August 1977 as a replacement for the Hamburg-bound Kevin Keegan. "King Kenny" cost Liverpool a then British record £440,000, and although many players fail to live up to the "most expensive player" tag, there is no doubt he did.

In Kenny's first season with the Reds, Liverpool won the European Cup for the second successive year, thanks to his superb chip over the FC Bruges goalkeeper in the final at Wembley. Then in 1980 Ian Rush signed for Liverpool, and throughout the 1980s the Dalglish-Rush partnership was unstoppable. While Dalglish was the creative genius, Rush was the lethal marksman. Liverpool dominated the 1980s, winning more trophies in the period than any club had ever managed before in a decade. But Dalglish was much more than a creative player, as his record of 172 goals in 515 Liverpool games proves.

In 1985 Kenny was appointed Liverpool's first ever player/manager and many people in the game considered it to be a huge gamble. However, this notion was completely dismissed when Liverpool won the League and FA Cup Double (only the fourth club ever to do so) in Dalglish's first season in charge. An astute man, Kenny also had an eye for a player, and when Ian Rush left the club for Juventus in 1987, Dalglish went out and bought John Aldridge, John Barnes and Peter Beardsley. The Liverpool team that captured the League Championship in the 1987–88 season is regarded by many fans as being among the best that Liverpool have ever produced. Kenny's trio of Aldridge, Barnes and Beardsley scored 64 goals between them that season (Aldridge 29, Beardsley 17 and Barnes 18), while the Reds lost only two League games, neither of which was at Anfield.

Following the Hillsborough Disaster on 15 April 1989, in which 96 Liverpool fans lost their lives on the Leppings Lane terrace, Dalglish spent much time attending funerals and trying to comfort the bereaved. In 1990 Liverpool went on to win the Championship (their last to date), but the stress brought on by the disaster was clearly taking its toll. On 22 February 1991, just a few days after the infamous 4–4 draw with Everton, Dalglish shocked the football world by resigning, announcing that he felt as though his "head was about to explode". During his time as a player and manager Liverpool won eight League Championships, three European Cups, two FA Cups, four League Cups and four Charity Shields. Kenny Dalglish was awarded the MBE in 1984 for services to football.

## ❖ GOING, GOING, GONE ❖

In October 1993, Christie's[†] sold a collection of Ray Kennedy's medals, caps and shirts for £101,200.

## ❖ IAN CALLAGHAN – A LIVERPOOL LEGEND ❖

Ian Callaghan's[††] football career spanned three decades, and during that time he won practically everything the game had to offer, including:

1 Second Division Championship
5 First Division Championships
2 FA Cups
2 UEFA Cups
1 European Cup
4 England caps*
1974 Football Writers' Footballer of the Year Award
*was a member of England's World Cup winning squad of 1966

Callaghan also holds five appearance records for Liverpool:

All games............................857
League games....................640
European games.................89
FA Cup games...................79
All Cup games..................210

## ❖ CLEAN-SHEET CLEMENCE ❖

Ray Clemence holds the Liverpool record for the highest number of clean sheets: 226 in 470 games. Ray also holds Liverpool's single season record of clean sheets with 28 in 1978–79.

## ❖ JOHNSON STRIKES FOR BOTH SIDES ❖

David Johnson, who had stints at Everton before and after his time at Anfield, was the first person to score for both sides in Merseyside derbies. Peter Beardsley is the only other player to have achieved the feat.

[†]On 28 September 2000, Phil Neal's yellow-metal 1977 European Cup winner's medal was sold at Christie's for £11,750.
[††]Ian Callaghan also played 87 matches for Swansea City and 17 matches for Crewe Alexandra, making a total of 968 games and 70 goals from the 1960s to the 1980s.

## ❖ WHAT THE REDS SAID (5) ❖

"The whole of my life, what they wanted was honesty. They were not so concerned with cultured football, but with triers who gave one hundred per cent."
**Bob Paisley**, *on the Kop*

## ❖ OWEN WINS BALLON D'OR ❖

In 2001 Michael Owen became the first Liverpool player to win the coveted European Player of the Year award. Commonly referred to as the *Ballon d'Or*[†] (Golden Ball), it was established in 1956 by *France Football*, the French football magazine, and is awarded to the footballer deemed to have been the best overall player in European football during the year. At first only European nationals playing in Europe qualified, but since 1995 all footballers playing in Europe have been eligible for the award, regardless of their birthplace. The winner is chosen by a vote of European football journalists, one from each of UEFA's member nations, which totalled 52 in 2003. Voters select their top five players in order of preference, and points are assigned to each player, five for a first-place vote, four for a second-place vote and so on down to one point for a fifth-place vote.

## ❖ OWN GOALS ❖

Only two Liverpool players have scored an own goal playing for England and they are two Phils:

Phil Neal.....................v Australia..........19 June 1983
Phil Thompson...........v Wales................17 May 1980

## ❖ DIXIE WHO? ❖

In September 1929 Liverpool paid Ayr United £5,500 for the services of their prolific centre-forward Jimmy Smith. In 1927–28, the same campaign in which Dixie Dean set the English season goalscoring record with 60 League goals for Everton, Smith set a new Scottish season record with 66 goals for Ayr United. During his time at Anfield, Smith managed 38 goals in 62 appearances, before signing for Tunbridge Wells in 1932.

---

*[†]Kevin Keegan twice won the* Ballon d'Or *when he was at Hamburg, in 1978 and again the following year.*

## ❖ WE ARE THE CHAMPIONS (6) ❖

Following their promotion to Division One in 1961–62, Liverpool finished the 1962–63 season in eighth place under the masterful guidance of Bill Shankly. The following season, Shanks took Liverpool to their sixth Division One Championship, the first of his three titles, in what became a purple period of success for the club. Just as they had done in 1946–47, Liverpool finished with their noses in front of Manchester United, the reigning champions. Uncharacteristically under Shanks, Liverpool's home form was quite erratic, with 5 losses and 16 wins from their 21 outings. The crunch game came on 4 April 1964 with the visit of United to Anfield. A 3–0 (Callaghan, Arrowsmith 2) win gave the Reds the two points, and despite drawing one and losing two of their final three League games, Liverpool won the title by four points.

### Football League Division 1
### 1963–64

| | | P | W | D | L | F | A | W | D | L | F | A | Pts |
|---|---|---|---|---|---|---|---|---|---|---|---|---|---|
| 1. | Liverpool | 42 | 16 | 0 | 5 | 60 | 18 | 10 | 5 | 6 | 32 | 27 | 57 |
| 2. | Manchester United | 42 | 15 | 3 | 3 | 54 | 19 | 8 | 4 | 9 | 36 | 43 | 53 |
| 3. | Everton | 42 | 14 | 4 | 3 | 53 | 26 | 7 | 6 | 8 | 31 | 38 | 52 |
| 4. | Spurs | 42 | 13 | 3 | 5 | 54 | 31 | 9 | 4 | 8 | 43 | 50 | 51 |
| 5. | Chelsea | 42 | 12 | 3 | 6 | 36 | 24 | 8 | 7 | 6 | 36 | 32 | 50 |
| 6. | Sheffield Wednesday | 42 | 15 | 3 | 3 | 50 | 24 | 4 | 8 | 9 | 34 | 43 | 49 |
| 7. | Blackburn Rovers | 42 | 10 | 4 | 7 | 44 | 28 | 8 | 6 | 7 | 45 | 37 | 46 |
| 8. | Arsenal | 42 | 10 | 7 | 4 | 56 | 37 | 7 | 4 | 10 | 34 | 45 | 45 |
| 9. | Burnley | 42 | 14 | 3 | 4 | 46 | 23 | 3 | 7 | 11 | 25 | 41 | 44 |
| 10. | West Bromwich Albion | 42 | 9 | 6 | 6 | 43 | 35 | 7 | 5 | 9 | 27 | 26 | 43 |
| 11. | Leicester City | 42 | 9 | 4 | 8 | 33 | 27 | 7 | 7 | 7 | 28 | 31 | 43 |
| 12. | Sheffield United | 42 | 10 | 6 | 5 | 35 | 22 | 6 | 5 | 10 | 26 | 42 | 43 |
| 13. | Nottingham Forest | 42 | 9 | 5 | 7 | 34 | 24 | 7 | 4 | 10 | 30 | 44 | 41 |
| 14. | West Ham United | 42 | 8 | 7 | 6 | 45 | 38 | 6 | 5 | 10 | 24 | 36 | 40 |
| 15. | Fulham | 42 | 11 | 8 | 2 | 45 | 23 | 2 | 5 | 14 | 13 | 42 | 39 |
| 16. | Wolverhampton W. | 42 | 6 | 9 | 6 | 36 | 34 | 6 | 6 | 9 | 34 | 46 | 39 |
| 17. | Stoke City | 42 | 9 | 6 | 6 | 49 | 33 | 5 | 4 | 12 | 28 | 45 | 38 |
| 18. | Blackpool | 42 | 8 | 6 | 7 | 26 | 29 | 5 | 3 | 13 | 26 | 44 | 35 |
| 19. | Aston Villa | 42 | 8 | 6 | 7 | 35 | 29 | 3 | 6 | 12 | 27 | 42 | 34 |
| 20. | Birmingham City | 42 | 7 | 7 | 7 | 33 | 32 | 4 | 0 | 17 | 21 | 60 | 29 |
| 21. | Bolton Wanderers | 42 | 6 | 5 | 10 | 30 | 35 | 4 | 3 | 14 | 18 | 45 | 28 |
| 22. | Ipswich Town | 42 | 9 | 3 | 9 | 38 | 45 | 0 | 4 | 17 | 18 | 76 | 25 |

## ❖ UP FOR THE CUP (1) ❖

Liverpool reached their third FA Cup final in 1965 and finally got their hands on the coveted trophy. In the third round Liverpool beat West Bromwich Albion 2–1 away and then in Round Four could only manage a 1–1 draw with Stockport County at Anfield before winning the replay 2–0. In the fifth round Liverpool beat Bolton Wanderers 1–0 at Burnden Park thanks to an Ian Callaghan goal. Liverpool met Leicester City in the sixth round and, after a 0–0 draw at Filbert Street, won the replay 1–0 at Anfield with a goal from Roger Hunt. In the semi-finals Liverpool eased past Chelsea 2–0 at Villa Park, then in the final beat Leeds United 2–1 after extra time at Wembley.

### FA CUP FINAL
*1 MAY 1965, WEMBLEY STADIUM*

**Liverpool** (0) 2     vs     **Leeds United** (0) 1
Hunt, St John                     Bremner
*After extra time*

*Att.* 100,000

*Liverpool:* Lawrence; Lawler, Byrne, Strong, Yeats; Stevenson, Ian Callaghan, Smith, Thompson; Hunt, St John

## ❖ DALGLISH THE CENTURION ❖

On 27 March 1986 Kenny Dalglish became the first player to win 100 caps for Scotland when he captained his country to a 3–0 friendly win over Romania at Hampden Park. Dalglish won 102 Scottish caps in total, a record that still stands today.

## ❖ BOYS FROM THE BLACKSTUFF ❖

In 1982 Graeme Souness appeared in an episode of Alan Bleasdale's *Boys from the Blackstuff*. Souness starred alongside his Liverpool team-mate Sammy Lee in the scene where Yosser Hughes (played by Bernard Hill) approaches Souness in a bar and says "You look like me."

## ❖ FIRST FOREIGN PLAYER ❖

Goalkeeper Arthur Riley was the first player from outside the UK and Ireland to play for the Reds. Liverpool manager Matt McQueen signed the South African in August 1925 after Riley took part in South Africa's 1924 tour of Britain.

## ❖ WELSH HAT-TRICK ❖

Kevin Keegan's first three games for England were all against Wales:

| | | |
|---|---|---|
| 15 November 1972 | Cardiff | 1–0 |
| 24 January 1973 | Wembley | 1–1 |
| 11 May 1974 | Cardiff | 2–0 |

## ❖ UNWANTED HISTORY ❖

In the 61st minute of the 1988 FA Cup final, Wimbledon's Dave Beasant saved a penalty from Liverpool's John Aldridge. It was the first penalty miss in an FA Cup final at Wembley, and Wimbledon went on to win the final 1–0.

## ❖ NINE STEPS TO GLORY ❖

On their way to winning the FA Cup in 1974, Liverpool played a total of nine games in the competition, with replays in round three against Doncaster Rovers, round four against Carlisle United and the semi-finals against Leicester City.

## ❖ "SIR" ROGER OF THE KOP ❖

Roger Hunt signed for Liverpool in 1959 from Stockton Heath and went on to make 492 appearances for the Reds, scoring 286 goals. In 1964 and 1966 his goals helped Liverpool to win the First Division Championship and in 1965 he scored the opening goal against Leeds United in the 1965 FA Cup final as Liverpool lifted the trophy for the first time. He played in England's 1966 World Cup-winning side and won a total of 34 caps, scoring 18 times. He joined Bolton Wanderers in 1969 and, in 2000, was awarded an MBE.

*Did You Know That?*
Only Ian Rush has socred more goals for Liverpool than Roger Hunt, although Hunt scored more League goals, 245 to 229.

## ❖ KEEGAN AND OWEN MAKE TOP 12 ❖

To celebrate UEFA's Golden Jubilee, each of the 52 member associations was invited to nominate its outstanding footballer of the past 50 years. Bobby Moore polled 50 per cent of the England vote, while Kevin Keegan came tenth in the voting and Michael Owen was 11th.

## ❖ WE ARE THE CHAMPIONS (7) ❖

In 1965–66 Liverpool once again prevented Manchester United from retaining the Division One Championship. However, it was another United, Leeds, who proved to be Liverpool's biggest rivals on their way to winning their seventh Division One title that season, England's World Cup winning year. Remarkably the fixtures schedule matched Liverpool and Leeds United for consecutive games on 27 and 28 December 1965. In the first encounter the Reds suffered a body blow, losing 1–0 at Anfield. However, the next day, Liverpool travelled to Elland Road and secured a 1–0 victory thanks to a Gordon Milne goal. In the end Liverpool won the title comfortably by six points.

### *Football League Division 1*
### 1965–66

|  |  | P | W | D | L | F | A | W | D | L | F | A | Pts |
|---|---|---|---|---|---|---|---|---|---|---|---|---|---|
| 1 | **Liverpool** | 42 | 17 | 2 | 2 | 52 | 15 | 9 | 7 | 5 | 27 | 19 | 61 |
| 2 | Leeds United | 42 | 14 | 4 | 3 | 49 | 15 | 9 | 5 | 7 | 30 | 23 | 55 |
| 3 | Burnley | 42 | 15 | 3 | 3 | 45 | 20 | 9 | 4 | 8 | 34 | 27 | 55 |
| 4 | Manchester United | 42 | 12 | 8 | 1 | 50 | 20 | 6 | 7 | 8 | 34 | 39 | 51 |
| 5 | Chelsea | 42 | 11 | 4 | 6 | 30 | 21 | 11 | 3 | 7 | 35 | 32 | 51 |
| 6 | West Bromwich Albion | 42 | 11 | 6 | 4 | 58 | 34 | 8 | 6 | 7 | 33 | 35 | 50 |
| 7 | Leicester City | 42 | 12 | 4 | 5 | 40 | 28 | 9 | 3 | 9 | 40 | 37 | 49 |
| 8 | Tottenham Hotspur | 42 | 11 | 6 | 4 | 55 | 37 | 5 | 6 | 10 | 20 | 29 | 44 |
| 9 | Sheffield United | 42 | 11 | 6 | 4 | 37 | 25 | 5 | 5 | 11 | 19 | 34 | 43 |
| 10 | Stoke City | 42 | 12 | 6 | 3 | 42 | 22 | 3 | 6 | 12 | 23 | 42 | 42 |
| 11 | Everton | 42 | 12 | 6 | 3 | 39 | 19 | 3 | 5 | 13 | 17 | 43 | 41 |
| 12 | West Ham United | 42 | 12 | 5 | 4 | 46 | 33 | 3 | 4 | 14 | 24 | 50 | 39 |
| 13 | Blackpool | 42 | 9 | 5 | 7 | 36 | 29 | 5 | 4 | 12 | 19 | 36 | 37 |
| 14 | Arsenal | 42 | 8 | 8 | 5 | 36 | 31 | 4 | 5 | 12 | 26 | 44 | 37 |
| 15 | Newcastle United | 42 | 10 | 5 | 6 | 26 | 20 | 4 | 4 | 13 | 24 | 43 | 37 |
| 16 | Aston Villa | 42 | 10 | 3 | 8 | 39 | 34 | 5 | 3 | 13 | 30 | 46 | 36 |
| 17 | Sheffield Wednesday | 42 | 11 | 6 | 4 | 35 | 18 | 3 | 2 | 16 | 21 | 48 | 36 |
| 18 | Nottingham Forest | 42 | 11 | 3 | 7 | 31 | 26 | 3 | 5 | 13 | 25 | 46 | 36 |
| 19 | Sunderland | 42 | 13 | 2 | 6 | 36 | 28 | 1 | 6 | 14 | 15 | 44 | 36 |
| 20 | Fulham | 42 | 9 | 4 | 8 | 34 | 37 | 5 | 3 | 13 | 33 | 48 | 35 |
| 21 | Northampton Town | 42 | 8 | 6 | 7 | 31 | 32 | 2 | 7 | 12 | 24 | 60 | 33 |
| 22 | Blackburn Rovers | 42 | 6 | 1 | 14 | 30 | 36 | 2 | 3 | 16 | 27 | 52 | 20 |

## ❖ CELEBRITY RAZOR ❖

Neil Ruddock appeared in *I'm a Celebrity, Get Me Out of Here!*

## ❖ BBC SPORTS TEAM OF THE YEAR AWARD ❖

Inaugurated in 1960, the BBC Sports Personality of the Year Team Award is given on an annual basis to the sporting team or partnership considered to have made the most substantive contribution to sport in that year. Liverpool have won the award on three occasions: in 1977, 1986 and 2001.

## ❖ REDS BEARING GIFTS ❖

The following table lists own goals scored by Liverpool players in an FA Premier League game (as at 15 January 2006):

| Date | Player | Opposition/Venue | Score |
|---|---|---|---|
| 13.3.93 | Steve Nicol | Middlesbrough | Away 2–1 *(w)* |
| 4.12.93 | Neil Ruddock | Sheffield Wednesday | Away 1–3 *(l)* |
| 4.12.93 | Mark Wright | Sheffield Wednesday | Away 1–3 *(l)* |
| 26.11.94 | Neil Ruddock | Tottenham Hotspur | Home 1–1 *(d)* |
| 26.8.95 | John Barnes | Tottenham Hotspur | Away 3–1 *(w)* |
| 18.10.97 | Neil Ruddock | Everton | Away 0–2 *(l)* |
| 5.12.98 | Jamie Carragher | Tottenham Hotspur | Away 1–2 *(l)* |
| 1.5.99 | Jamie Carragher | Tottenham Hotspur | Home 3–2 *(w)* |
| 2.8.99 | Rigobert Song | Leeds United | Away 2–1 *(w)* |
| 11.9.99 | Jamie Carragher* | Manchester Utd | Home 2–3 *(l)* |
| 1.10.00 | Sander Westerveld | Chelsea | Away 0–3 *(l)* |
| 9.1.02 | John Arne Riise | Southampton | Away 0–2 *(l)* |
| 4.10.03 | Sami Hyypia | Arsenal | Home 1–2 *(l)* |

*Jamie Carragher had the misfortune to score two own goals in the same game.*

## ❖ TOMMY SMITH, ALL-AMERICAN ❖

Tommy Smith, who won one cap for England in a 0–0 draw with Wales on 19 May 1971, played for Team America[†] in the 1976 USA Bicentennial Cup tournament matches against England and Brazil. At the time Tommy was playing for the Tampa Bay Rowdies.

## ❖ TRACTOR BOY ❖

John Wark, then at Ipswich Town, won the Professional Footballers' Association Player of the Year Award in 1981

[†]*Bobby Moore captained Team America to become the only player to have captained both England and a team that played England.*

# ❖ LIVERPOOL IRISH XI ❖

*Substitutes*
Jim *BEGLIN* • Kevin *SHEEDY* • Mark *KENNEDY*
Bill *LACEY* • Darren *POTTER*
*Player-Manager*
Steve *STAUNTON*

### Did You Know That?

Belfast-born Elisha Scott is the only member of this team to have played for Northern Ireland, making his international debut prior to the partition of Ireland. The legendary goalkeeper played five internationals for Ireland and a further 22 for Northern Ireland.

## ❖ THE EARLY YEARS ❖

Liverpool Football Club began life in the Lancashire League, which they won in their first season of existence, 1892–93. The club submitted an application to join the Football League and were admitted to the Second Division for 1893–94. Liverpool won the Second Division Championship that season, and so just two years after their formation the club were in the First Division, among the best England had to offer. However, at the end of their first season in the top flight, 1894–95, Liverpool were relegated to Division Two, only to bounce straight back up again as Division Two champions in 1895–96, remaining in the top flight until 1903–04.

## ❖ MOST APPEARANCES – ALL COMPETITIONS ❖

The following table lists the players who have made the most appearances for Liverpool in all competitions:

| No. | Player | Total Apps. | No. | Player | Total Apps. |
|---|---|---|---|---|---|
| 1. | Ian Callaghan | 857 | 7. | Bruce Grobbelaar | 628 |
| 2. | Ray Clemence | 665 | 8. | Alan Hansen | 620 |
| 3. | Emlyn Hughes | 665 | 9. | Chris Lawler | 549 |
| 4. | Ian Rush | 660 | 10. | Billy Liddell | 534 |
| 5. | Phil Neal | 650 | 11. | Kenny Dalglish | 515 |
| 6. | Tommy Smith | 638 | 12. | Ronnie Whelan | 493 |

## ❖ A QUESTION OF SPORT ❖

Emlyn Hughes is the only England footballer to have captained a team for a series of BBC TV's *A Question of Sport*, although Michael Owen captained a team for one programme in February 2004.

## ❖ ENGLAND'S RED WALL ❖

When England met Wales at Wembley on 19 May 1971, the entire Liverpool defence played – Emlyn Hughes, Chris Lawler, Larry Lloyd and Tommy Smith. England drew 0–0.

## ❖ RUSH RECORD ❖

Ian Rush holds the Liverpool record for scoring the most goals in all competitions in a single season. He scored 47 goals in 1983–84, including 32 in the League.

## ❖ GIVE ME FIVE! ❖

Only four players have scored five goals for Liverpool in a game:

Andy McGuigan 1901–02 ❖ John Evans 1954–55
Ian Rush 1983–84 ❖ Robbie Fowler 1993–94

## ❖ BBC SPORTS PERSONALITY OF THE YEAR ❖

Michael Owen is the only Liverpool player to have won the coveted BBC Sports Personality of the Year award. His 1998 award followed his outstanding performances for England at the World Cup finals.

### ❖ WHAT THE REDS SAID (6) ❖

"Mind, I've been here during the bad times too. One year we came second."
*Bob Paisley*

### ❖ THE SHANKLY GATES ❖

The Shankly Gates were unveiled at Anfield on 26 August 1982 to pay tribute to one of the greatest football managers ever. Bill Shankly single-handedly transformed Liverpool Football Club from a struggling Second Division side into one of the finest teams in Europe. Bill's widow, Nessie, formally unlocked the gates in a ceremony at which she was joined by Sir John W. Smith, Graeme Souness and Bob Paisley. Atop the gates are the words "You'll Never Walk Alone."

### ❖ *THIS IS YOUR LIFE* ❖

The popular TV show *This Is Your Life* has featured some famous Liverpool players and managers during its airing from 1969 to 1993[†]:

| Guest No. | Guest | Aired |
|---|---|---|
| 51 | Matt Busby | 12 May 1971 |
| 86 | Bill Shankly | 10 January 1973 |
| 209 | Bob Paisley | 28 December 1977 |
| 246 | Kevin Keegan | 14 February 1979 |
| 271 | Emlyn Hughes | 27 February 1980 |
| 329 | John Toshack | 17 February 1982 |
| 352 | Kenny Dalglish | 16 February 1983 |

### ❖ THREE THREES ❖

Jack Balmer[††] is the only player to have scored three consecutive hat-tricks for Liverpool. On 9 November 1946 Liverpool beat Portsmouth 3–0 at Anfield (one of Balmer's three goals was a penalty); on 16 November 1946 the Reds beat Derby County 4–1 at the Baseball Ground (Balmer netted all four); and on 23 November 1946 Liverpool beat Arsenal 4–2 at Anfield (Balmer scored three; Stubbins the other).

[†]*Liverpool fan and comedian Jimmy Tarbuck was the show's 359th guest on 13 April 1983.*
[††]*Balmer's consecutive hat-tricks were his only hat-tricks for the club.*

## ❖ WE ARE THE CHAMPIONS (8) ❖

In 1972–73 Liverpool won their eighth Division One title, Bill
Shankly's third and last in charge of the Reds. Liverpool began the
League campaign in red-hot form, beating Manchester City 2–0 (Hall,
Callaghan) on the opening day of the season at Anfield, then following
up with a 2–0 win over Manchester United, also at Anfield, just three
days later, thanks to goals from Toshack and Heighway. The season
was one long ding-dong battle with Arsenal, Double winners two
years earlier when they beat the Reds 2–1 (Heighway) after extra time
in the 1971 FA Cup final at Wembley. However, the crunch game was
the Reds' penultimate match of the season, when Leeds United visited
Anfield on a scorching Easter Monday. Goals from Peter Cormack and
Kevin Keegan for a 2–0 win on 23 April 1973 meant that barring a
mathematical miracle the Reds would win the Championship. In the
end Liverpool won the title race by three points.

### *Football League Division 1*
### 1972–73

|  | | P | W | D | L | F | A | W | D | L | F | A | Pts |
|---|---|---|---|---|---|---|---|---|---|---|---|---|---|
| 1. | Liverpool | 42 | 17 | 3 | 1 | 45 | 19 | 8 | 7 | 6 | 27 | 23 | 60 |
| 2. | Arsenal | 42 | 14 | 5 | 2 | 31 | 14 | 9 | 6 | 6 | 26 | 29 | 57 |
| 3. | Leeds United | 42 | 15 | 4 | 2 | 45 | 13 | 6 | 7 | 8 | 26 | 32 | 53 |
| 4. | Ipswich Town | 42 | 10 | 7 | 4 | 34 | 20 | 7 | 7 | 7 | 21 | 25 | 48 |
| 5. | Wolverhampton W. | 42 | 13 | 3 | 5 | 43 | 23 | 5 | 8 | 8 | 23 | 31 | 47 |
| 6. | West Ham United | 42 | 12 | 5 | 4 | 45 | 25 | 5 | 7 | 9 | 22 | 28 | 46 |
| 7. | Derby County | 42 | 15 | 3 | 3 | 43 | 18 | 4 | 5 | 12 | 13 | 36 | 46 |
| 8. | Tottenham Hotspur | 42 | 10 | 5 | 6 | 33 | 23 | 6 | 8 | 7 | 25 | 25 | 45 |
| 9. | Newcastle United | 42 | 12 | 6 | 3 | 35 | 19 | 4 | 7 | 10 | 25 | 32 | 45 |
| 10. | Birmingham City | 42 | 11 | 7 | 3 | 39 | 22 | 4 | 5 | 12 | 14 | 32 | 42 |
| 11. | Manchester City | 42 | 12 | 4 | 5 | 36 | 20 | 3 | 7 | 11 | 21 | 40 | 41 |
| 12. | Chelsea | 42 | 9 | 6 | 6 | 30 | 22 | 4 | 8 | 9 | 19 | 29 | 40 |
| 13. | Southampton | 42 | 8 | 11 | 2 | 26 | 17 | 3 | 7 | 11 | 21 | 35 | 40 |
| 14. | Sheffield United | 42 | 11 | 4 | 6 | 28 | 18 | 4 | 6 | 11 | 23 | 41 | 40 |
| 15. | Stoke City | 42 | 11 | 8 | 2 | 38 | 17 | 3 | 2 | 16 | 23 | 39 | 38 |
| 16. | Leicester City | 42 | 7 | 9 | 5 | 23 | 18 | 3 | 8 | 10 | 17 | 28 | 37 |
| 17. | Everton | 42 | 9 | 5 | 7 | 27 | 21 | 4 | 6 | 11 | 14 | 28 | 37 |
| 18. | Manchester United | 42 | 9 | 7 | 5 | 24 | 19 | 3 | 6 | 12 | 20 | 41 | 37 |
| 19. | Coventry City | 42 | 9 | 5 | 7 | 27 | 24 | 4 | 4 | 13 | 13 | 31 | 35 |
| 20. | Norwich City | 42 | 7 | 9 | 5 | 22 | 19 | 4 | 1 | 16 | 14 | 44 | 32 |
| 21. | Crystal Palace | 42 | 7 | 7 | 7 | 25 | 21 | 2 | 5 | 14 | 16 | 37 | 30 |
| 22. | West Bromwich Albion | 42 | 8 | 7 | 6 | 25 | 24 | 1 | 3 | 17 | 13 | 38 | 28 |

## ❖ PREMIER LEAGUE GOALS ❖

The inaugural FA Premier League season was 1992–93. Up to the end of the 2005–06 season the Reds had scored more than 800 Premiership goals. Here are some of the milestone strikes:

| Gl. | Player | Date | Venue | Opposition |
|---|---|---|---|---|
| 1 | Mark Walters | 19.8.1992 | Anfield | Sheffield United |
| 50 | Mark Walters | 17.4.1993 | Anfield | Coventry City |
| 100 | Nigel Clough | 4.1.1994 | Anfield | Manchester United |
| 150 | Robbie Fowler | 5.11.1994 | Anfield | Nottingham Forest |
| 200 | Robbie Fowler | 1.10.1995 | Old Trafford | Manchester Utd |
| 250 | Stan Collymore | 3.4.1996 | Anfield | Newcastle United |
| 300 | Stan Collymore | 19.2.1997 | Anfield | Leeds United |
| 350 | Michael Owen | 26.12.1997 | Anfield | Leeds United |
| 400 | Michael Owen | 24.10.1998 | Anfield | Nottingham Forest |
| 450 | Jamie Redknapp | 5.5.1999 | Anfield | Manchester United |
| 500 | Michael Owen | 1.4.2000 | Highfield Rd | Coventry City |
| 550 | Robbie Fowler | 3.3.2001 | Anfield | West Ham United |
| 600 | Michael Owen | 8.12.2001 | Anfield | Middlesbrough |
| 650 | Dietmar Hamann | 2.9.2002 | Anfield | Newcastle Utd |
| 700 | Michael Owen | 26.4.2003 | The Hawthorns | WBA |
| 750 | Emile Heskey | 4.4.2004 | Anfield | Blackburn Rovers |
| 800 | Milan Baros | 5.2.2005 | Anfield | Fulham |

## ❖ CHIEF EXECUTIVE SWAP ❖

In 1998 Rick Parry left his job as chief executive of the FA Premier League to take up the position of chief executive at Liverpool, of whom he is a lifelong fan. During his six years at the FA Premier League, Parry was instrumental in agreeing the ground-breaking deals with Sky TV for the screening of live matches.

## ❖ THE BIRTH OF LIVERPOOL ❖

Liverpool Football Club was founded in 1892 by John Houlding, the owner of Anfield. Prior to this, Anfield was occupied by Everton Football Club, but after a disagreement concerning the rent for the forthcoming season, 1892–93, between Houlding and the Everton board, Everton relocated to Goodison Park. Houlding now found himself with a football ground but without a team to play there. He decided to look north of the border. He signed ten Scotsmen for his new team, and on 15 March 1892 Liverpool Football Club was born.

## ❖ WE ALL LIVE IN A RED AND WHITE KOP ❖

### *(to the tune of "Yellow Submarine")*

On a Saturday afternoon
We support a team called Liverpool
And we sing until we drop
On the famous Spion Kop

We all live in a red and white Kop
A red and white Kop
A red and white Kop
We all live in a red and white Kop
A red and white Kop
A red and white Kop

*(Repeat)*

## ❖ LIVERPOOL PLAYERS IN TV ADS ❖

| | |
|---|---|
| Kevin Keegan | Brut Aftershave |
| | Dentyne Chewing Gum |
| | Sugar Puffs |
| Michael Owen | Lucozade |
| | Nationwide Building Society |
| | Walkers Crisps |
| Jamie Redknapp | Nationwide Building Society |
| | Sky TV |
| Steven Gerrard | Lucozade, Pringles |
| | JD Sports |
| | McDonalds |
| Alan Hansen | Carlsberg |
| | *The Daily Telegraph* |
| Jason McAteer | Wash & Go Shampoo |
| Nicolas Anelka | JD Sports |

## ❖ HAT-TRICK KINGS ❖

Gordon Hodgson has scored the highest number of hat-tricks for Liverpool: 17 from 1926 to 1936. Roger Hunt bagged five hat-tricks in the 1961–62 season. Only four Liverpool players: Phil Boersma, Ian Rush, Robbie Fowler and Michael Owen, have managed to score a hat-trick before the half-time whistle.

## ❖ ROBBIE FOWLER ❖

Robert "Robbie" Bernard Fowler was born on 9 April 1975 in Toxteth, Liverpool. He signed schoolboy forms with Liverpool, then became a YTS trainee with the club, before turning professional on his 17th birthday. On 22 September 1993 he made his debut for the Reds, scoring in a 3–1 away win over Fulham in the first leg of the first round of the Coca-Cola Cup, Nigel Clough and Ian Rush completing the Liverpool scoring. Two weeks later, Liverpool beat Fulham 5–0 at Anfield in the second leg with Fowler netting all five. He scored his first League hat-trick, against Southampton at Anfield on 30 October 1993, in only his fifth FA Premier League match. Overall he scored 12 times in his first 13 games for the Reds.

In November 1993 Fowler made his England Under-21 debut against San Marino and celebrated by scoring England's opener after only three minutes. At the end of that 1993–94 season, he was the Reds' leading scorer with 18 goals and in each of the following two seasons he broke the 30-goal barrier. In 1995 Robbie won his first trophy with Liverpool, the League Cup, and that year, and again in 1996, he was voted PFA Young Player of the Year. Fowler's goalscoring exploits for the Reds during the 1990s earned him iconic status among Anfield fans, who nicknamed him "God". In 1994–95 Fowler scored a hat-trick against Arsenal in only 4 minutes and 33 seconds, and on 14 December 1996 he found the net four times against Middlesbrough at Anfield to record his 100th goal for the Reds, achieving the milestone in one game fewer than his hero Ian Rush.

Robbie's career has been far from uneventful. After scoring a goal against Brann Bergen in a European Cup Winners' Cup game in March 1997, Robbie lifted his Liverpool shirt to reveal a tee-shirt in support of sacked Liverpool dockers. He was fined by UEFA for doing so but was adored on Merseyside. Ironically he won a UEFA Fair Play award later that year for insisting he had not been fouled in a game against Arsenal after the referee had awarded the Reds a penalty. In 1998 he suffered two serious injuries, which restricted him to a handful of games, and missed the 1998 World Cup Finals in France, in which his team-mate Michael Owen starred. Then in 1999 Robbie was fined £60,000 by Liverpool and the FA Premier League after he mimicked snorting cocaine off the back white line of the penalty box to celebrate a goal against Everton.

Robbie Fowler left Anfield on 30 November 2001 after 330 appearances and 171 goals for the Reds, only to return on 27 January 2006 via Leeds United and Manchester City. To date he has won 26 England caps and scored seven international goals for his country.

## ❖ 10 OUT OF 10 FOR THE REDS ❖

When Liverpool beat West Bromwich Albion 1–0 (Crouch) on 31 December 2005, it was the Reds' tenth consecutive victory in the FA Premier League during season 2005–06. Bolton Wanderers brought the Reds' winning streak to an end, when they held Liverpool 2–2 (Gerrard, Garcia) at the Reebok Stadium on 2 January 2006:

| Date | Opposition | Venue | Result | Attendance |
|------|-----------|-------|--------|-----------|
| Sat 29 Oct | West Ham United | H | 2–0 | 44,537 |
| Sat 5 Nov | Aston Villa | A | 2–0 | 42,551 |
| Sat 19 Nov | Portsmouth | H | 3–0 | 44,394 |
| Sat 26 Nov | Manchester City | A | 1–0 | 47,105 |
| Wed 30 Nov | Sunderland | A | 2–0 | 32,697 |
| Sat 3 Dec | Wigan Athletic | H | 3–0 | 44,098 |
| Sat 10 Dec | Middlesbrough | H | 2–0 | 43,510 |
| Mon 26 Dec | Newcastle United | H | 2–0 | 44,197 |
| Wed 28 Dec | Everton | A | 3–1 | 40,158 |
| Sat 31 Dec | West Bromwich Albion | H | 1–0 | 44,192 |

## ❖ KEEGAN'S CLUBS ❖

*Playing career*

| | |
|---|---|
| December 1968 to May 1971 | Scunthorpe United |
| May 1971 to May 1977 | Liverpool |
| May 1977 to July 1980 | SV Hamburg, Germany |
| July 1980 to August 1982 | Southampton |
| August 1982 to May 1984 | Newcastle United |

*Managerial career*

| | |
|---|---|
| February 1992 to January 1997 | Newcastle United |
| September 1997 to May 1998 | Fulham (Chief Operating Officer) |
| May 1998 to May 1999 | Fulham |
| May 1999 to October 2000 | England |
| June 2001 to May 2005 | Manchester City |

## ❖ THE COMEBACK OF ALL COMEBACKS? ❖

Although many Liverpool fans regard the 2005 European Champions League final comeback as the greatest in the club's history, it was not the Reds' first from three goals down. On 4 December 1909, Newcastle United led 5–2 at Anfield, but Liverpool stormed back to win 6–5. The Liverpool goalscorers were Stewart, Parkinson (2), Orr (2) and Goddard.

## ❖ MONEY MATTERS ❖

The following table charts the record transfer fee paid by Liverpool for a player:

| Player | Date | From | Fee |
|---|---|---|---|
| William Dunlop | Jan 1895 | Abercorn | £35 |
| Francis Becton | March 1895 | Preston North End | £100 |
| John Walker | April 1898 | Heart of Midlothian | £350 |
| Sam Hardy | May 1905 | Chesterfield | £500 |
| Fred Hopkin | May 1921 | Manchester United | £2,800 |
| Tom Morrison | Nov 1927 | St Mirren | £4,000 |
| Jim Smith | Sept 1929 | Ayr United | £5,500 |
| Tom Bradshaw | Jan 1930 | Bury | £8,000 |
| Albert Stubbins | Sept 1946 | Newcastle United | £12,500 |
| Kevin Lewis | June 1960 | Sheffield United | £13,000 |
| Gordon Milne | Aug 1960 | Preston North End | £16,000 |
| Ian St John | May 1961 | Motherwell | £35,000 |
| Peter Thompson | Aug 1963 | Preston North End | £40,000 |
| Emlyn Hughes | Feb 1967 | Blackpool | £65,000 |
| Tony Hateley | June 1967 | Chelsea | £96,000 |
| Alun Evans | Sept 1968 | Wolverhampton W. | £100,000 |
| John Toshack | Nov 1970 | Cardiff City | £110,000 |
| Ray Kennedy | July 1974 | Arsenal | £180,000 |
| David Johnson | Aug 1976 | Ipswich Town | £200,000 |
| Kenny Dalglish | Aug 1977 | Celtic | £440,000 |
| Craig Johnston | April 1981 | Middlesbrough | £575,000 |
| Mark Lawrenson | Aug 1981 | Brighton & Hove A. | £900,000 |
| Peter Beardsley | July 1987 | Newcastle United | £1,900,000 |
| Ian Rush | Aug 1988 | Juventus | £2,800,000 |
| Dean Saunders | July 1991 | Derby County | £2,900,000 |
| Phil Babb | Sept 1994 | Coventry City | £3,600,000 |
| Stan Collymore | July 1995 | Nottingham Forest | £8,500,000 |
| Emile Heskey | March 2000 | Leicester City | £11,000,000 |
| Djibril Cisse | July 2004 | Auxerre | £14,000,000 |

## ❖ HAT-TRICK SUB ❖

Steve Staunton is the only Liverpool player to score a hat-trick after coming on as a substitute. He replaced Ian Rush against Wigan Athletic in the second leg of the League Cup second-round tie at Anfield on 4 October 1989. The Reds won 3–0, Staunton netting all three. Wigan chose to play their home leg at Anfield.

## ❖ UP FOR THE CUP (2) ❖

In the 1974 FA Cup final at Wembley, Liverpool easily swept aside Newcastle United 3–0 to win the trophy for the second time in the club's history. Liverpool's 1973–74 road to FA Cup glory began with a disappointing 2–2 draw at Anfield with Doncaster Rovers in the third round. In the replay Liverpool won 2–0 but then in round four, the Reds could only manage a 0–0 draw with Carlisle United at Anfield before another 2–0 replay victory. In the fifth round Liverpool won 2–0 at home against Ipswich Town and then beat Bristol City 1–0 at Ashton Gate in the sixth. Leicester City were Liverpool's semi-final opponents and following a 0–0 draw at Old Trafford, Liverpool beat the Foxes 3–1 at Villa Park in their third replay of that season's competition.

### FA CUP FINAL
*4 MAY 1974, WEMBLEY*
**Liverpool** (0) 3     vs     **Newcastle United** (0) 0
Keegan (2), Heighway
*Att.* 100,000
*Liverpool:* Clemence; Smith, Lindsay, P. Thompson, Hughes; Cormack, Hall, Heighway, Callaghan; Toshack, Keegan

## ❖ PARTY POOPERS ❖

On 19 February 1910 Liverpool were Manchester United's first ever opponents at their new Old Trafford ground. Liverpool spoilt United's party by winning the game 4–3 (Goddard 2, Stewart 2) in front of a crowd of 45,000 fans. Archibald Leitch, who designed Anfield, was also the architect of Old Trafford.

## ❖ QUICK OFF THE MARK ❖

Robbie Fowler scored the fastest ever FA Premier League hat-trick when he bagged three against Arsenal at Anfield on 28 August 1994 in only 4 minutes and 33 seconds, just before the half-hour mark. Liverpool won the game 3–0.

## ❖ SUBBING THE SUBS ❖

Seven Reds have been subbed after coming on as substitutes themselves: Howard Gayle, Jimmy Carter, Dominic Matteo, Steven Gerrard, Davie Thompson, Vladimir Smicer (twice) and Nick Barmby.

## ❖ EUROPEAN GLORY NIGHTS (1) ❖

In the first leg of the 1973 UEFA Cup final, Liverpool crushed their German visitors at Anfield thanks to two goals from Kevin Keegan and a third from Larry Lloyd. Gunter Netzer and his teammates were simply overwhelmed by the Reds, who played with skill and passion in equally generous quantities. However, in the 65th minute the Reds had a scare, conceding a penalty, but Ray Clemence came to the rescue, saving Jupp Heynckes' kick. In the second leg, two weeks later, Liverpool were on the receiving end of wave after wave of attack from the Germans and went in at half-time 2–0 down, both goals scored by Heynckes. However, in the second half the home side looked like they had burnt themselves out and the Reds held on to claim a 3–2 aggregate victory.

### UEFA CUP FINAL
#### 1st LEG
*10 MAY 1973, ANFIELD, LIVERPOOL*

**Liverpool (2) 3**    vs    Borussia
Keegan (2), Lloyd      Moenchengladbach  (0) 0

*Att.* 41,168

*Liverpool:* Clemence, Lawler, Lindsay, Smith, Lloyd, Hughes, Keegan, Cormack, Toshack, Heighway (Hall), Callaghan

#### 2nd LEG
*23 MAY 1973, BORUSSIA-PARK, MOENCHENGLADBACH,*
*WEST GERMANY*

Borussia      vs    **Liverpool (0) 0**
Moenchengladbach (2) 2
Heynckes (2)

*Att.* 35,000

*Liverpool:* Clemence, Lawler, Lindsay, Smith, Lloyd, Hughes, Keegan, Cormack, Heighway (Boersma), Toshack, Callaghan

## ❖ A UNIQUE HAT-TRICK DOUBLE ❖

Sam Raybould was the first Liverpool player to score a hat-trick in both the Football League and FA Cup. On 1 March 1902 he scored three (Cox got the other) in the Reds' 4–0 win over Manchester City at Anfield in Division One, and on 10 March 1906 he scored a hat-trick in Liverpool's 3–0 win over Southampton, also at Anfield, in the FA Cup. Raybould was also the first Liverpool player to notch a hat-trick against Manchester United.

### ❖ WHAT THE REDS SAID (7) ❖

"One of my great regrets is that I got to speak to Bill Shankly only the once. After I signed for Liverpool, John Toshack took me to Shanks' house to meet him. He gave me two pieces of advice: don't overeat and don't lose your accent."
*Ally McCoist, whose lack of punctuality reached almost legendary status*

### ❖ MOVIE STAR SIGNS ❖

In 1984 John Wark left Ipswich Town and signed for Liverpool. In 1981 Wark had starred alongside Michael Caine, Bobby Moore, Pele and Sylvester Stallone in the movie *Escape to Victory*[†]. Wark played the Scottish international Arthur Hayes. Wark's fellow professionals Osvaldo Ardiles, Kazimierz Deyna, Kevin O'Callaghan, Russell Osman and Mike Summerbee also appeared in the film.

### ❖ THE PREDATOR ❖

When he was playing for Liverpool, Craig Johnston analysed the boots of his team-mates in an effort to identify how the design could be improved to enable the players to increase their control of the football. When he retired from football to care for his sister, who was ill at home in Australia at the time, he worked for Adidas on the development of the Predator, which is now the world's best-selling boot, worn by David Beckham, Zinedine Zidane and rugby player Jonny Wilkinson. In 2004 Johnston was shortlisted for the Design Museum's Designer of the Year prize for his latest football boot, the Pig, which he developed as a successor to the Predator. As well as designing football boots, Johnston has also developed the Supaskills system of measuring and improving football skills such as dribbling, heading and shooting.

### ❖ THE LONG AND SHORT OF IT ❖

Three players hold the distinction of being the club's shortest ever players: James McBride, Mervyn Jones and Robert Neil, who were all 5 feet 4 inches tall. Peter Crouch is the tallest player to have played for Liverpool at 6 feet 7 inches tall.

---

[†] *The movie was inspired by the real wartime exploits of Dynamo Kiev, who in 1942 played a German Luftwaffe XI in a series of matches in German-occupied Kiev and won them all. The Nazis took the defeats badly and murdered the entire team.*

## ❖ WE ARE THE CHAMPIONS (9) ❖

Just two years after taking over from Bill Shankly, Bob Paisley guided the Reds to their ninth Division One Championship success. Surprisingly it was a club that had never won the Division One title, Queens Park Rangers, who pushed the Reds right down to the wire in the race for the title. Indeed, on the opening day of the season QPR made their intentions known to everyone watching when they beat Liverpool 2–0 at Loftus Road. Liverpool did not manage to claim top spot in the League until they defeated the Londoners 2–0 (Toshack, Neal) at Anfield on 20 December 1975. Despite QPR winning more games during the campaign, 24 to the Reds' 23, Liverpool clinched the Championship by a single point after beating Wolverhampton Wanderers 3–1 (Keegan, Toshack, R. Kennedy) away in their last game of the season. Liverpool had now passed Arsenal's record of eight Division One titles to become "Champions of Champions".

### *Football League Division 1*
#### 1975–76

| | P | W | D | L | F | A | W | D | L | F | A | Pts |
|---|---|---|---|---|---|---|---|---|---|---|---|---|
| 1. Liverpool | 42 | 14 | 5 | 2 | 41 | 21 | 9 | 9 | 3 | 25 | 10 | 60 |
| 2. Queens Park Rangers | 42 | 17 | 4 | 0 | 42 | 13 | 7 | 7 | 7 | 25 | 20 | 59 |
| 3. Manchester United | 42 | 16 | 4 | 1 | 40 | 13 | 7 | 6 | 8 | 28 | 29 | 56 |
| 4. Derby County | 42 | 15 | 3 | 3 | 45 | 30 | 6 | 8 | 7 | 30 | 28 | 53 |
| 5. Leeds United | 42 | 1-3 | 3 | 5 | 37 | 19 | 8 | 6 | 7 | 28 | 27 | 51 |
| 6. Ipswich Town | 42 | 11 | 6 | 4 | 36 | 23 | 5 | 8 | 8 | 18 | 25 | 46 |
| 7. Leicester City | 42 | 9 | 9 | 3 | 29 | 24 | 4 | 10 | 7 | 19 | 27 | 45 |
| 8. Manchester City | 42 | 14 | 5 | 2 | 46 | 18 | 2 | 6 | 13 | 18 | 28 | 43 |
| 9. Tottenham Hotspur | 42 | 6 | 10 | 5 | 33 | 32 | 8 | 5 | 8 | 30 | 31 | 43 |
| 10. Norwich City | 42 | 10 | 5 | 6 | 33 | 26 | 6 | 5 | 10 | 25 | 32 | 42 |
| 11. Everton | 42 | 10 | 7 | 4 | 37 | 24 | 5 | 5 | 11 | 23 | 42 | 42 |
| 12. Stoke City | 42 | 8 | 5 | 8 | 25 | 24 | 7 | 6 | 8 | 23 | 26 | 41 |
| 13. Middlesbrough | 42 | 9 | 7 | 5 | 23 | 11 | 6 | 3 | 12 | 23 | 34 | 40 |
| 14. Coventry City | 42 | 6 | 9 | 6 | 22 | 22 | 7 | 5 | 9 | 25 | 35 | 40 |
| 15. Newcastle United | 42 | 11 | 4 | 6 | 51 | 26 | 4 | 5 | 12 | 20 | 36 | 39 |
| 16. Aston Villa | 42 | 11 | 8 | 2 | 32 | 17 | 0 | 9 | 12 | 19 | 42 | 39 |
| 17. Arsenal | 42 | 11 | 4 | 6 | 33 | 19 | 2 | 6 | 13 | 14 | 34 | 36 |
| 18. West Ham United | 42 | 10 | 5 | 6 | 26 | 23 | 3 | 5 | 13 | 22 | 48 | 36 |
| 19. Birmingham City | 42 | 11 | 5 | 5 | 36 | 26 | 2 | 2 | 17 | 21 | 49 | 33 |
| 20. Wolverhampton W. | 42 | 7 | 6 | 8 | 27 | 25 | 3 | 4 | 14 | 24 | 43 | 30 |
| 21. Burnley | 42 | 6 | 6 | 9 | 23 | 26 | 3 | 4 | 14 | 20 | 40 | 28 |
| 22. Sheffield United | 42 | 4 | 7 | 10 | 19 | 32 | 2 | 3 | 16 | 14 | 50 | 22 |

## ❖ LIVERPOOL ROBBED ❖

In 1892–93, their first year in existence, Liverpool won the Lancashire League Championship. On 1 September 1893, the championship trophy was stolen from a pawnbroker's shop where it was proudly on display. It was never recovered [†].

## ❖ THE £MILLION SELLERS ❖

The following players were sold by Liverpool for at least £1 million:

| Player | Date | To | Fee (£million) |
|---|---|---|---|
| Robbie Fowler | Nov 2001 | Leeds United | £11.0 |
| Stan Collymore | May 1997 | Aston Villa | £7.0 |
| Milan Baros | Aug 2005 | Aston Villa | £6.5 |
| Emile Heskey | July 2004 | Birmingham City | £6.0 |
| Dominic Matteo | Aug 2000 | Leeds United | £4.25 |
| Jason McAteer | Jan 1999 | Blackburn Rovers | £4.0 |
| Christian Ziege | Aug 2001 | Tottenham Hotspur | £4.0 |
| Sander Westerveld | Dec 2001 | Real Sociedad | £3.6 |
| Fernando Morientes | May 2006 | Valencia | £3.1 |
| Oyvind Leonhardsen | Aug 1999 | Tottenham Hotspur | £3.0 |
| Stephen Wright | Aug 2002 | Sunderland | £3.0 |
| Nick Barmby | Aug 2002 | Leeds United | £2.75 |
| John Scales | Dec 1996 | Tottenham Hotspur | £2.6 |
| Julian Dicks | Oct 1994 | West Ham United | £2.5 |
| David Thompson | Aug 2000 | Coventry City | £2.5 |
| Rigobert Song | Nov 2000 | West Ham United | £2.5 |
| Dean Saunders | Sept 1992 | Aston Villa | £2.3 |
| Alou Diarra | June 2005 | Lens | £2.0 |
| Mark Kennedy | March 1998 | Wimbledon | £1.75 |
| David James | June 1999 | Aston Villa | £1.7 |
| Sean Dundee | Aug 1999 | Vfb Stuttgart | £1.55 |
| Don Hutchison | Sept 1994 | West Ham United | £1.5 |
| Nigel Clough | Jan 1996 | Manchester City | £1.5 |
| Jean-Michel Ferri | July 1999 | Sochaux | £1.5 |
| Aboubacar Camara | Dec 2000 | West Ham United | £1.5 |
| John Aldridge | Sept 1989 | Real Sociedad | £1.1 |
| Steve Staunton | Aug 1991 | Aston Villa | £1.1 |
| Peter Beardsley | Aug 1991 | Everton | £1.0 |
| Paul Ince | July 1999 | Middlesbrough | £1.0 |

[†] *In 1895 Aston Villa won the FA Cup. Like Liverpool they allowed a local shop to place it on display. It was also stolen, from the window of a firm of football outfitters in Birmingham, and never traced.*

## ❖ GALACTICO REDS ❖

Four Liverpool players have played for Spanish giants Real Madrid:

Nicolas Anelka ❖ Steve McManaman
Fernando Morientes ❖ Michael Owen

## ❖ FIRST FA CUP FINAL ❖

Liverpool reached their first FA Cup final in 1913–14. On 25 April 1914 the Reds lost 1–0 to Burnley in the last FA Cup final to be played at the Crystal Palace ground.

## ❖ EVERTON PLAYS FOR LIVERPOOL ❖

Mark Everton Walters made his debut for the Reds in a 2–1 (Houghton, Barnes) home win over Oldham Athletic in the First Division on 17 August 1991.

## ❖ KIT MANUFACTURERS ❖

To date, Liverpool have had only three kit manufacturers:
Umbro ❖ Adidas ❖ Reebok
Adidas *(for the second time from summer of 2006)*

## ❖ THE SAINT ❖

On 2 May 1961 Bill Shankly paid Motherwell £37,500, a huge fee at the time, for the services of Ian St John. However, the money was well spent as St John went on to become a Liverpool hero, even after his playing days had ended. He made his debut for the club on 9 May 1961 against Everton in a Liverpool Senior Cup tie and scored a hat-trick. During his ten years at Anfield he made 419 appearances for the Reds, plus another five as a substitute, and scored 118 goals. His partnership with Roger Hunt in the Liverpool attack was as good as any in the history of the club. St John helped the Reds win Division Two in 1961–62, the League Championship in seasons 1963–64 and 1965–66, plus he scored the winning goal in the 2–1 extra-time win over Leeds United in the 1965 FA Cup final. When he left Anfield in August 1971, he signed for Coventry City as their assistant manager. He later found fame alongside the legendary Jimmy Greaves in the popular ITV football show *Saint and Greavsie*. Today Ian St John is a radio football commentator.

## ❖ EUROPEAN GLORY NIGHTS (2) ❖

Liverpool won their second European trophy in 1975–76 and just as in 1973, it was the UEFA Cup. The first leg at Anfield was a classic with Liverpool trailing Belgian side FC Bruges 2–0 at half-time. At half-time Bob Paisley brought on Jimmy Case for John Toshack and pushed Kevin Keegan up front. Suddenly the Reds looked more purposeful and three goals in the space of five minutes from Ray Kennedy, Case and Keegan set up an intriguing second leg. The return fixture was a dour affair as Liverpool stifled their stylish Belgian opponents for 90 minutes. In the 12th minute Raoul Lambert scored from the penalty spot to give Bruges the advantage on away goals. However, that position was wiped out with a typical Kevin Keegan strike just three minutes later. The game ended 1–1 and the Reds lifted their second UEFA Cup with a 4–3 aggregate victory.

### UEFA CUP FINAL
#### 1st LEG
*28 APRIL 1976, ANFIELD, LIVERPOOL*

**Liverpool** (2) 3    vs    FC Bruges (2) 2
Kennedy, Case, Keegan (pen)     Lambert, Cools

*Att.* 49,981

*Liverpool:* Clemence, Neal, Smith, Thompson, Kennedy, Hughes, Keegan, Fairclough, Heighway, Toshack (Case), Callaghan

#### 2nd LEG
*19 MAY 1976, JAN BREYDEL STADION, BRUGES, BELGIUM*

FC Bruges (1) 1    vs    **Liverpool** (1) 1
Lambert (pen)     Keegan

*Att.* 33,000

*Liverpool:* Clemence, Neal, Smith, Thompson, Kennedy, Hughes, Keegan, Case, Heighway, Toshack (Fairclough), Callaghan

## ❖ FIRST HAT-TRICK SCORER ❖

John Miller recorded the Reds' first hat-trick when he netted three times in Liverpool's first ever FA Cup game, a 4–0 (Wylie also scored) away win at Nantwich on 15 October 1892 in the first qualifying round of the 1892–93 competition. Seven days later Miller scored another hat-trick in Liverpool's 5–0 away win over Higher Walton in the Lancashire League, Wyllie (2) again joining him on the scoresheet.

## ❖ RESERVE ATTRACTION ❖

Albert Stubbins was a prolific goalscorer and very popular among the Liverpool fans. In 1948 he became involved in a contract dispute with the club that kept him out of action for three months. When the dispute was finally settled, he was given a run-out in the Reserves to gain match fitness and 20,000 fans turned up at Anfield to watch him.

## ❖ BIRTHPLACE OF THE REDS ❖

The Sandon Hotel is a large Victorian pub that used to be owned by the founder of Liverpool Football Club, John Houlding[†]. When the club was formed in 1892, the players used the pub as a changing room. The Sandon still stands today, more than a century later, on Oakfield Road just 50 yards from the Kop's flagpole corner. It is a popular meeting point and a hive of activity on match days.

## ❖ BIRTHDAY GOALS ❖

Seventeen Liverpool players have celebrated a birthday with a goal:

| Player | Date | Age | Opponent | Score | Comp |
|---|---|---|---|---|---|
| Tom Bromilow | 07.10.1922 | 28 | Everton | 5–1 | League |
| Gordon Hodgson (2) | 16.04.1927 | 23 | Bury | 2–2 | League |
| Robert Done | 27.04.1929 | 25 | Blackburn Rovers | 1–2 | League |
| Adolf Hanson | 27.02.1937 | 25 | Brentford | 2–2 | League |
| Berry Nieuwenhuys | 05.11.1938 | 27 | Portsmouth | 1–1 | League |
| Billy Liddell | 10.01.1948 | 26 | Nottingham Forest | 4–1 | FA Cup |
| John Evans | 28.08.1954 | 25 | Derby County | 2–3 | League |
| Jimmy Melia | 01.11.1958 | 21 | Stoke City | 2–0 | League |
| Steve Heighway | 25.11.1972 | 25 | Tottenham Hotspur | 2–1 | League |
| Phil Thompson | 21.01.1978 | 24 | Birmingham City | 2–3 | League |
| Terry McDermott | 08.12.1979 | 28 | Aston Villa | 3–1 | League |
| Craig Johnston | 08.12.1981 | 21 | Arsenal | 3–0 | Lge Cup |
| Terry McDermott | 08.12.1981 | 30 | Arsenal | 3–0 | Lge Cup |
| Ronnie Whelan (2) | 25.09.1982 | 21 | Southampton | 5–0 | League |
| Phil Neal | 20.02.1985 | 34 | York City | 7–0 | FA Cup |
| Steve McManaman | 11.02.1992 | 20 | Bristol Rovers | 2–1 | FA Cup |
| David Burrows | 25.10.1992 | 24 | Norwich City | 4–1 | League |
| Robbie Fowler | 09.04.2006 | 31 | Bolton Wanderers | 1–0 | League |

[†]*When Everton moved to Anfield in 1884, John Houlding was their chairman and he ran their affairs from an office upstairs at the Sandon Hotel.*

## ❖ LIVERPOOL'S EUROPEAN XI ❖

**1**
Pepe
*REINA*
*(SPAIN)*

**2**
Markus
*BABBEL*
*(GERMANY)*

**4**
Sami
*HYYPIA*
*(FINLAND)*
*(captain)*

**5**
Stephane
*HENCHOZ*
*(SWITZERLAND)*

**3**
John Arne
*RIISE*
*(NORWAY)*

**7**
Luis
*GARCIA*
*(SPAIN)*

**6**
Jan
*MOLBY*
*(DENMARK)*

**8**
Xabi
*ALONSO*
*(SPAIN)*

**9**
Karl-Heinz
*RIEDLE*
*(GERMANY)*

**10**
Jari
*LITMANEN*
*(FINLAND)*

**11**
Patrik
*BERGER*
*(CZECH REPUBLIC)*

### Substitutes
Sander *WESTERVELD* (HOLLAND) • Stig-Inge *BJORNEBYE* (NORWAY)
Igor *BISCAN* (CROATIA) • Vladimir *SMICER* (CZECH REPUBLIC)
Fernando *MORIENTES* (SPAIN)
### Manager
Rafael *BENITEZ* (SPAIN)

### *Did You Know That?*
Xabi Alonso's father, Miguel Angel "Periko" Alonso, played for FC Barcelona and won two La Liga Championship winners' medals with Real Sociedad, from whom Liverpool bought Xabi.

## ❖ OLYMPIC GOLD MEDALLISTS ❖

Two Liverpool players have won Olympic gold medals. Arthur Berry was a member of the successful Great Britain football side that claimed gold at both the 1908 (London) and 1912 (Stockholm) Olympic Games. Berry, whose father, Edwin, was Liverpool chairman from 1904 to 1909, made only four appearances for the Reds in two spells at Anfield, and at the end of the 1912–13 season the Oxford University graduate gave up football to become a barrister. Joe Dines was the second Liverpool player to win an Olympic gold medal. Dines, who made only one appearance for the Reds, against Chelsea on 9 September 1912, played alongside Berry at the 1912 games.

## ❖ WHAT THE REDS SAID (8) ❖

"It's there to remind our lads who they're playing for, and to remind the opposition who they're playing against."
***Bill Shankly***, *discussing the "This is Anfield" plaque in the players' tunnel*

## ❖ PENALTY KINGS ❖

The following table lists the first 15 penalties scored by Liverpool in the FA Premier League:

| Date | Player | Team | Venue | Score |
|------|--------|------|-------|-------|
| 25.8.1992 | Jan Molby | Ipswich Town | Away | 2–2 *(d)* |
| 29.8.1992 | Jan Molby | Leeds United | Away | 2–2 *(d)* |
| 26.9.1992 | Jan Molby | Wimbledon | Home | 2–3 *(l)* |
| 25.10.1992 | Mark Walters | Norwich City | Home | 4–1 *(w)* |
| 31.1.1993 | John Barnes | Arsenal | Away | 1–0 *(w)* |
| 17.4.1993 | Mark Walters | Coventry City | Home | 4–0 *(w)* |
| 21.4.1993 | Mark Walters | Leeds United | Home | 2–0 *(w)* |
| 8.5.1993 | Mark Walters | Tottenham Hotspur | Home | 6–2 *(w)* |
| 28.8.1993 | Jan Molby | Leeds United | Home | 2–0 *(w)* |
| 8.12.1993 | Jan Molby | Queens Park Rangers | Home | 3–2 *(w)* |
| 18.12.1993 | Robbie Fowler | Tottenham Hotspur | Away | 3–3 *(d)* |
| 14.2.1994 | Julian Dicks | Southampton | Away | 2–4 *(l)* |
| 9.4.1994 | Julian Dicks | Ipswich | Home | 1–0 *(w)* |
| 20.8.1994 | Jan Molby | Crystal Palace | Away | 6–1 *(w)* |
| 26.11.1994 | Robbie Fowler | Tottenham Hotspur | Home | 1–1 *(d)* |

## ❖ LIVERPOOL'S SHEPHERDS ❖

Liverpool signed Bill Shepherd from Elm Park in December 1945, and he played 57 games for the Reds at full-back without scoring. Bill's brothers, Arthur and Joe, also played for Liverpool. Arthur played ten games for the Reds during World War II, scoring eleven goals, including six in one game.

## ❖ LAST GOAL STANDING ❖

Julian Dicks has the honour of being the last Liverpool player to score in front of the standing Kop. On 9 April 1994, Dicks converted a penalty in Liverpool's 1–0 FA Premier League win over Ipswich Town. When the new Kop was opened, on 25 August 1928, it was the largest covered terrace in Europe.

# ❖ WE ARE THE CHAMPIONS (10) ❖

Liverpool were crowned Division One champions for the tenth time in the club's history in 1976–77, claiming their first back-to-back Championship successes since 1922–23. Bob Paisley had built a irresistible force from the winning side Shanks had left behind in 1974. In his first three seasons in charge, Paisley guided Liverpool to two Division One Championships, one UEFA Cup and the coveted European Cup. Liverpool's main adversaries in 1976–77 came from Manchester, but this time from the blue half – Manchester City. In the end Liverpool needed just a single point from their last two games to clinch the title. In their last home game Liverpool drew 0–0 with West Ham United to win the Championship in the game that marked Kevin Keegan's Anfield farewell before he joined SV Hamburg in Germany. Despite losing 2–1 (Johnson) away to Bristol City on the final day of the season, Liverpool finished the campaign one point ahead of Manchester City.

### *Football League Division 1*
#### 1976–77

| | P | W | D | L | F | A | W | D | L | F | A | Pts |
|---|---|---|---|---|---|---|---|---|---|---|---|---|
| 1. Liverpool | 42 | 18 | 3 | 0 | 47 | 11 | 5 | 8 | 8 | 15 | 22 | 57 |
| 2. Manchester City | 42 | 15 | 5 | 1 | 38 | 13 | 6 | 9 | 6 | 22 | 21 | 56 |
| 3. Ipswich Town | 42 | 15 | 4 | 2 | 41 | 11 | 7 | 4 | 10 | 25 | 28 | 52 |
| 4. Aston Villa | 42 | 17 | 3 | 1 | 55 | 17 | 5 | 4 | 12 | 21 | 33 | 51 |
| 5. Newcastle United | 42 | 14 | 6 | 1 | 40 | 15 | 4 | 7 | 10 | 24 | 34 | 49 |
| 6. Manchester United | 42 | 12 | 6 | 3 | 41 | 22 | 6 | 5 | 10 | 30 | 40 | 47 |
| 7. West Bromwich Albion | 42 | 10 | 6 | 5 | 38 | 22 | 6 | 7 | 8 | 24 | 34 | 45 |
| 8. Arsenal | 42 | 11 | 6 | 4 | 37 | 20 | 5 | 5 | 11 | 27 | 39 | 43 |
| 9. Everton | 42 | 9 | 7 | 5 | 35 | 24 | 5 | 7 | 9 | 27 | 40 | 42 |
| 10. Leeds United | 42 | 8 | 8 | 5 | 28 | 26 | 7 | 4 | 10 | 20 | 25 | 42 |
| 11. Leicester City | 42 | 8 | 9 | 4 | 30 | 28 | 4 | 9 | 8 | 17 | 32 | 42 |
| 12. Middlesbrough | 42 | 11 | 6 | 4 | 25 | 14 | 3 | 7 | 11 | 15 | 31 | 41 |
| 13. Birmingham City | 42 | 10 | 6 | 5 | 38 | 25 | 3 | 6 | 12 | 25 | 36 | 38 |
| 14. Queens Park Rangers | 42 | 10 | 7 | 4 | 31 | 21 | 3 | 5 | 13 | 16 | 31 | 38 |
| 15. Derby County | 42 | 9 | 9 | 3 | 36 | 18 | 0 | 10 | 11 | 14 | 37 | 37 |
| 16. Norwich City | 42 | 12 | 4 | 5 | 30 | 23 | 2 | 5 | 14 | 17 | 41 | 37 |
| 17. West Ham United | 42 | 9 | 6 | 6 | 28 | 23 | 2 | 8 | 11 | 18 | 42 | 36 |
| 18. Bristol City | 42 | 8 | 7 | 6 | 25 | 19 | 3 | 6 | 12 | 13 | 29 | 35 |
| 19. Coventry City | 42 | 7 | 9 | 5 | 34 | 26 | 3 | 6 | 12 | 14 | 33 | 35 |
| 20. Sunderland | 42 | 9 | 5 | 7 | 29 | 16 | 2 | 7 | 12 | 17 | 38 | 34 |
| 21. Stoke City | 42 | 9 | 8 | 4 | 21 | 16 | 1 | 6 | 14 | 7 | 35 | 34 |
| 22. Tottenham Hotspur | 42 | 9 | 7 | 5 | 26 | 20 | 3 | 2 | 16 | 22 | 52 | 33 |

### ❖ "JUDAS" SIGNS FOR THE REDS ❖

Prior to the start of the 2000–01 season, Nick Barmby became the first Everton player in more than 40 years to move across Stanley Park, when he joined the Reds in a £6 million transfer deal. At the time Barmby claimed he loved Liverpool more than Everton, which angered the Blues' fans. On 29 October 2000 Barmby ran out at Anfield to cries of "Judas" from the Everton fans. Barmby silenced the Blues, scoring in a 3–1 win for Liverpool; Heskey and Berger added the other two. In August 2002 Barmby was sold for £2.75 million to Leeds United.

### ❖ LIVERPOOL'S FIRST SUBSTITUTE ❖

The Reds' first substitute to replace a team-mate during a game was Geoff Strong, who replaced Chris Lawler against West Ham United in a First Division game at Anfield on 15 September 1965. The Reds were 1–0 down prior to Strong coming on. He made an impact, scoring the equalizing goal in a 1–1 draw in front of 44,397 fans. Strong played 201 games for the Reds, scoring 33 times.

### ❖ FATHER AND SON ❖

In May 1948 Roy Saunders signed for Liverpool as an amateur from Hull City. Roy played 144 games for the Reds, scoring once, before he was transferred to Swansea Town in March 1959. Thirty-two years later Liverpool signed Roy's son, Dean[†], from Derby County for £2.9 million. Dean made 61 appearances before he was sold to Aston Villa in September 1992 for £ 2.3 million.

### ❖ FIRST ENGLAND INTERNATIONAL ❖

On 25 March 1895, Liverpool signed Francis "Frank" Becton for £100 from Preston North End, and the inside-forward managed a goal every other game, scoring 37 times in 74 appearances for the Reds. Becton helped Liverpool to the Second Division Championship in 1895–96 before leaving for Sheffield United in 1898. During his career at Anfield, he also won one England cap (against Wales on 29 March 1897), making him Liverpool's first England international. Becton died in 1909 from tuberculosis, aged just 36.

---

[†]*Dean Saunders scored a record four goals for Liverpool in a European game when the Reds beat Kuusysi Lahti 6–1 in the first leg of a UEFA Cup first round tie at Anfield on 18 September 1991.*

## ❖ EUROPEAN GLORY NIGHTS (3) ❖

Ever since Liverpool first entered European competition in 1964, the club and the fans had dreamed that one day they would win the top prize, the European Cup. In 1976–77 the dream became a reality when Liverpool beat Borussia Moenchengladbach in the final in the Stadio Olimpico, Rome, on 25 May 1977. Goals from Terry McDermott, Tommy Smith and a Phil Neal penalty were enough to see off the Germans in a 3–1 victory. On their way to the final, Liverpool beat Crusaders in the first round 7–0 on aggregate, defeated Trabzonspor 3–1 in Round Two, squeezed past Saint Etienne 3–2 in the third round and beat FC Zurich home and away in the semi-finals for a comfortable 6–1 aggregate victory.

### EUROPEAN CUP FINAL
*25 MAY 1977, STADIO OLIMPICO, ROME*

**Liverpool** (1) **3**    vs    Borussia
McDermott, Smith,        Moenchengladbach (0) 1
Neal (pen)        Simonsen

*Att.* 52,000

*Liverpool:* Clemence; Neal, Jones, Smith, Hughes; Case, Kennedy, Callaghan, McDermott; Keegan, Heighway

## ❖ UNITED LEGEND WAS A LIVERPOOL RED ❖

The most famous Manchester United manager, Sir Matt Busby, played for Liverpool. Liverpool signed Busby from Manchester City on 11 March 1936 in a deal worth £8,000. A fine left-half, Busby made 125 appearances for the Reds, scoring three goals. After World War II, Liverpool offered Busby a job on the Anfield coaching staff, but while he was contemplating the proposal, Manchester United offered him their vacant manager's job and he accepted.

## ❖ THE BOOT ROOM ❖

The Boot Room at Anfield was one of the most famous locations in football. It was where Liverpool plotted their years of success and was the brainchild of Bill Shankly. Many opposing managers were invited to the Boot Room after a game for a drink and chat, and legend has it that it was during these little get-togethers that the Liverpool backroom staff used to try and gain information on opposition teams for future use. Soon after Graeme Souness arrived as Liverpool manager in 1993 it was demolished.

## ❖ THE £MILLION MEN ❖

In July 1987 Peter Beardsley became the first player to cost Liverpool £1 million or more, when the club paid Newcastle United £1.9 million for his services, at the time a record fee between two British clubs. Since then Liverpool have splashed out seven- and eight-figure sums on the following players:

| Player | Date | From | Fee (£million) |
|---|---|---|---|
| Djibril Cisse | July 2004 | Auxerre | £14 |
| Emile Heskey | March 2000 | Leicester City | £11 |
| Xabi Alonso | August 2004 | Real Sociedad | £10.75 |
| El Hadji Diouf | July 2002 | Lens | £10 |
| Stan Collymore | July 1995 | Nottingham Forest | £8.5 |
| Dietmar Hamann | July 1999 | Newcastle United | £8 |
| Peter Crouch | July 2005 | Southampton | £7 |
| Jose Reina | July 2005 | Villareal | £6 |
| Sanz Luis Garcia | August 2004 | Barcelona | £6 |
| Nick Barmby | July 2000 | Everton | £6 |
| Daniel Agger | January 2006 | Brondby | £5.8 |
| Fernando Morientes | January 2005 | Real Madrid | £5.5 |
| Christian Ziege | August 2000 | Middlesbrough | £5.5 |
| Igor Biscan | December 2000 | Croatia Zagreb | £5.5 |
| Mohamed Sissoko | July 2005 | Valencia | £5 |
| Jason McAteer | September 1995 | Bolton Wanderers | £4.5 |
| Paul Ince | July 1997 | Inter Milan | £4.2 |
| Oyvind Leonhardsen | June 1997 | Wimbledon | £4 |
| Sander Westerveld | June 1999 | Vitesse Arnhem | £4 |
| Vladimir Smicer | July 1999 | Lens | £3.75 |
| Phil Babb | September 1994 | Coventry City | £3.6 |
| Vegard Heggem | July 1998 | Rosenborg | £3.5 |
| Stephane Henchoz | July 1999 | Blackburn Rovers | £3.5 |

| | | | |
|---|---|---|---|
| Patrik Berger | August 1996 | Borussia Dortmund | £3.25 |
| Bernard Diomede | June 2000 | Auxerre | £3 |
| John Scales | September 1994 | Wimbledon | £3 |
| Dean Saunders | July 1991 | Derby County | £2.9 |
| Ian Rush | August 1988 | Juventus | £2.8 |
| Aboubacar Camara | June 1999 | Marseille | £2.8 |
| Nigel Clough | June 1993 | Nottingham Forest | £2.75 |
| Rigobert Song | January 1999 | Salernitana | £2.6 |
| Sami Hyypia | July 1999 | Willem II Tilburg | £2.6 |
| Neil Ruddock | July 1993 | Tottenham Hotspur | £2.5 |
| Paul Stewart | July 1992 | Tottenham Hotspur | £2.3 |
| Mark Wright | July 1991 | Derby County | £2.2 |
| Josemi | July 2004 | Malaga | £2 |
| Sean Dundee | June 1998 | Karlsruhe | £2 |
| Karl-Heinz Riedle | July 1997 | Borussia Dortmund | £1.8 |
| Michael Thomas | December 1991 | Arsenal | £1.5 |
| Julian Dicks | September 1993 | West Ham United | £1.5 |
| Mark Kennedy | March 1995 | Millwall | £1.5 |
| Danny Murphy | July 1997 | Crewe Alexandra | £1.5 |
| Jen-Michel Ferri | December 1998 | Istanbulspor | £1.5 |
| Mark Walters | August 1991 | Rangers | £1.2 |
| Ronny Rosenthal | June 1990 | Standard Liege | £1 |
| David James | June 1992 | Watford | £1 |
| Brad Friedel | December 1997 | Columbus Crew | £1 |
| Daniel Sjolund | November 2000 | West Ham United | £1 |

## ❖ ALAN HANSEN ❖

Alan Hansen was born on 13 June 1955 in Sauchie, Scotland. In 1973 he joined his brother John at Partick Thistle and played more than 100 games for "The Jags", impressing many teams north and south of the border with his calm, cool, assured displays in defence. In May 1977 he signed for Liverpool for £100,000.

On 24 September 1977, he made his Liverpool debut in the 1–0 (McDermott) Division One win over Derby County at Anfield. Hansen was put into the first team sporadically during the 1977–78 season, making only 18 League appearances as the Reds lost the League Championship and the League Cup final to the emerging force in English football, Nottingham Forest, but managed to retain the European Cup. In 1978–79 Hansen established himself as a regular in the heart of the Liverpool defence and helped the Reds regain the First Division Championship. He also made his full international debut for Scotland.

In 1979–80 Hansen won his second League Championship winners' medal with Liverpool, and 1980–81 ended with a League Cup winners' medal when he scored the winner against West Ham United at Villa Park in the replay of the final. Hansen also collected a European Cup winners' medal in 1981 following the Reds' 1–0 (A. Kennedy) victory over Real Madrid in the final in Paris. A fourth Championship winners' medal followed in 1981–82, and at the end of the season he travelled to Spain with Scotland for the 1982 World Cup Finals. He won another League Cup winners medal in 1984, this time after beating Merseyside rivals Everton The first game, at Wembley, ended 0–0, but Liverpool won the replay 1–0 (Souness).

Hansen's proudest moment came in 1986, when as captain he lifted the FA Cup at Wembley to add to the 1985–86 League Championship, making Liverpool only the third team to win the Double in the twentieth century. Alan retired in 1990 after 616 appearances and 14 goals for the Reds. He won eight League Championships, two FA Cups, three League Cups, five FA Charity Shields and three European Cups with Liverpool. Since retiring Alan has been a regular on the BBC's *Match of the Day* programme, a role, he noted, which has seen him stopped more in the street than he ever was as a player.

## ❖ CALL THE DOC ❖

During his Liverpool days David Johnson was nicknamed "Doc" by his team-mates because he had a habit of carrying a bag that contained just about every type of cream and pill imaginable.

## ❖ MEDALLION MAN ❖

Not only is Kenny Dalglish the only player to have won all three domestic competitions in both England and Scotland, he was also the first to player score 100 goals in both English and Scottish Leagues. These are Kenny's major medals, won as a player or manager:

### The Player
*Celtic*
Scottish Championship winner
1971–72, 1972–73, 1973–74, 1976–77
Scottish Cup winner
1971–72, 1973–74, 1974–75, 1976–77
Scottish League Cup winner 1974–75

*Liverpool*
Division One Championship winner
1978–79, 1979–80, 1981–82, 1982–83, 1983–84, 1985–86, 1987–88
FA Cup winner 1986 *(as player-manager)*
League Cup winner
1980–81, 1981–82, 1982–83, 1983–84
European Cup winner
1977–78, 1980–81, 1983–84
European Super Cup winner 1977

### The Manager
*Liverpool*
Division One Championship winner
1985–86, 1987–88, 1989–90
FA Cup winner 1986, 1989

*Blackburn Rovers*
FA Premier League winner 1994–95

*Celtic (caretaker manager)*
Scottish League Cup winner 2000

### Awards
PFA Players' Player of the Year 1983
Football Writers' Association Player of the Year 1979, 1983
Member of the Scotland Football Hall of Fame
Member of the FIFA 100
Freedom of the City of Glasgow 1986

## ❖ EUROPEAN GLORY NIGHTS (4) ❖

In 1977–78, Liverpool retained the European Cup despite losing their talisman, Kevin Keegan, to SV Hamburg in the summer. However, "The King Is Dead, Long Live The King" was the cry from the Liverpool fans when a certain Kenny Dalglish arrived at Anfield at the beginning of the season. Dalglish spearheaded the Liverpool attack throughout the defence of the trophy as Liverpool cruised through the competition. Following a first-round bye, Liverpool beat Dynamo Dresden 6–3 on aggregate in Round Two, SL Benfica 6–2 in the third round and then were paired in the semi-finals with the team they had beaten in the final the previous May – Borussia Moenchengladbach. Liverpool lost the first leg 2–1 in Germany but won 3–0 at Anfield in the return leg. In the final, played at Wembley Stadium, Liverpool beat FC Bruges 1–0 thanks to a Dalglish goal in the 65th minute.

### EUROPEAN CUP FINAL
*10 MAY 1978, WEMBLEY STADIUM*
**Liverpool** (0) 1     vs     FC Bruges (0) 0
Dalglish 65
*Att.* 92,000
*Liverpool:* Clemence; Neal, Thompson, Hansen, Hughes; McDermott, Kennedy, Souness; Case (Heighway), Fairclough, Dalglish

## ❖ WHAT THE REDS SAID (9) ❖

"If you think this club is in crisis, you've never been to some of the places I have."
**David Speedie**, *putting some perspective on a dip in Liverpool's fortunes*

## ❖ SHIRT SPONSORS ❖

Four companies that have sponsored the Liverpool shirt:

Hitachi ❖ Crown Paints ❖ Candy ❖ Carlsberg

## ❖ THE CENTENARY STAND ❖

In 1992 Liverpool celebrated their centenary. In September of that year they officially opened the Centenary Stand, which was built on the site of the old Kemlyn Road Stand.

## ❖ BRAVEHEART ❖

During the 1965 FA Cup final Liverpool's Gerry Byrne broke his collarbone after just three minutes' play and because substitutes were not permitted at this time he bravely carried on. Liverpool went on to lift the Cup that day, beating Leeds United 2–1 (Hunt, St John) after extra time. Byrne joined Liverpool, his home-town club, in 1955 and went on to make 273 appearances for the Reds before retiring in 1969 because of injury. He also had a brief spell on the coaching staff at Anfield.

## ❖ A CENTURY OF HAT-TRICKS ❖

On 6 March 1948 Albert Stubbins recorded the Reds' 100th competitive hat-trick when he scored all four goals in a 4–0 Division One win over Huddersfield Town at Anfield.

## ❖ EIGHT-GOAL CUP THRILLER ❖

On Saturday 7 January 2006 Liverpool travelled to Kenilworth Road to play Championship club Luton Town in the FA Cup third round. By the hour mark, the Reds were 3–1 down and facing a second successive early Cup exit, following the defeat by Burnley at the same stage of the competition the previous season. However, Liverpool staged a remarkable comeback to win 5–3, the pick of the goals coming from Xabi Alonso[†], who scored with a 30-yard effort to level the game at 3–3. Then, with his side trailing 4–3, Luton goalkeeper Beresford went forward for a stoppage-time corner. The ball broke to Alonso who, despite screams from Gerrard for a pass, fired the ball all of 60 yards from inside his own half into the back of the Hatters' net. Gerrard and Sinama-Pongolle (2) scored the Reds' other three goals.

## ❖ A FORGOTTEN MAN ❖

Liverpool's reserve goalkeeper in the 1977 European Cup final win in Rome, Peter McDonnell was signed from Bury in 1974 and moved on to Oldham Athletic in 1978 without managing a senior outing for the Reds.

[†]Liverpool fan Adrian Hayward placed a bet at the beginning of the 2005–06 season that Xabi Alonso would score a goal from his own half during the season. He staked £200 at 125–1, and when Alonso scored Liverpool's fifth goal against Luton, the Red was in the black to the tune of £25,000. Hayward placed the bet after noticing that Alonso had tried several long-range efforts at goal the previous season.

## ❖ WE ARE THE CHAMPIONS (11) ❖

In 1978–79 Liverpool prevented Brian Clough's Nottingham Forest from retaining their Division One Championship title in a season that saw the Midlanders become the third English club to lift the European Cup. During the season Liverpool could not stop scoring goals, hitting 85 in the League at an average of better than two per game, including a 7–0 (Dalglish 2, R. Kennedy, Johnson 2, Neal, McDermott) hammering of Tottenham Hotspur and a 6–0 (Dalglish 2, Johnson 2, A. Kennedy, R. Kennedy) thrashing of Norwich City, both at Anfield. Amazingly the Reds conceded just 16 goals, with only QPR, West Bromwich, Leeds and Everton finding the net at Anfield. Although Forest pushed Liverpool hard all season, the Reds' firepower was just too much for the opposition and Liverpool claimed their eleventh Division One title, their fourth of the decade. Emlyn Hughes left the Reds at the end of the season for Wolves.

### *Football League Division 1*
### 1978–79

| | P | W | D | L | F | A | W | D | L | F | A | Pts |
|---|---|---|---|---|---|---|---|---|---|---|---|---|
| 1. **Liverpool** | 42 | 19 | 2 | 0 | 51 | 4 | 11 | 6 | 4 | 34 | 12 | 68 |
| 2. Nottingham Forest | 42 | 11 | 10 | 0 | 34 | 10 | 10 | 8 | 3 | 27 | 16 | 60 |
| 3. West Bromwich Albion | 42 | 13 | 5 | 3 | 38 | 15 | 11 | 6 | 4 | 34 | 20 | 59 |
| 4. Everton | 42 | 12 | 7 | 2 | 32 | 17 | 5 | 10 | 6 | 20 | 23 | 51 |
| 5. Leeds United | 42 | 11 | 4 | 6 | 41 | 25 | 7 | 10 | 4 | 29 | 27 | 50 |
| 6. Ipswich Town | 42 | 11 | 4 | 6 | 34 | 21 | 9 | 5 | 7 | 29 | 28 | 49 |
| 7. Arsenal | 42 | 11 | 8 | 2 | 37 | 18 | 6 | 6 | 9 | 24 | 30 | 48 |
| 8. Aston Villa | 42 | 8 | 9 | 4 | 37 | 26 | 7 | 7 | 7 | 22 | 23 | 46 |
| 9. Manchester United | 42 | 9 | 7 | 5 | 29 | 25 | 6 | 8 | 7 | 31 | 38 | 45 |
| 10. Coventry City | 42 | 11 | 7 | 3 | 41 | 29 | 3 | 9 | 9 | 17 | 39 | 44 |
| 11. Tottenham Hotspur | 42 | 7 | 8 | 6 | 19 | 25 | 6 | 7 | 8 | 29 | 36 | 41 |
| 12. Middlesbrough | 42 | 10 | 5 | 6 | 33 | 21 | 5 | 5 | 11 | 24 | 29 | 40 |
| 13. Bristol City | 42 | 11 | 6 | 4 | 34 | 19 | 4 | 4 | 13 | 13 | 32 | 40 |
| 14. Southampton | 42 | 9 | 10 | 2 | 35 | 20 | 3 | 6 | 12 | 12 | 33 | 40 |
| 15. Manchester City | 42 | 9 | 5 | 7 | 34 | 28 | 4 | 8 | 9 | 24 | 28 | 39 |
| 16. Norwich City | 42 | 7 | 10 | 4 | 29 | 19 | 0 | 13 | 8 | 22 | 38 | 37 |
| 17. Bolton Wanderers | 42 | 10 | 5 | 6 | 36 | 28 | 2 | 6 | 13 | 18 | 47 | 35 |
| 18. Wolverhampton W. | 42 | 10 | 4 | 7 | 26 | 26 | 3 | 4 | 14 | 18 | 42 | 34 |
| 19. Derby County | 42 | 8 | 5 | 8 | 25 | 25 | 2 | 6 | 13 | 19 | 46 | 31 |
| 20. Queens Park Rangers | 42 | 4 | 9 | 8 | 24 | 33 | 2 | 4 | 15 | 21 | 40 | 25 |
| 21. Birmingham City | 42 | 5 | 9 | 7 | 24 | 25 | 1 | 1 | 19 | 13 | 39 | 22 |
| 22. Chelsea | 42 | 3 | 5 | 13 | 23 | 42 | 2 | 5 | 14 | 21 | 50 | 20 |

## ❖ MONEY BAGS ❖

On 16 February 2006 Real Madrid were officially proclaimed the richest football club in the world based on revenues from the 2004–05 season. Real Madrid deposed the perennial "money bags", Manchester United, who had ruled the rich list for the previous eight years. The Deloitte table does not take account of the cost of transfer fees or players' wages and is focused solely on each club's day-to-day income from football business such as corporate hospitality, merchandising, television revenue and match ticket sales. Liverpool, thanks to their 2005 UEFA Champions League success, moved up two places in the table listing the top 20 richest clubs in the world. (Previous season's figures in brackets):

| | | | |
|---|---|---|---|
| 1 | (2) | Real Madrid | £186.2m |
| 2 | (1) | Manchester United | £166.4m |
| 3 | (3) | AC Milan | £158m |
| 4 | (5) | Juventus | £154.9m |
| 5 | (4) | Chelsea | £149.1m |
| 6 | (7) | Barcelona | £140.4m |
| 7 | (9) | Bayern Munich | £128m |
| 8 | (10) | Liverpool | £122.4m |
| 9 | (8) | Inter Milan | £119.7m |
| 10 | (6) | Arsenal | £115.7m |
| 11 | (12) | Roma | £89m |
| 12 | (11) | Newcastle United | £87.1m |
| 13 | (14) | Tottenham Hotspur | £70.6m |
| 14 | (17) | Schalke | £65.8m |
| 15 | (-) | Lyon | £62.7m |
| 16 | (13) | Glasgow Celtic | £62.6m |
| 17 | (16) | Manchester City | £60.9m |
| 18 | (-) | Everton | £60m |
| 19 | (-) | Valencia | £57.2m |
| 20 | (15) | SS Lazio | £56.1m |

*Source: Deloitte*

## ❖ OCEANIA FOOTBALLER OF THE YEAR ❖

The Oceania Footballer of the Year award is chosen by a forum of southern hemisphere journalists and is presented to the best footballer from the Oceania region. Harry Kewell (Australia) is the only Liverpool player to have won the award, winning it in 2003, having also won it in 1999 when he was at Leeds United.

### ❖ SUPERMAC ❖

Andy McGuigan made only 35 appearances for Liverpool over two seasons, but he was the first player to score five goals in a single game for the Reds. On 4 January 1902, he netted five times in a 7–0 First Division win over Stoke City at Anfield, Sam Raybould scoring the other two. McGuigan had also been a member of Liverpool's first Division One Championship winning side the previous season. McGuigan joined Liverpool from Hibernian, and went from Anfield to Middlesbrough, Accrington Stanley and Exeter before returning to help coach the Reds to two League titles in the early 1920s.

### ❖ CAN I HAVE KENNY'S SHIRT PLEASE? ❖

When Jari Litmanen arrived at Liverpool he asked if he could wear the number 7 shirt worn so famously for the club by a boyhood idol of his, Kenny Dalglish. When he was politely told it was taken, he asked for any shirt with the number 7 on it. He settled for number 37!

### ❖ WAR HERO ❖

Liverpool player Len Carney won the Military Cross during World War II. As a player, he made six appearances for the Reds, scoring the only goal of the game on 31 August 1946 when Liverpool beat Sheffield United at Bramall Lane in the opening match of their 1946–47 Championship winning season.

### ❖ RED THREADS ❖

Djibril Cisse held a party a party at the end of March 2006 to launch his new range of designer clothing under his own label "Klubb Nine". The bash was held at Liverpool's Isis Club and was attended by his team-mates, Peter Crouch, Jamie Carragher and Steven Gerrard.

### ❖ THE GREAT EASTERN ❖

The flagpole at Anfield's Kop end was the topmast from Isambard Kingdom Brunel's[†] ambitious ship *Great Eastern*, a giant of its time. The vessel was broken up at the end of the nineteenth century at Rock Ferry, which lies across the Mersey from Anfield. The mast was floated across the river, then drawn up to the ground by four horses.

[†] *In a 2002 BBC poll, Brunel was voted the second greatest ever Briton, behind Winston Churchill.*

## ❖ FA CUP FINAL KING ❖

Ian Rush[†] has the most goals in FA Cup finals. He scored five times: two in 1986, two in 1989 and one in 1992 – all for Liverpool.

## ❖ PENALTY SCORERS IN DERBY GAMES ❖

The following players have converted from the penalty spot for Liverpool in a Merseyside derby game:

| Player | Season | Venue | Competition |
|---|---|---|---|
| Jimmy Ross | 1895–96 | Anfield | League |
| Andrew McCowie | 1898–99 | Goodison Park | League |
| Thomas Robertson | 1901–02 | Anfield | FA Cup |
| Sam Raybould | 1902–03 | Goodison Park | League |
| Alfred West | 1905–06 | Anfield | League |
| Gordon Hodgson | 1934–35 | Anfield | League |
| Willie Fagan | 1938–39 | Goodison Park | League |
| Willie Stevenson | 1964–65 | Goodison Park | League |
| Phil Neal | 1976–77 | Anfield Park | League |
| Phil Neal | 1976–77 | Maine Road | FA Cup |
| Phil Neal | 1979–80 | Goodison Park | League |
| Peter Beardsley | 1989–90 | Anfield | League |
| John Barnes | 1990–91 | Goodison Park | League |
| Robbie Fowler | 1998–99 | Anfield | Premiership |
| Patrik Berger | 2000–01 | Anfield | Premiership |
| Michael Owen | 2001–02 | Goodison Park | Premiership |

## ❖ ALDRIDGE THE BASQUE ❖

During the 1989–90 season John Aldridge could not get a starting position in the Liverpool line-up and agreed to join the Spanish side Real Sociedad. However, before he left the club, Aldridge was given a special run-out as a substitute against Crystal Palace on 12 September 1989 in what turned out to be Liverpool's record First Division win. Aldridge signed off his Liverpool career in style by scoring a penalty in front of the Kop in the Reds' 9–0 victory, in which Nicol (2), McMahon, Rush, Gillespie, Beardsley, Barnes and Hysen also scored. When the final whistle blew, Aldo threw his shirt and boots into the crowd and signed for Real Sociedad the next day, becoming the first non-Basque player ever signed by the club.

[†]Ian Rush scored 10 times in 18 games at Wembley for the Reds.

## ❖ WHAT THE REDS SAID (10) ❖

"Don't worry, Alan. At least you'll be able to play close to a great team."
**Bill Shankly**, *to Alan Ball, who had joined Everton in 1966*

## ❖ HAT-TRICK OF HAT-TRICKS ❖

Ian Rush was the first player to score a hat-trick for Liverpool in all three major domestic competitions:

| Date | Opposition | Competition | Score |
|------|-----------|-------------|-------|
| 26 January 1982 | Notts County | Division One | 4–0 |
| 10 March 1985 | Barnsley | FA Cup | 4–0 |
| 9 October 1990 | Crewe Alexandra | League Cup | 4–1 |

Rush also scored hat-tricks for the Reds in the following major cup competitions:

| Date | Opposition | Competition | Score |
|------|-----------|-------------|-------|
| 24 October 1984 | Benfica | European Cup | 3–1 |
| 30 September 1986 | Everton | Screen Sport Super Cup | 4–1 |
| 16 September 1992 | Apollon Limassol | European Cup Winners' Cup | 6–1 |

## ❖ TWO CAPS BUT NO GAMES FOR REDS ❖

On 4 May 1979 Liverpool signed Frank McGarvey from St Mirren for £250,000. Although he won two Scottish caps during his brief spell at Anfield, Frank never managed a first-team game for the Reds. At the end of the 1979–80 season he was sold on to Celtic for £325,000.

## ❖ HAT-TRICK OF PENALTIES ❖

On 26 November 1986 Jan Molby scored a hat-trick of penalties against Coventry City at Anfield in a League Cup fourth-round replay. Molby took 45 penalties for the Reds overall, converting 42 of them.

## ❖ DERBY GOAL KING ❖

When Ian Rush left Anfield in 1996, he had scored 25 goals for Liverpool against Everton, more than any other player in the history of Merseyside derbies.

## ❖ WE ARE THE CHAMPIONS (12) ❖

Liverpool won their third set of back-to-back Division One titles in 1979–80, Bob Paisley, remarkably, using just 18 players in the 84 League games played over the two seasons. It was Liverpool's twelfth Division One Championship and pushed them further ahead of their nearest "Champions of Champions" challengers, Arsenal, who were still stuck on eight titles. Manchester United, managed by Dave Sexton, pushed Liverpool hard all season, and defeated them 2–1 (Dalglish) at Old Trafford on 5 April 1980. However, the Reds held their nerve in the final six matches of the season, winning three and drawing two, to clinch the championship by two points. Two factors proved cruicial in the final analysis: first, Liverpool collected 24 points on their travels, compared to United's 21; second, the Reds' scored 16 more goals than United and let in eight fewer, resulting in relative goal differences of +51 for Liverpool and +30 for United.

### *Football League Division 1*
1979–80

|  | P | W | D | L | F | A | W | D | L | F | A | Pts |
|---|---|---|---|---|---|---|---|---|---|---|---|---|
| 1. **Liverpool** | 42 | 15 | 6 | 0 | 46 | 8 | 10 | 4 | 7 | 35 | 22 | 60 |
| 2. Manchester United | 42 | 17 | 3 | 1 | 43 | 8 | 7 | 7 | 7 | 22 | 27 | 58 |
| 3. Ipswich Town | 42 | 14 | 4 | 3 | 43 | 13 | 8 | 5 | 8 | 25 | 26 | 53 |
| 4. Arsenal | 42 | 8 | 10 | 3 | 24 | 12 | 10 | 6 | 5 | 28 | 24 | 52 |
| 5. Nottingham Forest | 42 | 16 | 4 | 1 | 44 | 11 | 4 | 4 | 13 | 19 | 32 | 48 |
| 6. Wolverhampton W. | 42 | 9 | 6 | 6 | 29 | 20 | 10 | 3 | 8 | 29 | 27 | 47 |
| 7. Aston Villa | 42 | 11 | 5 | 5 | 29 | 22 | 5 | 9 | 7 | 22 | 28 | 46 |
| 8. Southampton | 42 | 14 | 2 | 5 | 53 | 24 | 4 | 7 | 10 | 12 | 29 | 45 |
| 9. Middlesbrough | 42 | 11 | 7 | 3 | 31 | 14 | 5 | 5 | 11 | 19 | 30 | 44 |
| 10. West Bromwich Albion | 42 | 9 | 8 | 4 | 37 | 23 | 2 | 11 | 8 | 17 | 27 | 41 |
| 11. Leeds United | 42 | 10 | 7 | 4 | 30 | 17 | 3 | 7 | 11 | 16 | 33 | 40 |
| 12. Norwich City | 42 | 10 | 8 | 3 | 38 | 30 | 3 | 6 | 12 | 20 | 36 | 40 |
| 13. Crystal Palace | 42 | 9 | 9 | 3 | 26 | 13 | 3 | 7 | 11 | 15 | 37 | 40 |
| 14. Tottenham Hotspur | 42 | 11 | 5 | 5 | 30 | 22 | 4 | 5 | 12 | 22 | 40 | 40 |
| 15. Coventry City | 42 | 12 | 2 | 7 | 34 | 24 | 4 | 5 | 12 | 22 | 42 | 39 |
| 16. Brighton & Hove A | 42 | 8 | 8 | 5 | 25 | 20 | 3 | 7 | 11 | 22 | 37 | 37 |
| 17. Manchester City | 42 | 8 | 8 | 5 | 28 | 25 | 4 | 5 | 12 | 15 | 41 | 37 |
| 18. Stoke City | 42 | 9 | 4 | 8 | 27 | 26 | 4 | 6 | 11 | 17 | 32 | 36 |
| 19. Everton | 42 | 7 | 7 | 7 | 28 | 25 | 2 | 10 | 9 | 15 | 26 | 35 |
| 20. Bristol City | 42 | 6 | 6 | 9 | 22 | 30 | 3 | 7 | 11 | 15 | 36 | 31 |
| 21. Derby County | 42 | 9 | 4 | 8 | 36 | 29 | 2 | 4 | 15 | 11 | 38 | 30 |
| 22. Bolton Wanderers | 42 | 5 | 11 | 5 | 19 | 21 | 0 | 4 | 17 | 19 | 52 | 25 |

# ❖ LIVERPOOL WORLD XI ❖

**1**
Bruce
*GROBBELAAR*
(ZIMBABWE)

**2**
Salif
*DIAO*
(SENEGAL)

**3**
Avi
*COHEN*
(ISRAEL)

**4**
Mauricio
*PELLEGRINO*
(ARGENTINA)

**5**
Rigobert
*SONG*
(CAMEROON)

**6**
Momo
*SISSOKO*
(MALI)

**7**
Berry
*NIEUWENHUYS*
(SOUTH AFRICA)

**8**
Craig
*JOHNSTON*
(AUSTRALIA)
*(captain)*

**9**
Gordon
*HODGSON*
(SOUTH AFRICA)

**10**
El Hadji
*DIOUF*
(SENEGAL)

**11**
Harry
*KEWELL*
(AUSTRALIA)

*Substitutes*
Brad *FRIEDEL* (USA) • Djimi *TRAORE* (MALI) • Robert *PRIDAY* (SOUTH AFRICA)
Titi *CAMARA* (GUINEA) • Ronny *ROSENTHAL* (ISRAEL)
*Manager*
Gerard *HOULLIER* (FRANCE)

*Did You Know That?*
Craig Johnston was born in South Africa to Australian parents and grew up in Australia. Craig never played at international level for either country but did represent England at both Under-21 and "B" team level.

## ❖ FIRST EVER LEAGUE GOALSCORER ❖

On 2 September 1893 Malcolm McVean scored Liverpool's first ever League goal in the 2–0 away win at Middlesbrough Ironopolis, Joe McQue slotting the other. An original member of the "Team of the Macs", McVean was signed from Third Lanark in 1892 and made 126 appearances for the club, scoring 40 goals.

## ❖ PLAYING IN PAIN ❖

Phil Neal hated missing training and matches so much that when he broke his foot he had a specially adapted football boot made so that it eased the pain when he was playing.

## ❖ NICKNAMES ❖

The following is a list of selected Anfield personnel and their nicknames:

| | | | |
|---|---|---|---|
| John Barnes | Digger | Henry Lewis | Harry |
| Thomas Bradshaw | Tiny | Jason McAteer | Dave |
| Aboubacar Camara | Titi | William McConnell | Billy Mac |
| Harry Chambers | Sharky/Smiler | Steve McManaman | Shaggy |
| Kenny Dalglish | Super | Ronnie Moran | Bugsy |
| Peter Crouch | Coathanger | Phil Neal | Zico |
| J Edward Doig | Ned | Steve Nicol | Chico |
| David Fairclough | Supersub | Berry Nieuwenhuys | Nivvy |
| Dietmar Hamann | Didi | Ronald Orr | Wee |
| Alan Hansen | Jockey | Bob Paisley | Gunner |
| Emlyn Hughes | Crazy Horse | Fred Rodgers | The Bullet |
| Robbie Fowler | God | Ronny Rosenthal | Rocket |
| Adolf Hanson | Alf | Neil Ruddock | Razor |
| Fred Hopkin | Polly | Kenneth Rudham | Doug |
| John Hughes | Geezer | Ian Rush | Omar |
| John Hunter | Sailor | Ian St John | Saint |
| James Jackson | The Parson | John Scales | Bond |
| David Johnson | Doc | Bill Shankly | Shanks |
| Thomas Johnson | Tosh | Steve Staunton | Stan |
| Rob Jones | Trigger | Graeme Souness | Charlie |
| Alan Kennedy | Barney Rubble | Ron Yeats | Rowdy |

## ❖ SPURS MANAGER WAS A RED ❖

Keith Burkinshaw, who managed Tottenham Hotspur to FA Cup wins in 1981 and 1982 and to UEFA Cup success in 1984, made one appearance for the Reds during the 1954–55 season. In 1982 he became the only former Liverpool player to lead a team out against the Reds at Wembley, when Liverpool met Tottenham Hotspur in the League Cup final. That day, the Reds came out on top, winning 3–1 (Whelan 2, Rush).

## ❖ KOP SEE FA CUP FOR THE FIRST TIME ❖

On 4 May 1965, three days after lifting the FA Cup for the first time with their 2–1 win over Leeds United at Wembley, Liverpool paraded the trophy in front of the Kop prior to the first leg of their European Cup semi-final against Inter Milan.

## ❖ UP FOR THE CUP (3) ❖

In 1980–81 Liverpool won the League Cup for the first time. In round two they beat Bradford City 4–1 on aggregate before seeing off Swindon Town at Anfield in the third round with a comfortable 5–0 victory. In round four Liverpool beat Portsmouth 4–1 at Anfield and in round five disposed of Birmingham City 3–1 in another home win. Manchester City provided the Reds' semi-final opposition over two legs. In the first, Liverpool won 1–0 at Maine Road, then drew 1–1 at Anfield in the return. An Alan Kennedy goal in the 118th minute against West Ham United at Wembley earned Liverpool a draw in the final. But, on 1 April 1981, Liverpool finally got their hands on the League Cup, beating the Hammers 2–1 (Dalglish, Hansen) in the replay at Villa Park.

### LEAGUE CUP FINAL
*14 MARCH 1981, WEMBLEY*

**Liverpool** (0) 1    vs    **West Ham United** (0) 1
A. Kennedy          Stewart (pen)
*After extra time*

*Att.* 100,000
*Liverpool:* Clemence; Neal, A. Kennedy, Hansen, Irwin;
R. Kennedy, McDermott, Souness; Lee, Dalglish, Heighway (Case)

#### REPLAY
*1 APRIL 1981, VILLA PARK, BIRMINGHAM*

**Liverpool** (2) 2    vs    **West Ham United** (1) 1
Dalglish, Hansen       Goddard
*Att.* 36,693
*Liverpool:* Clemence; Neal, A. Kennedy, Hansen, Thompson;
R. Kennedy, McDermott, Lee, Souness; Dalglish, Rush

## ❖ 100 EUROPEAN CUP GOALS AT ANFIELD ❖

On 20 March 1985 Liverpool beat Austrian champions Austria Vienna 4–1 at Anfield in the third round of the 1984–85 European Cup. Going into the game Liverpool needed just three goals to reach the landmark figure of 100 European Cup goals at Anfield. In the 16th minute Paul Walsh scored number 98 and in the 39th minute Steve Nicol made it 2–0 with goal number 99. The landmark goal duly arrived one minute into the second half – it was an own goal by Austria Vienna defender Obermayer. Walsh netted Liverpool's fourth (and 101st).

### ❖ DALGLISH IS ONE IN THREE ❖

Kenny Dalglish is one of only three men to have won the Championship as a manager with two different clubs: the Division One Championship with Liverpool in 1985–86, 1987–88, 1989–90; the FA Premier League with Blackburn Rovers in 1994–95.

### ❖ DOUBLE LEAGUE-WINNING CAPTAIN ❖

Don MacKinlay was born in Newton Mearns, near Glasgow, on 25 July 1891. He made his Liverpool debut on 20 April 1910, in a 7–3 (Parkinson 4, Bowyer 2, Stewart) First Division home win over Nottingham Forest, and went on to captain the Reds to successive First Division Championships in 1921–22 and 1922–23. MacKinlay made 434 appearances for the Reds, scoring 34 goals, before leaving Anfield in July 1929. Amazingly he only won two caps for Scotland.

### ❖ FOREIGN FA CUP WINNERS ❖

When Liverpool beat Everton 3–1 (Rush 2, Johnston) after extra time in the 1986 FA Cup final, they did not have a single Englishman in their starting eleven.

### ❖ ENGLISH MAC AMONG A TEAM OF MACS ❖

Goalkeeper William "Bill" McOwen was the sole English "Mac" among the Liverpool "Team of the Macs" (there were eight of them) that lifted the Second Division Championship in 1893–94. During that championship-winning season, McOwen conceded just 16 goals in 23 matches as Liverpool went undefeated in the League[††]. When he retired from playing football, McOwen resumed his earlier career as a dentist.

### ❖ STAN'S THE MAN ❖

Steve Staunton, nicknamed "Stan" by his team-mates, was installed as the new manager of the Republic of Ireland on 12 January 2006. His first match in charge was a friendly international against Sweden at Lansdowne Road on 1 March. Ireland won 3–0.

---

[†]*Steve McMahon was Liverpool's substitute for the match but did not get on to the pitch.*
[††]*Defender Matt McQueen played in goal for the five League matches McOwen missed in 1893–94.*

### ❖ STEVE HEIGHWAY ❖

Steve Heighway was born in Dublin on 25 November 1947. In 1970 Steve was at university studying for his final exams for a degree in ecomomics. At the same time he was playing for Skelmersdale United, where he was spotted by a Reds scout and quickly signed by the club. On 22 September 1970 Heighway made his Liverpool debut against Mansfield Town in a League Cup tie at Anfield.

Heighway was a strong, athletic and quick winger who provided many pinpoint crosses into the box for the likes of Kevin Keegan and John Toshack to put away. In 1971, he helped Liverpool to the FA Cup final, where League champions Arsenal were aiming to become only the second club to do the Double in the twentieth century. Despite the humid conditions inside Wembley that day, Heighway played well for the Reds and was as energetic as any player on the pitch. In the second minute of extra time Heighway raced down the wing and cut inside Pat Rice at full-back to fire a shot past Bob Wilson into the Arsenal net. However, Arsenal then proceeded to score twice to deny Steve his first FA Cup winners' medal.

In 1972–73, Heighway won the first of four League Championships with the Reds and a UEFA Cup winners' medal. In 1973–74 his outstanding performances took the club back to Wembley for the FA Cup final and an encounter with Newcastle United. This time Liverpool lifted the Cup after a 3–0 victory, with Heighway and Keegan (2) the goalscorers. In 1975-76, he completed a second League and UEFA Cup double, while the following season saw Liverpool conquer almost all before them to just miss out on a unique treble of of League, FA Cup and European Cup, going down to Manchester United in the FA Cup final. In the European Cup final, though, Heighway set up two of Liverpool's three goals in their 3–1 (McDermott, Smith, Neal) victory over Borussia Moenchengladbach.

Steve Heighway won two more European Cup winners' medals (1978 and 1981), another League Championship (1979), the European Super Cup (1978) and a League Cup winners' medal (1981). In 1981 Steve left Anfield, having made 475 appearances for the club, scoring 76 goals, as well as having won 33 caps for the Republic of Ireland during his Liverpool career. Eight years later, Steve returned to Anfield to take up a coaching role at the Academy.

### *Did You Know That?*
It was Bob Paisley's sons who first spotted Steve Heighway playing for Skelmersdale United against South Liverpool in 1970 and recommended him to their father.

### ❖ REDS' FIRST AMERICAN ❖

In 1948 during Liverpool's tour of the USA, Joseph Cadden, who was born in Scotland but grew up in America, played for the Brooklyn Wanderers. He impressed the Anfield coaching staff so much that they offered him a contract. Cadden, a central defender, became the first player signed by Liverpool from an American club. However, things never really worked out for him at Liverpool, for whom he made only four appearances before moving on to Grimsby Town.

### ❖ 16 YEARS TOO LATE ❖

On 12 September 2004 a "Wimbledon 1988" side took on a "Liverpool 1988" side to celebrate the greatest ever day in Wimbledon's history – their 1–0 defeat of the Reds in the 1988 FA Cup final at Wembley. The 2004 rematch ended 1–1 with John Aldridge scoring the Liverpool goal from the penalty spot. Aldo famously missed a penalty, the first ever missed in an FA Cup final, during the 1988 Wembley encounter.

### ❖ CAPPED WITHOUT A KICK ❖

In the 1982 World Cup finals in Spain, Phil Neal earned an England cap without even touching the ball. The Liverpool full-back replaced Kenny Sansom late in the game against France, but he didn't have time to get to his position when the referee blew the final whistle.

### ❖ THE REDS USED TO BE THE BLUES ❖

Liverpool originally played in Everton's blue-and-white quarters after the Toffees left Anfield in 1892. They changed to their now traditional red kit in 1895. The club badge first appeared a shirt at the 1950 FA Cup final – and Liverpool wore white that day. The Reds' first shirt bearing a sponsor's name was worn in 1978

### ❖ LIVERPOOL ANGRY OVER ASHES HEROES ❖

Liverpool FC voiced their disillusionment after the entire England cricket team was honoured in the 2006 New Year's Honours List after winning back the Ashes from Australia. Liverpool pointed out that home-grown UEFA Champions League winners, Jamie Carragher and Steven Gerrard, were overlooked while Paul Collingwood, who only played in one Ashes match scoring just 17 runs without taking any wickets, was awarded an MBE.

## ❖ REDS PLAYER JOINS THE BEATLES ❖

On 1 June 1967 the Beatles released their *Sgt. Pepper's Lonely Hearts Club Band* album. The sleeve carries illustrations of many famous people, including Bob Dylan, Stan Laurel and Oliver Hardy, The Beatles themselves – and Albert Stubbins (Liverpool striker 1946–53).

## ❖ KEEPING UP A FINE TRADITION ❖

Only 19 goalkeepers have started a game for Liverpool since 1963:

| | | |
|---|---|---|
| Jim Furnell | 1962–63 | 28 games |
| Tommy Lawrence | 1959–71 | 390 games |
| William Molyneux | 1961–67 | 1 games |
| John Ogston | 1965–68 | 1 game |
| Ray Clemence | 1967–81 | 665 games |
| Frank Lane | 1971–75 | 2 games |
| Steve Ogrizovic | 1977–82 | 5 games |
| Bruce Grobbelaar | 1981–94 | 628 games |
| Mike Hooper | 1985–93 | 73 games |
| David James | 1992–99 | 277 games |
| Brad Friedel | 1997–2000 | 31 games |
| Sander Westerveld | 1999–2001 | 103 games |
| Pegguy Arphexad | 2000–2003 | 6 games |
| Jerzy Dudek | 2001–date | 179 games |
| Chris Kirkland | 2001–date | 45 games |
| Patrice Luzi | 2002–05 | 1 game |
| Paul Jones | 2004–04 | 2 games |
| Scott Carson | 2005–date | 9 games |
| Jose Reina | 2005–date | 53 games |

## ❖ RED IN WINTER, WHITE IN SUMMER ❖

A number of Liverpool players have played cricket during the close season. Perhaps the most successful Liverpool cricketing footballer was Gordon Hodgson, who combined scoring goals for Liverpool with taking wickets for Lancashire. The South African made more than 50 first-class appearances for Lancashire and was part of their County Championship winning sides of 1930 and 1931. Other Liverpool cricketing footballers include goalkeeper Harry Storer, who played for Derbyshire in 1895; Cyril Done, who was a regular with Bootle; former manager Phil Taylor, who once played for Gloucestershire; and goalkeeper Steve Ogrizovic, who played for Shropshire and dismissed West Indies ace Alvin Kallicharran.

## ❖ EUROPEAN GLORY NIGHTS (5) ❖

Liverpool's 1980–81 European Cup campaign got off to a poor start when they could only draw 1–1 with Finnish amateurs Oulu Palloseura in their first-round, first-leg encounter in Finland. However, Liverpool won the second leg 10–1. In the second round Liverpool beat Alex Ferguson's industrious Aberdeen side home and away for a 5–0 aggregate win, and in round three eased past CSKA Sofia with home and away wins (6–1 on aggregate). Now only Bayern Munich, European champions in 1974, 1975 and 1976, stood between Liverpool and a place in the final. Liverpool drew the home leg 0–0, but a Ray Kennedy goal in the 1–1 draw in Munich was enough to see Liverpool progress on the away goals rule. Liverpool beat Real Madrid 1–0 (Alan Kennedy) in the final in Paris on 27 May 1981 to claim their third European crown.

### EUROPEAN CUP FINAL
*27 MAY 1981, PARC DES PRINCES, PARIS*
**Liverpool** (0) 1      vs      Real Madrid (0) 0
A. Kennedy

*Att.* 48,360

*Liverpool:* Clemence; Neal, Thompson, Hansen, A. Kennedy; Lee, McDermott, Souness, R. Kennedy; Dalglish (Case), Johnson

## ❖ MR VERSATILE ❖

In October 1892 Liverpool signed Matt McQueen[†] from Leith Athletic. He made his debut on 2 September 1893 in a 2–0 (McQue, McVean) away win at Middlesbrough Ironopolis, and from then until he left Liverpool in 1899 he played in every position on the field for the club, including making 12 appearances in goal. After leaving Anfield, McQueen became a referee, then in 1918 he was appointed a director of Liverpool. In January 1923 his fellow directors asked him to become manager following the shock resignation of David Ashworth. Although the Reds won the First Division Championship that year, most of the points that earned them the title had been won while McQueen's predecessor was in charge. McQueen did not enjoy any major success as a manager in his own right, but he did sign the legendary striker Gordon Hodgson. In 1928 McQueen was forced to retire after losing a leg in a car crash but continued to live in Kemlyn Road next to the ground.

[†] *When John McKenna signed Matt McQueen from Leith Athletic in 1892, he signed his brother, Hugh, at the same time.*

### ❖ DON'T SWEAR AT ME ❖

In 1925 Liverpool signed Jimmy "The Parson" Jackson from Aberdeen. A man of the cloth, Jackson combined his life as a clergyman with his football career and was one of the first players to supplement his income by writing. He was a regular columnist in the *Liverpool Weekly Post*. Jackson took over the captaincy of the club from the legendary Don McKinlay and, befitting a man of God, he did not take kindly to swearing from his team-mates or opposing players. His run-ins with Liverpool's iconic Irish goalkeeper Elisha Scott are the stuff of folklore, since Scott reportedly swore constantly. Jackson officiated at the funeral of former Liverpool chairman W.C. McConnell and remained at the club until 1933.

### ❖ CRAZY HORSE OVERTAKEN ❖

Michael Owen won the most caps for England while at Liverpool with 60 appearances for his country. He passed Emlyn Hughes's record of 59 on 24 June 2004 in England's penalty shoot-out defeat to Portugal in Lisbon in the quarter-finals of the 2004 European Championships.

### ❖ ANFIELD SOUTH ❖

Former Liverpool chairman Sir John Smith dubbed Wembley Stadium "Anfield South", such was the frequency of the club's visits to the Twin Towers during his stewardship of the Reds.

### ❖ LIVERPOOL EMPLOY A DIGGER ❖

John Barnes's nickname at Liverpool was "Digger" – not to imply that his displays in the heart of midfield were workmanlike but because his initials are "JCB" for John Charles Barnes.

### ❖ AFRICAN PLAYER OF THE YEAR ❖

After the 2002 World Cup Finals in Japan/South Korea, Liverpool signed the Senegalese striker El Hadji Diouf. Diouf won the African Player of the Year award in 2002 and again in 2003.

### ❖ FIRST EIRE INTERNATIONAL ❖

Steve Heighway was the first Liverpool player capped at international level by the Republic of Ireland.

### ❖ UP FOR THE CUP (4) ❖

In 1982 Liverpool beat Tottenham Hotspur 3–1 at Wembley to win their second successive League Cup (at that point called the "Milk Cup"). In the second round Liverpool beat Exeter City 5–0 at home and 6–0 away before disposing of Middlesbrough in round three with a comfortable 4–1 win at Anfield. In the fourth round three extra-time goals sank Arsenal 3–0 at Anfield after the two sides had drawn 0–0 at Highbury a week earlier. Barnsley threatened to prove a stumbling block in round five, as Liverpool could only manage a 0–0 home draw, but they then won 3–1 at Oakwell in the return. Ipswich Town were Liverpool's semi-final opponents. The Reds won the first leg 2–0 at Portman Road and drew the return 2–2 at Anfield. It took 30 minutes of extra time before Liverpool could edge out Spurs 3–1 in the final. Two months later Spurs lifted the FA Cup for the second successive year.

**MILK CUP FINAL**
*13 MARCH 1982, WEMBLEY*
**Liverpool** (0) 3    **vs**    **Tottenham Hotspur** (1) 1
Whelan 2, Rush      Archibald
*After extra time*
*Att*. 100,000
*Liverpool:* Grobbelaar; Neal, A. Kennedy, Lawrenson, Thompson; Johnston, Lee, McDermott (Johnson), Souness; Dalglish, Rush

### ❖ RELEGATED LIVERPOOL BEAT CHAMPS ❖

In 1903–04 Liverpool, First Division champions only three years before, were relegated to Division Two. Remarkably Liverpool scored more goals overall (49) than 1903–04 champions Sheffield Wednesday (48). Away from home Liverpool scored 25 goals to Wednesday's 14.

### ❖ LIVERPOOL'S ENGLAND HAT-TRICK MEN ❖

When England beat Jamaica 6–0 at Old Trafford in their last World Cup finals warm-up friendly on 3 June 2006, Peter Crouch scored a hat-trick. It gave him five goals in his last three international appearances. Before Crouch, the last Reds player to get three goals for England was Michael Owen, against Germany at Munich on 1 September 2001. Crouch's Liverpool team-mate Jamie Carragher assisted on his second goal, while former Kop hero Owen made the third.

## ❖ WE ARE THE CHAMPIONS (13) ❖

Ipswich Town – nicknamed "The Tractor Boys", and UEFA Cup winners in 1980–81 – ran Liverpool a close second in the race for the 1981–82 Division One Championship. Liverpool got off to a disastrous start that season, winning just three of their opening 11 League games. When Manchester City went away from Anfield having won 3–1 (Whelan) on Boxing Day, the Reds lay in 12th position in the table with hopes of winning a 13th title a mere pipe dream. But suddenly the Dalglish–Rush partnership ignited and Bruce Grobbelaar stopped making the mistakes that had cost the Reds so dearly in their early games. The Reds set off on a 25-match run that netted 20 wins, 3 draws and 2 defeats. In the end Liverpool won the Division One Championship title by four points. Amazingly, it was Liverpool's away form that guaranteed them the title, winning 12 times on the road.

### *Football League Division 1*
### 1981–82

| | P | W | D | L | F | A | W | D | L | F | A | Pts |
|---|---|---|---|---|---|---|---|---|---|---|---|---|
| 1. **Liverpool** | 42 | 14 | 3 | 4 | 39 | 14 | 12 | 6 | 3 | 41 | 18 | 87 |
| 2. Ipswich Town | 42 | 17 | 1 | 3 | 47 | 25 | 9 | 4 | 8 | 28 | 28 | 83 |
| 3. Manchester United | 42 | 12 | 6 | 3 | 27 | 9 | 10 | 6 | 5 | 32 | 20 | 78 |
| 4. Tottenham Hotspur | 42 | 12 | 4 | 5 | 41 | 26 | 8 | 7 | 6 | 26 | 22 | 71 |
| 5. Arsenal | 42 | 13 | 5 | 3 | 27 | 15 | 7 | 6 | 8 | 21 | 22 | 71 |
| 6. Swansea City | 42 | 13 | 3 | 5 | 34 | 16 | 8 | 3 | 10 | 24 | 35 | 69 |
| 7. Southampton | 42 | 15 | 2 | 4 | 49 | 30 | 4 | 7 | 10 | 23 | 37 | 66 |
| 8. Everton | 42 | 11 | 7 | 3 | 33 | 21 | 6 | 6 | 9 | 23 | 29 | 64 |
| 9. West Ham United | 42 | 9 | 10 | 2 | 42 | 29 | 5 | 6 | 10 | 24 | 28 | 58 |
| 10. Manchester City | 42 | 9 | 7 | 5 | 32 | 23 | 6 | 6 | 9 | 17 | 27 | 58 |
| 11. Aston Villa | 42 | 9 | 6 | 6 | 28 | 24 | 6 | 6 | 9 | 27 | 29 | 57 |
| 12. Nottingham Forest | 42 | 7 | 7 | 7 | 19 | 20 | 8 | 5 | 8 | 23 | 28 | 57 |
| 13. Brighton & Hove A. | 42 | 8 | 7 | 6 | 30 | 24 | 5 | 6 | 10 | 13 | 28 | 52 |
| 14. Coventry City | 42 | 9 | 4 | 8 | 31 | 24 | 4 | 7 | 10 | 25 | 38 | 50 |
| 15. Notts County | 42 | 8 | 5 | 8 | 32 | 33 | 5 | 3 | 13 | 29 | 36 | 47 |
| 16. Birmingham City | 42 | 8 | 6 | 7 | 29 | 25 | 2 | 8 | 11 | 24 | 36 | 44 |
| 17. West Bromwich Albion | 42 | 6 | 6 | 9 | 24 | 25 | 5 | 5 | 11 | 22 | 32 | 44 |
| 18. Stoke City | 42 | 9 | 2 | 10 | 27 | 28 | 3 | 6 | 12 | 17 | 35 | 44 |
| 19. Sunderland | 42 | 6 | 5 | 10 | 19 | 26 | 5 | 6 | 10 | 19 | 32 | 44 |
| 20. Leeds United | 42 | 6 | 11 | 4 | 23 | 20 | 4 | 1 | 16 | 16 | 41 | 42 |
| 21. Wolverhampton W. | 42 | 8 | 5 | 8 | 19 | 20 | 2 | 5 | 14 | 13 | 43 | 40 |
| 22. Middlesbrough | 42 | 5 | 9 | 7 | 20 | 24 | 3 | 6 | 12 | 14 | 28 | 39 |

### ❖ WHAT THE REDS SAID (11) ❖

"If you're in the penalty area and don't know what to do with the ball, put it in the net and we'll discuss the options later."
**Bob Paisley**

### ❖ RED GERMAN LIONS ❖

On 8 May 2006, Sven Goran Eriksson included three current and two former Liverpool players in his 23-man England squad for the 2006 World Cup finals in Germany: Jamie Carragher, Peter Crouch and Steven Gerrard. Ex Reds Michael Owen and David James were also included by the England coach.

### ❖ FIRST TO RETAIN THE EUROPEAN CUP ❖

Liverpool became the first English side to retain the European Cup when they beat FC Bruges 1–0 (Dalglish) at Wembley in 1978.

### ❖ HANSEN GETS JOB AS A BUTLER ❖

In an advertisement for Carlsberg, Liverpool legend Alan Hansen played a butler to a fictitious footballer. In the advertisement Hansen is seen cleaning the player's football boots.

### ❖ LUCKY LEAGUE CUP VENUES ❖

Liverpool have won the League Cup[†] at four different stadia:

Maine Road, Manchester ❖ Millennium Stadium, Cardiff
Villa Park, Birmingham ❖ Wembley Stadium, London

### ❖ ABANDONED GAMES ❖

In more than 118 years of football at Anfield, only two matches have been abandoned. In 1903 a First Division game against Wolverhampton Wanderers had to be called off because of a heavy downpour of rain. Then in 1973 torrential rain stopped the first leg of the UEFA Cup final between Liverpool and Borussia Moenchengladbach after just 17 minutes.

---

[†]*Liverpool lost the 1978 League Cup final to Nottingham Forest after a replay at Old Trafford, Manchester.*

### ❖ UP FOR THE CUP (5) ❖

In 1982–83 Liverpool won their third consecutive League Cup, beating Manchester United 2–1 after extra time in the final at Wembley. Liverpool's defence of the trophy began with a 2–1 away win and a 2–0 home win over Ipswich Town in the second round. Liverpool beat Rotherham United 1–0 at Anfield in Round Three and Norwich City 2–0 at Anfield in Round Four. A fifth-round home draw resulted in a 2–1 victory over West Ham United before Liverpool notched up a 3–1 two-leg aggregate win over Burnley in the semi-finals. Following United's defeat to Liverpool in the final they went on to win the FA Cup.

**MILK CUP FINAL**
*26 MARCH 1983, WEMBLEY STADIUM*
**Liverpool (0) 2**    vs    **Manchester United (1) 1**
A. Kennedy, Whelan    Whiteside
*After extra time*
*Att.* 100,000

*Liverpool:* Grobbelaar; Neal, A. Kennedy, Hansen, Lawrenson; Whelan, Johnston (Fairclough), Lee, Souness; Dalglish, Rush

### ❖ PFA YOUNG PLAYER OF THE YEAR ❖

All professional footballers, regardless of nationality, playing in the English leagues and who are under the age of 23 are eligible for the PFA Young Player of the Year award[†]. Since its inception, and up to 2005, only four Liverpool players have won it:

| Year | Player |
|------|--------|
| 2001 | Steven Gerrard |
| 1998 | Michael Owen |
| 1996 | Robbie Fowler |
| 1995 | Robbie Fowler |
| 1983 | Ian Rush |

### ❖ HEAD OVER HEELS IN LOVE ❖

On 9 June 1979 Kevin Keegan released a single entitled "Head Over Heels In Love", a song written by Chris Norman and Pete Spencer. The single reached number 31 in the charts.

[†]*Paul Walsh won the award in 1983 when he was at Luton Town, Nicolas Anelka in 1999 when he was at Arsenal, and Harry Kewell in 2000 when he was a Leeds United player.*

### ❖ LAST ONE FOR SHANKS ❖

Bill Shankly led Liverpool out on to the pitch for the final time on 10 August 1974 in the FA Charity Shield at Wembley. Although he had resigned four weeks earlier, Shankly was asked to take charge as Bob Paisley would not be officially installed until the following Tuesday. As it happens Leeds United had also just changed managers, Don Revie having been offered the England post, but their new boss, Brian Clough, stepped aside to allow Revie to lead Leeds out one last time. The game was significant in several other ways: it was first time the Charity Shield had been played at Wembley Stadium; it was Liverpool's first victory in a penalty shoot-out; and Kevin Keegan and Billy Bremner became the first British players to be sent off at Wembley. The game ended 1–1 (Boersma) and in the penalty shoot-out, Alec Lindsay, Emlyn Hughes, Brian Hall, Tommy Smith, Peter Cormack and Ian Callaghan converted their kicks as the Reds won 6–5.

### ❖ FATHER AND SON MISS FINAL ❖

Bill Shankly signed Gordon Milne[†] from Preston North End for £16,000 in August 1960 and he was a vital member of the Reds team that won the Second Division Championship in 1961–62 and two First Division titles in 1963–64 and 1965–66. However, injury ruled him out of Liverpool's first FA Cup triumph in 1965. Strangely enough, Milne's father, Jimmy, missed Preston North End's 1938 FA Cup triumph, also through injury. Milne Jnr went on to play 280 games for Liverpool, scoring 18 times. In 1967 he left Anfield and joined Blackpool for £30,000, later going on to manage Wigan Athletic, Coventry City, Leicester City and Besiktas in Turkey.

### ❖ THE GUNNER ❖

Bob Paisley was nicknamed "Gunner" at Liverpool. The tag derived from his rank in the army.

### ❖ MERSEYSIDE DOUBLE ❖

Liverpool won the First Division Championship in 1905–06 after their Second Division Championship success the previous season. Everton completed a 1905–06 double for Merseyside by beating Newcastle United 1–0 in the FA Cup final.

[†]Gordon Milne's father, Jimmy, was a team-mate of Bill Shankly's at Preston North End.

## ❖ CRAZY HORSE HOLDS UP GAME ❖

On 9 November 2004 Emlyn Hughes lost his brave battle for life after fighting a brain tumour for 15 months. Prior to Liverpool's Carling Cup fourth round 2–0 win over Middlesbrough on 10 November 2004, a minute's silence was held for him.

## ❖ NEAL EVER PRESENT ❖

Phil Neal holds the Liverpool record for the most consecutive appearances. Unbelievably he was an ever-present for eight successive League seasons and in all competitions he played 417 games consecutively. Three other Liverpool players have made more than 300 consecutive appearances for the club: Ray Clemence (336), Chris Lawler (316) and Bruce Grobbelaar (310).

## ❖ ON THE SPOT ❖

As of 15 January 2006, Liverpool had been awarded 73 penalties in FA Premier League games. The table shows the Reds' conversion record:

|  | Scored | Missed | Conversion Rate |
|---|---|---|---|
| Home | 31 | 12 | 72.09% |
| Away | 23 | 7 | 76.67% |

## ❖ MISPLACED GENEROSITY ❖

Cardiff City's Danny Malloy is the only player to have scored two own goals in the same match for the Reds. He did so in the opening game of the 1959–60 season on 22 August 1959 at Anfield. The Reds still managed to lose the game 3–2.

## ❖ HOMESICK RUSH ❖

During his one year with Juventus in Serie A, it was reported that Ian Rush was homesick and requested food parcels from home containing baked beans.

## ❖ REDS HUMBLED IN THE CUP ❖

On 10 January 1953 Liverpool, then in Division One, visited Gateshead in the third round of the FA Cup and were dispatched 1–0 by the non-league side.

# ❖ THE ALL-TIME LIVERPOOL XI ❖

**1**
Elisha
*SCOTT*

**2**
Phil
*NEAL*

**6**
Alan
*HANSEN*

**5**
Ron
*YEATS*

**3**
Ephraim
*LONGWORTH*

**6**
Billy
*LIDDELL*
*(captain)*

**8**
Graeme
*SOUNESS*

**11**
Ian
*CALLAGHAN*

**9**
Ian
*RUSH*

**10**
Robbie
*FOWLER*

**7**
Kenny
*DALGLISH*

*Substitutes*
Ray *CLEMENCE* • Mark *LAWRENSON* • Terry *McDERMOTT*
Ray *KENNEDY* • Roger *HUNT*
*Manager*
Bill *SHANKLY*

---

### *Did You Know That?*

When Bill Shankly bought Scottish international Ron "Rowdy" Yeats from Dundee United in July 1961, he declared: "I've bought a Colossus. Come into the dressing room and have a walk around him."

## ❖ AN EARLY MISTAKE ❖

The very first own goal in Liverpool's favour came in the club's first season, 1892–93. It was scored by Alfred Townsend as Liverpool beat Newton 9–0 in the second qualifying round of the FA Cup. The other scorers that day were McCartney, Wyllie (3), Cameron, McVean (2) and McQueen.

## ❖ SIX RULED OUT ❖

On 5 September 1896 Liverpool lost 1–0 to Blackburn Rovers at Ewood Park in a First Division game that saw no fewer than six goals disallowed by the referee.

## ❖ QUICKEST STRIKE ❖

On 16 February 1938 Jack Balmer scored against Everton at Goodison Park after just ten seconds to register Liverpool's fastest ever goal. The Reds won the Merseyside derby 3–1 (Balmer, Shafto 2) that day.

## ❖ THE PERM BRIGADE ❖

Terry McDermott lays claim to having begun the Liverpool perm craze in the early 1970s: "I was the first to get my perm done. The lads all laughed, but one by one they started having it done themselves. I kept mine for five years," said McDermott as the likes of Phil Neal, Graeme Souness and Phil Thompson joined the perm brigade.

## ❖ THE SHANKLY YEARS ❖

T.V. Williams appointed Bill Shankly manager of Liverpool in December 1959. Here is a breakdown of all the games the club played during Shankly's reign up to his resignation in July 1974:

|   | All | Home | Away |
|---|---|---|---|
| P | 784 | 387 | 397 |
| W | 408 | 271 | 137 |
| D | 198 | 75 | 123 |
| L | 178 | 41 | 137 |
| F | 1308 | 828 | 480 |
| A | 767 | 313 | 454 |

## ❖ MILITARY MEDAL WINNER ❖

William "Bill" Jones was signed by the Reds from Hayfield St Matthews in September 1938. After winning the Military Medal during the Allied crossing of the Rhine in World War II, he made his Reds debut on 31 August 1946 in a 1–0 (Carney) away win over Sheffield United. Jones played 26 times in the Reds' 1946–47 First Division Championship winning season and went on to make a total of 277 appearances for the club, scoring 17 times. He left Liverpool in 1954 to become player-manager at Ellesmere Port but later returned to Anfield as a scout in the 1960s and 1970s. The grandfather of Rob Jones, who played for the club from 1991 to 1999, Bill Jones was the man responsible for signing Roger Hunt for Liverpool.

## ❖ WE ARE THE CHAMPIONS (14) ❖

The strongest challenge to Liverpool in the Division One Championship title race in 1982–83 came from an unlikely source. Watford had just been promoted from Division Two and were still enjoying the backing of the charismatic Elton John as chairman, and could have only dreamed about the season they went on to enjoy. Liverpool, on the other hand, wanted to end the campaign in style for Bob Paisley, who had announced that he was retiring at the end of the season after ten years in charge. Liverpool won their 14th Division One title by 11 points from Watford, with Manchester United one point further behind in third place. In a season when no team lost more at home than they won – and Luton's 28 home points were comfortably the lowest in the division – Liverpool was the only club to actually win more on the road than they lost. Paisley also lifted the League Cup to bring a fitting end to his Anfield career.

### *Football League Division 1*
#### 1982–83

| | | P | W | D | L | F | A | W | D | L | F | A | Pts |
|---|---|---|---|---|---|---|---|---|---|---|---|---|---|
| 1. | Liverpool | 42 | 16 | 4 | 1 | 55 | 16 | 8 | 6 | 7 | 32 | 21 | 82 |
| 2. | Watford | 42 | 16 | 2 | 3 | 49 | 20 | 6 | 3 | 12 | 25 | 37 | 71 |
| 3. | Manchester United | 42 | 14 | 7 | 0 | 39 | 10 | 5 | 6 | 10 | 17 | 28 | 70 |
| 4. | Tottenham Hotspur | 42 | 15 | 4 | 2 | 50 | 15 | 5 | 5 | 11 | 15 | 35 | 69 |
| 5. | Nottingham Forest | 42 | 12 | 5 | 4 | 34 | 18 | 8 | 4 | 9 | 28 | 32 | 69 |
| 6. | Aston Villa | 42 | 17 | 2 | 2 | 47 | 15 | 4 | 3 | 14 | 15 | 35 | 68 |
| 7. | Everton | 42 | 13 | 6 | 2 | 43 | 19 | 5 | 4 | 12 | 23 | 29 | 64 |
| 8. | West Ham United | 42 | 13 | 3 | 5 | 41 | 23 | 7 | 1 | 13 | 27 | 39 | 64 |
| 9. | Ipswich Town | 42 | 11 | 3 | 7 | 39 | 23 | 4 | 10 | 7 | 25 | 27 | 58 |
| 10. | Arsenal | 42 | 11 | 6 | 4 | 36 | 19 | 5 | 4 | 12 | 22 | 37 | 58 |
| 11. | West Bromwich Albion | 42 | 11 | 5 | 5 | 35 | 20 | 4 | 7 | 10 | 16 | 29 | 57 |
| 12. | Southampton | 42 | 11 | 5 | 5 | 36 | 22 | 4 | 7 | 10 | 18 | 36 | 57 |
| 13. | Stoke City | 42 | 13 | 4 | 4 | 34 | 21 | 3 | 5 | 13 | 19 | 43 | 57 |
| 14. | Norwich City | 42 | 10 | 6 | 5 | 30 | 18 | 4 | 6 | 11 | 22 | 40 | 54 |
| 15. | Notts County | 42 | 12 | 4 | 5 | 37 | 25 | 3 | 3 | 15 | 18 | 46 | 52 |
| 16. | Sunderland | 42 | 7 | 10 | 4 | 30 | 22 | 5 | 4 | 12 | 18 | 39 | 50 |
| 17. | Birmingham City | 42 | 9 | 7 | 5 | 29 | 24 | 3 | 7 | 11 | 11 | 31 | 50 |
| 18. | Luton Town | 42 | 7 | 7 | 7 | 34 | 33 | 5 | 6 | 10 | 31 | 51 | 49 |
| 19. | Coventry City | 42 | 10 | 5 | 6 | 29 | 17 | 3 | 4 | 14 | 19 | 42 | 48 |
| 20. | Manchester City | 42 | 9 | 5 | 7 | 26 | 23 | 4 | 3 | 14 | 21 | 47 | 47 |
| 21. | Swansea City | 42 | 10 | 4 | 7 | 32 | 29 | 0 | 7 | 14 | 19 | 40 | 41 |
| 22. | Brighton & Hove A. | 42 | 8 | 7 | 6 | 25 | 22 | 1 | 6 | 14 | 13 | 46 | 40 |

## ❖ SUPER CUP SUCCESS ❖

The European Super Cup was created in 1972, when Ajax Amsterdam won the trophy, beating Rangers 6–3 over two legs. That first Super Cup was an unofficial contest, but UEFA has officially recognized the competiton since 1973 and it continued to be held over two legs until 1998[†]. The contest was originally between the holders of the European Cup and of the European Cup Winners' Cup but, since 1999, it has been the Champions League and UEFA Cup winners who have played a one-off match in Monaco. Liverpool have played in five European Super Cup finals, winning three and losing two.

### 1977 1st LEG
*VOLKSPARKSTADION, HAMBURG, 22 NOVEMBER 1977*

Hamburg SV (1) 1    vs    **Liverpool** (0) 1
Keller (29)               Fairclough (65)

*Att.* 16,000

*Liverpool:* Clemence; Neal, Jones (Smith), Thompson, Hughes; R. Kennedy, Case (Johnson), Callaghan, Heighway; Dalglish, Fairclough

### 2nd LEG
*ANFIELD, LIVERPOOL, 6 DECEMBER 1977*

**Liverpool** (2) 6    vs    Hamburg SV (0) 0
Thompson (21)
McDermott (40, 56, 57)
Fairclough (84)
Dalglish (88)

*Liverpool won 7–1 on aggregate*

*Att.* 34,931

*Liverpool:* Clemence; Neal, Smith, Thompson, Hughes; R. Kennedy, McDermott, Heighway (Johnson), Case; Dalglish, Fairclough

### 1978 1st LEG
*PARC ASTRID, BRUSSELS, 4 DECEMBER 1978*

Anderlecht (2) 3    vs    **Liverpool** (1) 1
Vercauteren (17)        Case (27)
Vander Elst (38),
Rensenbrink (87)

*Att.* 35,000

*Liverpool:* Clemence; Neal, A. Kennedy, Hughes, Hansen; R. Kennedy, Case, McDermott, Souness; Dalglish, Johnson (Heighway)

2nd LEG

*ANFIELD, LIVERPOOL, 19 DECEMBER 1978*

**Liverpool** (1) **2**   vs   Anderlecht (0) 1
Hughes (13)          Vander Elst (71)
Fairclough (87)

*Liverpool lost 4–3 on aggregate*

*Att.* 23,598

*Liverpool:* Ogrizovic; Neal, Hughes, Thompson, Hansen;
R. Kennedy, Case, McDermott, Souness; Dalglish, Fairclough

**1984**

*STADIO COMMUNALE, TURIN, 16 JANUARY 1985*

Juventus (1) 2   vs   **Liverpool** (0) **0**
Boniek (39, 79)

*Att.* 55,384

*Liverpool:* Grobbelaar; Neal, Kennedy, Lawrenson, Hansen;
Nicol, Whelan, McDonald, Wark; Rush, Walsh

**2001**

*STADE LOUIS II, MONACO, 24 AUGUST 2001*

**Liverpool** (2) **3**   vs   Bayern Munich (0) 2
Riise (23), Heskey (45)     Salihamidzic (57)
Owen (46)           Jancker (82)

*Att.* 15,000

*Liverpool:* Westerveld, Babbel, Henchoz, Hyypia, Carragher,
Gerrard (Biscan), Hamann, McAllister, Riise (Murphy),
Owen (Fowler), Heskey

**2005**

*STADE LOUIS II, MONACO, 26 AUGUST 2005*

**Liverpool** (0) **3**   vs   CSKA Moscow (1) 1
Cisse (82, 103)       Carvalho (28)
Luis Garcia (109)

*Att.* 16,000

*Liverpool:* Reina, Finnan (Sinama-Pongolle), Hyypia, Riise (Cisse),
Luis Garcia, Alonso (Sissoko), Hamann, Josemi, Morientes,
Carragher, Zenden

*'No final was held in 1981 because Liverpool were unable to agree a suitable date to play the European Cup-Winners' Cup winners Dinamo Tbilisi.*

## ❖ EMLYN HUGHES OBE ❖

Emlyn Walter Hughes was born on 28 August 1947 in Barrow-in-Furness. Hughes came from a sporting family – his father was former Barrow and Great Britain rugby league star Fred Hughes, both his brother and uncle were rugby league professionals, while one of his aunts was an England hockey international. In February 1967 Bill Shankly signed the 19-year-old Hughes from Blackpool for £65,000. He had only played 31 League and Cup games for the Tangerines, but his strength, skill and bravery led Bill Shankly to boldly declare, "This boy is the future captain of England." How right Shankly was! Hughes went on to win 62 England caps, 59 of them while a Liverpool player, and to captain his country on 23 occasions.

Hughes made his debut for the Reds on 4 March 1967 in a 2–1 (Lawler, Hunt) First Division home win over Stoke City. He proved to be a major asset to the Liverpool side, adding a new dimension to their play. He could break up an opposition attack and then surge upfield, sometimes finishing a move off with a cannonball shot. His team-mates quickly named him "Crazy Horse", since his infectious enthusiasm for the game lit up the Liverpool dressing room, while out on the pitch he just never seemed to tire. Emlyn played for Liverpool at full-back, centre-half and in midfield and has earned his place as one of the greatest of Liverpool captains, the first to hold aloft the European Cup, after the 3–1 (McDermott, Smith, Neal) win over Borussia Moenchengladbach in 1977.

Hughes won his first England cap against Holland on 5 November 1969 in a 1–0 win in Amsterdam. In 1970 he was a non-playing member of the England squad that travelled to Mexico for the World Cup Finals. In 1974 he replaced Bobby Moore as England captain, but with England missing out on qualification for three consecutive major tournaments, Emlyn never played for his country in a World Cup Finals nor in a European Championship Finals tournament.

Emlyn won his first medal with Liverpool in 1973 when the Reds lifted the First Division Championship, and that same season he added a UEFA Cup winners' medal. In total with Liverpool he won four League Championships, one FA Cup, two UEFA Cups and two European Cups. In 1977 Hughes was voted the Football Writers' Footballer of the Year, and in August 1979 he joined Wolverhampton Wanderers for £90,000 after 665 games and 49 goals for the Reds, going on to success with Wolves, in 1980, in the one trophy he never won during his Anfield days, the League Cup. In 1983 he was awarded the OBE for his services to football. Emlyn Hughes died of a brain tumour on 9 November 2004 at his home in Sheffield.

## ❖ WHAT THE REDS SAID (12) ❖

"I'm on top of the world. This is the best night of my life."
***Steven Gerrard**, on the night Liverpool won the 2005 Champions League*

## ❖ 60-YEAR SERVANT ❖

Joe Hewitt signed for the Reds from Sunderland on 11 February 1904. In 1910, after 164 games and 71 goals for the club, he left Anfield to join Bolton Wanderers. The following year, though, he returned to the Reds to take up a coaching position, and his career at Anfield spanned a further 60 years, until his death in 1971.

## ❖ ANFIELD SET ALIGHT ❖

On 3 March 1923 Fred "Polly" Hopkin scored his first goal for the Reds. Liverpool, the reigning champions, were riding high in the League and Hopkin's goal was the last in a 3–0 home win over Bolton Wanderers, in which Forshaw and Johnson also scored. As soon as Hopkin's goal went in, riotous celebrations broke out on the terraces and the main stand caught fire. The ground had to be evacuated, but the result stood and Liverpool went on to retain the League title.

## ❖ LIVERPOOL FORCE NEW TROPHY ❖

When Liverpool lifted the 2005 European Champions Cup in Istanbul after a dramatic penalty shoot-out win over AC Milan, UEFA permitted the Reds to retain the trophy since it was their fifth victory in the competition[†]. UEFA ordered a new trophy to be forged for the 2005–06 competition.

## ❖ THE MACCA AND GROWLER PARTNERSHIP ❖

Robbie Fowler, whose nickname is Growler, and Steve McManaman, aka Macca, had a horseracing business, known as "The Macca and Growler Partnership". They owned a number of horses, trained by Martin Pipe, and they were very successful, too, winning more than £600,000 in win and place prize money between 2001 and 2005.

---

[†]*Four other clubs have been awarded a European Cup trophy permanently: Real Madrid, who won the first five competitions from 1956 to 1960; Ajax, who won consecutively in 1971, 1972 and 1973; Bayern Munich, who won consecutively in 1974, 1975 and 1976; and AC Milan, who won the competition for the fifth time in 1994.*

## ❖ WORLD SOCCER'S TOP 100 ❖

In its December 1999 issue *World Soccer*, English international football magazine established in 1960, conducted a poll of its readers to choose the 100 greatest players of the twentieth century. Readers selected their top ten players in order of preference. Points were assigned to each vote a player gained, ten points for a first-place vote, nine points for a second-place vote and so on down to one point for a tenth-place vote. Pele ran away with first place, but 15 England players featured in the top 100, including two Liverpool stars:

| Ranking | Player | Pts |
|---|---|---|
| 44 | Michael Owen | 90 |
| 56 | Kevin Keegan | 60 |

## ❖ FAIRFOUL FALLS FOUL OF LAW ❖

After Manchester United beat Liverpool 2–0 at Old Trafford on Good Friday 1915, the press reported how some Liverpool players had appeared to lose interest in the game. When bookmakers reported that they had taken numerous bets that United would win 2–0, the football authorities launched an inquiry. The investigation found that Tom Fairfoul and three of his Liverpool team-mates (Tom Miller, Bob Pursell and Jackie Sheldon), along with four United players, had conspired to fix the result. All eight were suspended for life. Nevertheless at the end of World War I, the players had their bans rescinded in recognition of their contribution to the war effort. Three of the four Liverpool players, Sheldon, Pursell and Miller, played for the club after the war, but Fairfoul retired.

## ❖ FA YOUTH CUP WINNERS ❖

Liverpool's first win in the FA Youth Cup came in 1996 with a team that included Jamie Carragher and Michael Owen. The young Reds beat West Ham United's junior side 4–1 on aggregate in the two-leg final. In 2005–06, Liverpool overcame Manchester City 3–2 on aggregate to win the FA Youth Cup for the second time.

## ❖ FIRST SIX-FIGURE RED ❖

In September 1968 Alun Evans became Liverpool's first six-figure purchase when he arrived from Wolverhampton Wanderers for £100,000. He scored 33 goals in 111 games for the Reds.

## ❖ UP FOR THE CUP (6) ❖

Liverpool won the League Cup for the fourth consecutive year in 1984. In round two the Reds had a comfortable 8–1 two-leg aggregate win over Brentford. However, it took three attempts to squeeze past Fulham in the third round, with Liverpool finally winning the second replay 1–0 away after extra time. Birmingham City then proved an obstacle in round four, Liverpool winning a replay 3–0 at Anfield. A marathon campaign continued, Liverpool needing yet another replay to see off Sheffield Wednesday, who eventually succumbed 3–0 at Anfield. Walsall then stood between Liverpool and a fifth consecutive appearance in the final. Liverpool drew the first leg 2–2 at Anfield before winning the return leg 2–0. In the 1983–84 final Liverpool drew 0–0 with Everton at Wembley before beating their Merseyside rivals 1–0 at Maine Road in the replay.

**MILK CUP FINAL**
*25 MARCH 1984, WEMBLEY STADIUM*
**Liverpool** (0) **0**     vs     **Everton** (0) **0**
*Att.* 100,000
*Liverpool:* Grobbelaar; Neal, A. Kennedy, Lawrenson, Hansen; Whelan, Lee, Johnston (Robinson), Souness; Dalglish, Rush

**REPLAY**
*28 MARCH 1984, MAINE ROAD, MANCHESTER*
**Liverpool** (1) **1**     vs     **Everton** (0) **0**
Souness
*Att.* 52,089
*Liverpool:* Grobbelaar; Neal, A. Kennedy, Lawrenson, Hansen; Whelan, Souness, Lee, Johnston; Rush, Dalglish

## ❖ WE ALL LIVE IN A ROBBIE FOWLER HOUSE ❖

Robbie Fowler is reputedly the wealthiest sportsman in Britain. A racehorse owner and property tycoon besides being a footballer, his wealth is estimated at £28 million.[†] Robbie's property portfolio is believed to contain in the region of 100 properties in and around the Liverpool area. Fans often tease him by singing, to the tune of "Yellow Submarine", "We all live in a Robbie Fowler house".

---

[†] *When Robbie Fowler re-signed for Liverpool from Manchester City in January 2006, wages were not discussed.*

## ❖ WE ARE THE CHAMPIONS (15) ❖

At the start of the 1983–84 season Joe Fagan moved from the Boot Room to the Manager's Office at Anfield to replace Bob Paisley, who had retired. What a season it was for the mild-mannered Fagan as he guided Liverpool to League Cup success, their fifth Division One Championship title (their third in succession) and their fourth European Cup triumph. Southampton pressed the Reds hard all season, with Liverpool managing only one point from the six on offer against the south coast club. However, whereas the Reds lost six League games in of the season, the Saints lost nine, including seven on the road. In the end Liverpool won the title by three points.

### *Football League Division 1*
### 1983–84

| | P | W | D | L | F | A | W | D | L | F | A | Pts |
|---|---|---|---|---|---|---|---|---|---|---|---|---|
| 1. Liverpool | 42 | 14 | 5 | 2 | 50 | 12 | 8 | 9 | 4 | 23 | 20 | 80 |
| 2. Southampton | 42 | 15 | 4 | 2 | 44 | 17 | 7 | 7 | 7 | 22 | 21 | 77 |
| 3. Nottingham Forest | 42 | 14 | 4 | 3 | 47 | 17 | 8 | 4 | 9 | 29 | 28 | 74 |
| 4. Manchester United | 42 | 14 | 3 | 4 | 43 | 18 | 6 | 11 | 4 | 28 | 23 | 74 |
| 5. Queens Park Rangers | 42 | 14 | 4 | 3 | 37 | 12 | 8 | 3 | 10 | 30 | 25 | 73 |
| 6. Arsenal | 42 | 10 | 5 | 6 | 41 | 29 | 8 | 4 | 9 | 33 | 31 | 63 |
| 7. Everton | 42 | 9 | 9 | 3 | 21 | 12 | 7 | 5 | 9 | 23 | 30 | 62 |
| 8. Tottenham Hotspur | 42 | 11 | 4 | 6 | 31 | 24 | 6 | 6 | 9 | 33 | 41 | 61 |
| 9. West Ham United | 42 | 10 | 4 | 7 | 39 | 24 | 7 | 5 | 9 | 21 | 31 | 60 |
| 10. Aston Villa | 42 | 14 | 3 | 4 | 34 | 22 | 3 | 6 | 12 | 25 | 39 | 60 |
| 11. Watford | 42 | 9 | 7 | 5 | 36 | 31 | 7 | 2 | 12 | 32 | 46 | 57 |
| 12. Ipswich Town | 42 | 11 | 4 | 6 | 34 | 23 | 4 | 4 | 13 | 21 | 34 | 53 |
| 13. Sunderland | 42 | 8 | 9 | 4 | 26 | 18 | 5 | 4 | 12 | 16 | 35 | 52 |
| 14. Norwich City | 42 | 9 | 8 | 4 | 34 | 20 | 3 | 7 | 11 | 14 | 29 | 51 |
| 15. Leicester City | 42 | 11 | 5 | 5 | 40 | 30 | 2 | 7 | 12 | 25 | 38 | 51 |
| 16. Luton Town | 42 | 7 | 5 | 9 | 30 | 33 | 7 | 4 | 10 | 23 | 33 | 51 |
| 17. West Bromwich Albion | 42 | 10 | 4 | 7 | 30 | 25 | 4 | 5 | 12 | 18 | 37 | 51 |
| 18. Stoke City | 42 | 11 | 4 | 6 | 30 | 23 | 2 | 7 | 12 | 14 | 40 | 50 |
| 19. Coventry City | 42 | 8 | 5 | 8 | 33 | 33 | 5 | 6 | 10 | 24 | 44 | 50 |
| 20. Birmingham City | 42 | 7 | 7 | 7 | 19 | 18 | 5 | 5 | 11 | 20 | 32 | 48 |
| 21. Notts County | 42 | 6 | 7 | 8 | 31 | 36 | 4 | 4 | 13 | 19 | 36 | 41 |
| 22. Wolverhampton W. | 42 | 4 | 8 | 9 | 15 | 28 | 2 | 3 | 16 | 12 | 52 | 29 |

### *Did You Know That?*
Joe Fagan had to be persuaded to take a Jaguar as a club car in favour of his modest Ford.

## ❖ LIVERPOOL CLUB CAPTAINS 1892–2006 ❖

| Captain | Years |
|---|---|
| Andrew Hannah | 1892–1895 |
| Jimmy Ross | 1895–1897 |
| John McCartney | 1897–1898 |
| Harry Storer | 1898–1899 |
| Alex Raisbeck | 1899–1909 |
| Arthur Goddard | 1909–1912 |
| Ephraim Longworth | 1912–1913 |
| Harry Lowe | 1913–1915 |
| Ephraim Longworth/Don MacKinlay | 1919–1920 |
| Ephraim Longworth | 1920–1921 |
| Don MacKinlay | 1921–1928 |
| Tom Bromilow | 1928–1929 |
| James Jackson | 1929–1930 |
| Tom Morrison | 1930–1931 |
| Tom Bradshaw | 1931–1934 |
| Ernie Blenkinsop/Tom Cooper | 1934–1935 |
| Ernie Blenkinsop | 1935–1936 |
| Ernie Blenkinsop/Tom Cooper | 1936–1937 |
| Tom Cooper | 1937–1939 |
| Matt Busby | 1939–1940 |
| Willie Fagan | 1945–1947 |
| Jack Balmer | 1947–1950 |
| Phil Taylor | 1950–1953 |
| Bill Jones | 1953–1954 |
| Laurie Hughes | 1954–1955 |
| Billy Liddell | 1955–1958 |
| Johnny Wheeler | 1958–1959 |
| Ronnie Moran | 1959–1960 |
| Dick White | 1960–1961 |
| Ron Yeats | 1961–1970 |
| Tommy Smith | 1970–1973 |
| Emlyn Hughes | 1973–1979 |
| Phil Thompson | 1979–1982 |
| Graeme Souness | 1982–1984 |
| Phil Neal | 1984–1985 |
| Alan Hansen | 1985–1988 |
| Ronnie Whelan | 1988–1989 |
| Alan Hansen | 1989–1990 |
| Ronnie Whelan | 1990–1991 |
| Steve Nicol | 1990–1991 |
| Mark Wright | 1991–1993 |
| Ian Rush | 1993–1996 |
| John Barnes | 1996–1997 |
| Paul Ince | 1997–1999 |
| Jamie Redknapp | 1999–2002 |
| Sami Hyypia | 2001–2003 |
| Steven Gerrard | 2003– |

## ❖ EUROPEAN GLORY NIGHTS (6) ❖

In the first round of the 1983–84 European Cup, Liverpool beat BK Odense home and away for a comfortable 6–0 aggregate victory. In the second round a hard-fought tie with Spanish champions Athletic Bilbao ended in a 1–0 win in Spain thanks to an Ian Rush goal after a 0–0 draw at Anfield. In the third round Liverpool were drawn against Portuguese champions Benfica. Liverpool won the first leg 1–0 at Anfield and then hammered Benfica 4–1 in the Stadium of Light a fortnight later. Dinamo Bucharest were Liverpool's last obstacle on the way to their fourth final appearance, and the Reds won both legs for a 3–1 aggregate victory. In the final Liverpool met AS Roma in their own backyard, the Stadio Olimpico in Rome. The game ended 1–1 after extra time but Bruce Grobbelaar's antics in the penalty shoot-out unnerved the Italians, and Liverpool lifted the cup with a 4–2 win on spot-kicks.

**EUROPEAN CUP FINAL**
*30 MAY 1984, STADIO OLIMPICO, ROME*
**Liverpool** (1) 1    vs    AS Roma (1) 1
Neal    Pruzzo 42
*After extra time*
*Liverpool won 4–2 on penalties*
*Att. 69,693*
*Liverpool:* Grobbelaar; Neal, Lawrenson, Hansen, A.Kennedy; Johnston (Nicol), Lee, Souness, Whelan; Dalglish (Robinson), Rush

## ❖ WHAT THE REDS SAID (13) ❖

"I probably deserve the man of the match ball after that. Me scoring a goal? It's like someone else scoring a hat-trick."
**Jamie Carragher**, *after scoring against FBK Kaunas in July 2005*

## ❖ DERBY UNDER LIGHTS ❖

Everton were the first team Liverpool played under floodlights at Anfield. Liverpool's new floodlights cost £15,000 to install in 1957, and the game, played on 30 October to commemorate the 75th anniversary of the Liverpool County FA, was won 3–2 by the Reds, with Billy Liddell striking twice. Those first Anfield floodlights, which were mounted on pylons set in each of the ground's four corners, were removed in 1973 and replaced with two new sets across the roof of the Kemlyn Stand and the Main Stand.

## ❖ JOE DID IT ALL ❖

Joe Fagan is an Anfield legend, a stalwart of the old Boot Room and a manager who was the first ever English club boss to win a treble of major honours. He arrived at Anfield as a trainer in 1958, 18 months before Bill Shankly, after a career as a player with Manchester City and Bradford Park Avenue and latterly a spell as a trainer at Rochdale. Joe served as Shankly's number two and was Bob Paisley's right-hand man from 1977 to 1983. When Paisley retired, Liverpool turned to Joe for stability and he didn't let the club down. His first game in charge of the Reds was a 1–1 draw (Rush) away at Wolverhampton Wanderers in the First Division on 27 August 1983. In his first season in charge he guided Liverpool to League Cup glory, League Championship success and he captured the European Cup for the fourth time in the club's history. Fagan rounded off the year by collecting the Manager of the Year award. Following the Heysel Disaster[†], he stepped down as Liverpool boss. Joe Fagan passed away in July 2001, aged 80.

## ❖ 85-YEAR HOODOO ENDED ❖

On 18 February 2006, Liverpool beat Manchester United 1–0 at Anfield in the FA Cup fifth round thanks to a Peter Crouch goal after 19 minutes. It was the Reds' first FA Cup win over United since their 2–1 success (Lacey, Chambers) at Old Trafford on 12 January 1921.

## ❖ SHANKLY QUITS ❖

On 12 July 1974[††], Bill Shankly, aged 60, announced his retirement as the manager of Liverpool after almost 15 years in charge of the club. He had made the decision to leave five weeks previously, but club directors tried to persuade him to stay. Shankly said that he was starting to feel the strain after so long in the job and that he had to take his family into consideration. "The pressures have built up so much during my 40 years in the game that I felt it was time to have a rest," he said.

---

[†]*Liverpool's 1–0 European Cup final defeat against Juventus at the Heysel Stadium, Brussels, on 29 May 1985 was the last time a competitive fixture was played in the stadium, until it was completely renovated and renamed the King Badouin II Stadium.*

[††]*After Bill Shankly retired as Liverpool manager in July 1974, he was often seen at Liverpool training sessions. However, it was felt his presence undermined new manager Bob Paisley, and the Liverpool board banned him from the training ground.*

## ❖ PHIL THOMPSON ❖

Phil Thompson was born on 21 January 1954 in Liverpool and supported Liverpool as a boy, standing on the Kop. Phil joined the club as a professional on 22 January 1971 from Kirkby Schools and made his debut on 3 April 1972 in a 3–0 (Lawler, Toshack, Hughes) away win at Manchester United.

In his first season at Anfield, 1972–73, Thompson won the First Division Championship, a UEFA Cup winners' medal and even a Reserve Team Championship winners' medal under the management of Bill Shankly. When 1973–74 arrived, Phil had dislodged Larry Lloyd, with Tommy Smith moving to full-back. Thompson now stood at the heart of the Liverpool defence alongside legendary Liverpool captain Emlyn Hughes. That season, Phil won an FA Cup winners' medal, having successfully man-marked the powerful and prolific Newcastle United striker Malcolm Macdonald out of the Wembley showpiece. In 1975–76, Thompson was an integral part of the Liverpool side that lifted the Double of League Championship and UEFA Cup.

On 24 March 1976 Don Revie awarded Phil Thompson his first international cap in England's 2–1 win over Wales in Wrexham. Phil was very much at home on his international debut, playing alongside club team-mates Ray Clemence, Phil Neal, Kevin Keegan and Ray Kennedy. During a mini-tournament in the United States at the end of the 1975–76 season, Phil scored his first and only international goal in a 3–2 win over Italy in New York. In 1976–77 Phil played enough games to win his third League Championship winners' medal but missed the 1977 FA Cup final defeat to Manchester United and the 1977 European Cup victory over Borussia Moenchengladbach through injury. Phil returned to the Liverpool side the following season and won his first European Cup winners' medal in the 1–0 (Dalglish) win over FC Bruges at Wembley. A year later he won his fourth League Championship winners' medal, and when Emlyn Hughes left Liverpool in August 1979, Bob Paisley made Thompson club captain. Phil's proudest moment as skipper came in the 1981 European Cup final win over Real Madrid in Paris. He later took the trophy to bed and then down to his local pub, *The Falcon*, in Kirkby, so his mates could have their photographs taken with it.

When Thompson lost the club captaincy and his place in the team, he moved to Sheffield United, in March 1985, after 477 appearances and 13 goals for the Reds. Phil won seven League Championships, one FA Cup, two League Cups, six FA Charity Shields, two European Cups, one UEFA Cup and one European Super Cup. He also played for England 43 times. Phil later returned to Anfield for spells as a coach and assistant manager.

## ❖ REDS AT THE WORLD CUP ❖

| Year | Location | Player | Country | Matches | Goals |
|---|---|---|---|---|---|
| 1950 | Brazil | Laurie Hughes | England | 3 | 0 |
| 1958 | Sweden | Alan A'Court | England | 3 | 0 |
| | | Tommy Younger | Scotland | 2 | 0 |
| 1966 | England | Roger Hunt | England | 6 | 3 |
| | | Ian Callaghan | England | 1 | 0 |
| 1978 | Argentina | Kenny Dalglish | Scotland | 3 | 1 |
| | | Graeme Souness | Scotland | 1 | 0 |
| 1982 | Spain | Phil Thompson | England | 5 | 0 |
| | | Phil Neal | England | 2 | 0 |
| | | Alan Hansen | Scotland | 3 | 0 |
| | | Graeme Souness | Scotland | 3 | 1 |
| | | Kenny Dalglish | Scotland | 2 | 1 |
| 1986 | Mexico | Jan Molby | Denmark | 4 | 0 |
| | | Steve Nicol | Scotland | 3 | 0 |
| 1990 | Italy | John Barnes | England | 5 | 0 |
| | | Peter Beardsley | England | 4 | 0 |
| | | Steve McMahon | England | 3 | 0 |
| | | Steve Staunton | Ireland | 5 | 0 |
| | | Ray Houghton | Ireland | 5 | 0 |
| | | Ronnie Whelan | Ireland | 1 | 0 |
| | | Gary Gillespie | Scotland | 1 | 0 |
| | | Glenn Hysen | Sweden | 2 | 0 |
| 1994 | USA | Stig Inge Bjornebye | Norway | 3 | 0 |
| 1998 | France | Paul Ince | England | 4 | 0 |
| | | Michael Owen | England | 4 | 2 |
| | | Steve McManaman | England | 1 | 0 |
| | | Stig Inge Bjornebye | Norway | 4 | 0 |
| | | Oyvind Leonhardsen | Norway | 3 | 0 |
| | | Brad Friedel | USA | 1 | 0 |
| 2002 | Japan/Korea | Michael Owen | England | 5 | 2 |
| | | Emile Heskey | England | 5 | 1 |
| | | Dietmar Hamann | Germany | 6 | 0 |
| | | Jerzy Dudek | Poland | 2 | 0 |
| | | Abel Xavier | Portugal | 1 | 0 |
| | | El Hadji Diouf | Senegal | 5 | 0 |

*Salif Diao did not sign a contract with Liverpool until after the 2002 World Cup.*

### Did You Know That?
Gerry Byrne was a member of England's 1966 World Cup winning squad, but he did not play in a single game.

## ❖ EUROPEAN NIGHT OF TRAGEDY ❖

The 1985 European Cup final will always be marred by the truly awful events that unfolded in the Heysel Stadium, Brussels, prior to kick-off that late May night, as 39 fans lost their lives when a wall collapsed. Back in the autumn of 1984, though, Liverpool had begun their defence of the European Cup with home and away wins over Lech Poznan for a 5–0 aggregate score in Round One. In the second round Liverpool faced Benfica in the competition for the second successive year and squeezed through 3–2 on aggregate. Austrian champions Austria Vienna were disposed of 5–2 in the third round, and in the semi-finals Liverpool beat Greece's Panathinaikos 4–0 at Anfield and 1–0 in Athens. At Heysel in the final, Liverpool went down 1–0 to Juventus, but the result pales into insignificance alongside the human tragedy that took place.

### EUROPEAN CUP FINAL
*29 MAY 1985, HEYSEL STADIUM, BRUSSELS*
**Liverpool** (0) 0      vs      Juventus (0) 1
Boniek (pen)
*Att.* 58,000
*Liverpool:* Grobbelaar; Neal, Beglin, Lawrenson (Gillespie), Hansen; Nicol, Dalglish, Whelan, Wark; Rush, Walsh (Johnson)

## ❖ SCOTLAND'S FIRST RED ❖

In 1897 George Allan became the first Liverpool player to be capped by Scotland. Liverpool had signed Allan from Leith Athletic in 1895 and he was the Reds' top goalscorer as they won the Division Two Championship in 1895–96[†]. That season he also became the first player to score four goals in a game for Liverpool in the 10–1 win over Rotherham at Anfield on 18 February 1896. Besides Allan, McVean (3), Ross (2) and Becton also made the scoresheet.

## ❖ PAISLEY WINS LEAGUE TITLE AS A PLAYER ❖

The first season after the war (1946–47) saw the First Division Championship title return to Anfield. The team containing Bob Paisley, Jack Balmer and the legendary Billy Liddell swept all before them in the League, losing just once in their last 16 games.

[†]*In 1895–96, Liverpool beat Rotherham 10–1 at home and 5–0 away in Division Two.*

## ❖ FOOTBALL WRITERS' TRIBUTE AWARD ❖

The Football Writers' Tribute Award is presented on an annual basis to an individual who the Football Writers' Committee feels has made an outstanding contribution to the national game. The trophy is presented at a gala dinner at The Savoy Hotel in London every January. Two Liverpool legends have won the award:

| Year | Award winner |
|------|------|
| 1987 | Kenny Dalglish |
| 1984 | Bob Paisley |

## ❖ EUROPEAN TRAVELS IN BRITAIN ❖

Besides Anfield, Liverpool have played European games in a number of British stadia, including:

Wembley Stadium ❖ Celtic Park *(Celtic)* ❖ Easter Road *(Hibernian)*
Elland Road *(Leeds United)* ❖ Seaview *(Crusaders)*
Stamford Bridge *(Chelsea)* ❖ White Hart Lane *(Tottenham Hotspur)*

## ❖ MANAGER OF THE YEAR ❖

Four different Liverpool managers have won the Manager of the Year award. Both Joe Fagan and Kenny Dalglish won in their first year.

| | |
|------|------|
| Bill Shankly | 1973 |
| Bob Paisley | 1976, 1977, 1979, 1980, 1982, 1983 |
| Joe Fagan | 1984 |
| Kenny Dalglish | 1986, 1988, 1990 |

## ❖ INAUSPICIOUS START ❖

On 19 December 1959 Bill Shankly took charge of Liverpool for the first time. Cardiff City were the visitors to Anfield for a Division Two game and humiliated the Reds, winning 4–0.

## ❖ SIX IN SIX FOR CROUCH ❖

Peter Crouch's debut derby goal against Everton at Goodison Park on 28 December 2005 was his sixth goal in six games after a sequence of nine games when he couldn't buy a goal. Liverpool won the game 3–1, the other goals coming from Steven Gerrard and Djibril Cisse.

# ❖ LIVERPOOL MANAGERS XI ❖

**1**
Matt
*McQUEEN*
*(LIVERPOOL)*

**2**
Phil
*NEAL*
*(BOLTON WANDERERS)*

**4**
Emlyn
*HUGHES*
*(ROTHERHAM UNITED)*
*(captain)*

**5**
Ron
*YEATS*
*(TRANMERE ROVERS)*

**3**
Steve
*STAUNTON*
*(REPUBLIC OF IRELAND)*

**6**
Peter
*CORMACK*
*(PARTICK THISTLE)*

**8**
Graeme
*SOUNESS*
*(RANGERS)*

**11**
John
*BARNES*
*(CELTIC)*

**7**
Kevin
*KEEGAN*
*(NEWCASTLE UNITED)*

**9**
John
*TOSHACK*
*(REAL MADRID)*

**10**
John
*ALDRIDGE*
*(TRANMERE ROVERS)*

*Substitutes*
Ian *ST JOHN* *(MOTHERWELL)* • Mark *LAWRENSON* *(PETERBOROUGH UNITED)*
Keith *BURKINSHAW* *(TOTTENHAM HOTSPUR)* • Matt *BUSBY* *(MANCHESTER UNITED)*
Mark *WRIGHT* *(CHESTER)*
*Manager*
Bob *PAISLEY* *(LIVERPOOL)*

### *Did You Know That?*
John Aldridge joined Tranmere Rovers in 1991 and, in his first season there, equalled the club's goalscoring record of 40. Aldo later managed the club guiding them to the 2000 Worthington Cup final.

# ❖ LIVERPOOL'S FIRST MANAGER ❖

Between 1892 and 1896, "Honest John" McKenna, Liverpool's first manager (actually co-manager with William Barclay), guided the Reds to the Lancashire League title (1892–93) and the Second Division Championship twice (1893–94 and 1895–96). As a result of his frequent trips to Scotland, the first ever Liverpool team – against Higher Walton in the Lancashire League on 3 September 1892 (they won 8–0 at Anfield) – did not contain a single Englishman. Known as the "Team of the Macs", that first season's squad contained eight "Macs": James McBride, John McCartney, Duncan McLean, Bill McOwen (an Englishman), Joe McQue, Matt and Hugh McQueen and Malcolm McVean).

## ❖ UNLUCKY 13 FOR REDS IN 200TH DERBY ❖

The Merseyside derby[†] is, to date, the most played derby match in English football history. The 200th Merseyside derby was played at Goodison Park on 11 December 2004 in front of 40,552 fans. It was the 99th meeting between the two sides at Goodison and the 25th meeting in the FA Premier League. Liverpool's 13th away Premiership derby against Everton proved unlucky as the Toffees won the game 1–0 with a Lee Carsley goal in the 68th minute. Following the game, Liverpool's full record against Everton was:

|                        | P   | W  | D  | L  | F   | A   |
|------------------------|-----|----|----|----|-----|-----|
| FA Premier League      | 24  | 8  | 10 | 7  | 27  | 25  |
| Division One           | 146 | 54 | 44 | 48 | 203 | 181 |
| FA Cup                 | 20  | 9  | 5  | 6  | 34  | 24  |
| League Cup             | 4   | 2  | 1  | 1  | 2   | 1   |
| FA Charity Shield      | 3   | 1  | 1  | 1  | 2   | 2   |
| Screen Sport Super Cup | 2   | 2  | 0  | 0  | 7   | 2   |
| Totals                 | 200 | 76 | 61 | 63 | 275 | 235 |

## ❖ ABLETT DOUBLES UP ❖

Gary Ablett won an FA Cup winners' medal with Liverpool in 1989 and repeated the achievement with Everton in 1995.

## ❖ MENACE FROM SUBS ❖

Liverpool's Ian Rush and Everton's Stuart McCall scored two goals each, having both come on as substitutes in the 1989 FA Cup final. Ian Rush's first strike in Liverpool's 3–2 win broke Dixie Dean's Merseyside derby goalscoring record. John Aldridge provided Liverpool's other goal.

## ❖ RUSH STRIKES IN BILBAO ❖

Liverpool travelled to Spain to face Athletic Bilbao in the second leg of their second round European Cup tie on 2 November 1983 after managing only a 0–0 draw at Anfield. However, an Ian Rush strike in the 66th minute in the San Mamés Stadium was enough to send the Reds into the next round.

[†]*Liverpool failed to record a single derby victory in the five years between 1994 and 1999, whilst Everton broke a decade-long hoodoo by winning at Anfield in November 1995.*

## ❖ WHAT THE REDS SAID (14) ❖

"My philosophy is that the club is more important than anyone."
*Gerard Houllier*

## ❖ BILL SHANKLY OBE ❖

William "Bill" Shankly was born on 2 September 1913 in East Ayrshire, Scotland. Bill was one of five brothers who all played professional football. His brother Robert was also a successful manager, guiding Dundee Football Club to the Scottish First Division Championship in 1961–62. Bill played for Carlisle United and Preston North End and appeared for Partick Thistle during World War II. In 1949 he was appointed manager of Carlisle United before moving to Grimsby Town in 1951, Workington in 1953, Huddersfield Town in 1956 and finally Liverpool in 1959. At the end of the 1973–74 season Bill Shankly retired and was awarded the OBE for his services to football. Bill Shankly died on 29 September 1981, aged 68. In 2002 he was made an Inaugural Inductee of the English Football Hall of Fame in recognition of his contribution to the English game as manager of Liverpool[†]. Here is a record of Bill Shankly's major honours as player and manager:

### As a player
*Preston North End*
1933–34: Division Two runners-up
1936–37: FA Cup finalists
1937–38: FA Cup winners
7 international caps for Scotland

### As a manager
*Liverpool*
1961–62: Division Two champions
1963–64: Division One champions
1964–65: FA Cup winners
1965–66: Division One champions,
European Cup Winners' Cup finalists
1968–69: Division One runners-up
1970–71: FA Cup finalists
1972–73: Division One champions, UEFA Cup winners
1973–74: FA Cup winners, Division One runners-up

---

[†]*Today, the "Shankly Gates" at Anfield are a lasting memorial to a true Liverpool icon and one of the club's most successful managers.*

# ❖ WE ARE THE CHAMPIONS (16) ❖

The 1985–86 season was a head-to-head race for the Division One Championship between Liverpool, now under the leadership of player-manager Kenny Dalglish, and Everton. Liverpool drew first blood, beating Everton 3–2 (Dalglish, Rush, McMahon) at Goodison Park in their ninth League game of the campaign. However, when Everton beat the Reds 2–0 at Anfield on 22 February 1986, the pressure was on for Liverpool. The Reds responded by winning 11 of their remaining 12 League fixtures, taking 34 out of the 36 points available to clinch their sixteenth Division One Championship. Both Merseyside clubs won 16 of their 21 home League games and 10 of their 21 away League games, but whereas the Toffees lost eight League games, the Reds lost just six. To rub salt into the wound, Liverpool won their first ever domestic "Double" in 1986, beating Everton 3–1 (Rush 2, Johnston) in the FA Cup final.

## *Canon League Division 1*
### 1985–86

|  | P | W | D | L | F | A | W | D | L | F | A | Pts |
|---|---|---|---|---|---|---|---|---|---|---|---|---|
| 1. Liverpool | 42 | 16 | 4 | 1 | 58 | 14 | 10 | 6 | 5 | 31 | 23 | 88 |
| 2. Everton | 42 | 16 | 3 | 2 | 54 | 18 | 10 | 5 | 6 | 33 | 23 | 86 |
| 3. West Ham United | 42 | 17 | 2 | 2 | 48 | 16 | 9 | 4 | 8 | 26 | 24 | 84 |
| 4. Manchester United | 42 | 12 | 5 | 4 | 35 | 12 | 10 | 5 | 6 | 35 | 24 | 76 |
| 5. Sheffield Wednesday | 42 | 13 | 6 | 2 | 36 | 23 | 8 | 4 | 9 | 27 | 31 | 73 |
| 6. Chelsea | 42 | 12 | 4 | 5 | 32 | 27 | 8 | 7 | 6 | 25 | 29 | 71 |
| 7. Arsenal | 42 | 13 | 5 | 3 | 29 | 15 | 7 | 4 | 10 | 20 | 32 | 69 |
| 8. Nottingham Forest | 42 | 11 | 5 | 5 | 38 | 25 | 8 | 6 | 7 | 31 | 28 | 68 |
| 9. Luton Town | 42 | 12 | 6 | 3 | 37 | 15 | 6 | 6 | 9 | 24 | 29 | 66 |
| 10. Tottenham Hotspur | 42 | 12 | 2 | 7 | 47 | 25 | 7 | 6 | 8 | 27 | 27 | 65 |
| 11. Newcastle United | 42 | 12 | 5 | 4 | 46 | 31 | 5 | 7 | 9 | 21 | 41 | 63 |
| 12. Watford | 42 | 11 | 6 | 4 | 40 | 22 | 5 | 5 | 11 | 29 | 40 | 59 |
| 13. Queens Park Rangers | 42 | 12 | 3 | 6 | 33 | 20 | 3 | 4 | 14 | 20 | 44 | 52 |
| 14. Southampton | 42 | 10 | 6 | 5 | 32 | 18 | 2 | 4 | 15 | 19 | 44 | 46 |
| 15. Manchester City | 42 | 7 | 7 | 7 | 25 | 26 | 4 | 5 | 12 | 18 | 31 | 45 |
| 16. Aston Villa | 42 | 7 | 6 | 8 | 27 | 28 | 3 | 8 | 10 | 24 | 39 | 44 |
| 17. Coventry City | 42 | 6 | 5 | 10 | 31 | 35 | 5 | 5 | 11 | 17 | 36 | 43 |
| 18. Oxford United | 42 | 7 | 7 | 7 | 34 | 27 | 3 | 5 | 13 | 28 | 53 | 42 |
| 19. Leicester City | 42 | 7 | 8 | 6 | 35 | 35 | 3 | 4 | 14 | 19 | 41 | 42 |
| 20. Ipswich Town | 42 | 8 | 5 | 8 | 20 | 24 | 3 | 3 | 15 | 12 | 31 | 41 |
| 21. Birmingham City | 42 | 5 | 2 | 14 | 13 | 25 | 3 | 3 | 15 | 17 | 48 | 29 |
| 22. West Bromwich Albion | 42 | 3 | 8 | 10 | 21 | 36 | 1 | 4 | 16 | 14 | 53 | 24 |

## ❖ KEVIN KEEGAN OBE ❖

Joseph Kevin Keegan was born on 14 February 1951 in Armthorpe, Yorkshire. As a teenager, Keegan was rejected by his local team, Doncaster Rovers, but Scunthorpe United recognized he had talent and signed him. Keegan made 120 appearances for "The Iron" before moving to Liverpool in May 1971 for £33,000. On 14 August 1971 Keegan made a scoring debut for the Reds in a 3–1 home win over Nottingham Forest (Tommy Smith and Emlyn Hughes also got on the scoresheet). Kevin had been on the pitch only 12 minutes before he found the back of the net. Speaking of his new recruit, Bill Shankly described the £33,000 fee as "daylight robbery" and could not believe his luck at having acquired such a bargain.

For the following six seasons Keegan stamped his personality all over the club. He was a bundle of dynamite who inspired the Reds to victory after victory at home in England and all across Europe. He and his strike partner, John Toshack, caused mayhem among opposing defenders as they scored goal on goal. In 1972–73 they helped Liverpool win their first Championship in seven years plus their first European trophy, the UEFA Cup. Kevin's workrate was so high that he would be found winning the ball in midfield, running back to his own half to defend and leading the Liverpool attack when going forward. Keegan was the Reds' joint top goalscorer in the League in 1972–73 with 13 goals, and he bagged two in the UEFA Cup final win over Borussia Moenchengladbach. He was already an international, having made his debut for England in their 1–0 win over Wales in Cardiff on 15 November 1972.

In 1974 Liverpool reached the FA Cup final and ironically their third-round opponents were Doncaster Rovers. Keegan scored twice in the 2–2 draw at Anfield before the Reds' won the replay 2–0 (Heighway, Cormack), and scored twice more on the way to Wembley. In the final he once more scored two in Liverpool's 3–0 win over Newcastle United, Steve Heighway getting the other. The 1974–75 season began badly for Kevin, however, when he was sent off along with Billy Bremner of Leeds United in the FA Charity Shield, and Liverpool finished the season trophyless. Fortunes improved the following season as Keegan won his second League Championship winners' medal and his second UEFA Cup winners' medal, as well as being the 1976 FWA Footballer of the Year and England captain.

The 1976–77 season was Kevin's last at Anfield, adding victory in the European Cup final to a further League Championship title. After 323 appearances and exactly 100 goals, Keegan left Liverpool in the summer of 1977 and joined SV Hamburg for £500,000.

## ❖ LIVERPOOL MANAGERS ❖

*1892–1896*    **John McKenna/William Barclay**
*1896–1915*    **Tom Watson**
       2 League titles
*1920–1923*    **David Ashworth**
       1 League title
*1923–1928*    **Matt McQueen**
       1 League title
*1928–1936*    **George Patterson**
*1936–1951*    **George Kay**
       1 League title
*1951–1956*    **Don Welsh**
*1956–1959*    **Phil Taylor**
*1959–1974*    **Bill Shankly**
       3 League titles
       2 FA Cups
       1 UEFA Cup
*1974–1983*    **Bob Paisley**
       6 League titles
       3 League Cups
       3 European Cups
       1 UEFA Cup
       1 European Super Cup
*1983–1985*    **Joe Fagan**
       1 League title
       1 League Cup
       1 European Cup
*1985–1991*    **Kenny Dalglish**
       3 League titles
       2 FA Cups
*1991–1994*    **Graeme Souness**
       1 FA Cup
*1994–1998*    **Roy Evans**
       1 League Cup
*1998*    **Roy Evans/Gerard Houllier**
*1998–2004*    **Gerard Houllier**
       1 UEFA Cup
       1 FA Cup
       1 League Cup
*2004–*    **Rafael Benitez**
       1 European Cup (Champions League)
       1 FA Cup

## ❖ UP FOR THE CUP (7) ❖

In 1986 the first Merseyside derby FA Cup final took place and Liverpool won it, beating Everton 3–1 at Wembley. Liverpool went 1–0 down in the final after only five minutes but stormed back to claim their third FA Cup success. On their way to the final Liverpool beat Norwich City 5–0 at Anfield in the third round and Chelsea 2–1 at Stamford Bridge in the fourth. In round five Liverpool could only manage a 1–1 draw away to York City but won the replay 3–1 at Anfield. Watford provided Liverpool's sixth-round opponents and once again a replay was required following a 0–0 draw at Anfield. In the replay Liverpool won 2–1 at Vicarage Road before going on to beat Southampton 2–0 at White Hart Lane in the semi-finals.

### FA CUP FINAL
*10 MAY 1986, WEMBLEY STADIUM*

**Liverpool (0) 3**  vs  **Everton (0) 1**
Rush (2), Johnston      Lineker

*Att.* 98,000

*Liverpool:* Grobbelaar; Beglin, Nicol, Lawrenson, Hansen; Molby, Whelan, Johnston, MacDonald; Rush, Dalglish

## ❖ PFA MERIT AWARD ❖

At the end of every season the members of the Professional Footballers' Association give out their PFA Merit Award to a person or persons who have made an outstanding contribution to football. It was first awarded in 1974, since when four former Liverpool personnel have been honoured:

| Year | Award winner |
|------|-------------|
| 1998 | Steve Ogrizovic |
| 1997 | Peter Beardsley |
| 1983 | Bob Paisley |
| 1978 | Bill Shankly |

## ❖ THE PAISLEY GATEWAY ❖

On 8 April 1999 Jessie, widow of the legendary Bob Paisley, unveiled the Paisley Gateway situated in front of the Kop entrance at Anfield. The gates depict the three European Cups won by Liverpool under Paisley and the coat of arms for Hetton-le-Hole, his birthplace in County Durham.

### ❖ BOB PAISLEY OBE ❖

Robert "Bob" Paisley was born on 23 January 1919 in Hetton-le-Hole, County Durham. He was a member of the Bishop Auckland side that won the FA Amateur Cup in 1939 and joined Liverpool in May that year. World War II delayed his debut for the Reds until 5 January 1946, in which game Liverpool won 2–0 (Liddell, Fagan) away to Chester in the third round of the FA Cup. Paisley went on to make 277 appearances for the Reds, scoring 12 goals. He made his final appearance at the end of the 1953–54 season before joining the Liverpool backroom staff. When Bill Shankly retired in July 1974, Paisley assumed the Liverpool icon's mantle as manager. Paisley himself retired at the end of the 1982–83 season and was replaced by another Boot Room boy, Joe Fagan. Bob Paisley died on 14 February 1996. In 2002 he was made an Inaugural Inductee of the English Football Hall of Fame in recognition of his contribution to the English game as manager of Liverpool. Here is a record of Bob Paisley's major honours as player and manager with Liverpool:

#### As a player
1947: Division One Championship winners
1950: FA Cup runners-up

#### As a manager
1974: FA Charity Shield winners
1976: Division One champions, UEFA Cup winners,
FA Charity Shield winners
1977: Division One champions, European Cup winners,
European Super Cup winners, FA Charity Shield *(shared)*
1978: European Cup winners
1979: Division One champions
1980: Division One champions, FA Charity Shield winners
1981: League Cup winners, European Cup winners
1982: Division One champions, League Cup winners,
FA Charity Shield winners
1983: Division One champions, League Cup winners

### ❖ THE REDS BEATEN BY THE REDS ❖

In the quarter-finals of the 1980–81 European Cup, Liverpool beat Bulgarian champions CSKA Sofia 5–1 at Anfield (Souness 3, Lee, McDermott) and 1–0 in Sofia (Johnson). Like Liverpool, CSKA, who were founded in 1948, are nicknamed "The Reds".

## ❖ WE ARE THE CHAMPIONS (17) ❖

The 1987–88 season brought Liverpool's seventeenth Division One crown but also brought disappointment when the Reds lost the 1988 FA Cup final to Wimbledon, who denied the Merseysiders their second Double in three years. Throughout the League campaign Liverpool were simply awesome. They won 26 of their 42 games, drew 12 and lost just twice, to Everton and Nottingham Forest, with both defeats coming away from Anfield. The Liverpool defence were Scrooge-like, conceding only 24 goals, just 9 of them at home. Liverpool won the title by a comfortable nine points from Alex Ferguson's Manchester United, with whom they drew both League games that season.

### *Barclays League Division 1*
### 1987–88

| | | P | W | D | L | F | A | W | D | L | F | A | Pts |
|---|---|---|---|---|---|---|---|---|---|---|---|---|---|
| 1. | **Liverpool** | 40 | 15 | 5 | 0 | 49 | 9 | 11 | 7 | 2 | 38 | 15 | 90 |
| 2. | Manchester United | 40 | 14 | 5 | 1 | 41 | 17 | 9 | 7 | 4 | 30 | 21 | 81 |
| 3. | Nottingham Forest | 40 | 11 | 7 | 2 | 40 | 17 | 9 | 6 | 5 | 27 | 22 | 73 |
| 4. | Everton | 40 | 14 | 4 | 2 | 34 | 11 | 5 | 9 | 6 | 19 | 16 | 70 |
| 5. | Queens Park Rangers | 40 | 12 | 4 | 4 | 30 | 14 | 7 | 6 | 7 | 18 | 24 | 67 |
| 6. | Arsenal | 40 | 11 | 4 | 5 | 35 | 16 | 7 | 8 | 5 | 23 | 23 | 66 |
| 7. | Wimbledon | 40 | 8 | 9 | 3 | 32 | 20 | 6 | 6 | 8 | 26 | 27 | 57 |
| 8. | Newcastle United | 40 | 9 | 6 | 5 | 32 | 23 | 5 | 8 | 7 | 23 | 30 | 56 |
| 9. | Luton Town | 40 | 11 | 6 | 3 | 40 | 21 | 3 | 5 | 12 | 17 | 37 | 53 |
| 10. | Coventry City | 40 | 6 | 8 | 6 | 23 | 25 | 7 | 6 | 7 | 23 | 28 | 53 |
| 11. | Sheffield Wednesday | 40 | 10 | 2 | 8 | 27 | 30 | 5 | 6 | 9 | 25 | 36 | 53 |
| 12. | Southampton | 40 | 6 | 8 | 6 | 27 | 26 | 6 | 6 | 8 | 22 | 27 | 50 |
| 13. | Tottenham Hotspur | 40 | 9 | 5 | 6 | 26 | 23 | 3 | 6 | 11 | 12 | 25 | 47 |
| 14. | Norwich City | 40 | 7 | 5 | 8 | 26 | 26 | 5 | 4 | 11 | 14 | 26 | 45 |
| 15. | Derby County | 40 | 6 | 7 | 7 | 18 | 17 | 4 | 6 | 10 | 17 | 28 | 43 |
| 16. | West Ham United | 40 | 6 | 9 | 5 | 23 | 21 | 3 | 6 | 11 | 17 | 31 | 42 |
| 17. | Charlton Athletic | 40 | 7 | 7 | 6 | 23 | 21 | 2 | 8 | 10 | 15 | 31 | 42 |
| 18. | Chelsea | 40 | 7 | 11 | 2 | 24 | 17 | 2 | 4 | 14 | 26 | 51 | 42 |
| 19. | Portsmouth | 40 | 4 | 8 | 8 | 21 | 27 | 3 | 6 | 11 | 15 | 39 | 35 |
| 20. | Watford | 40 | 4 | 5 | 11 | 15 | 24 | 3 | 6 | 11 | 12 | 27 | 32 |
| 21. | Oxford United | 40 | 5 | 7 | 8 | 24 | 34 | 1 | 6 | 13 | 20 | 46 | 31 |

### ❖ ROBBIE RICH ❖

On 1 November 1994, Liverpool gave Robbie Fowler, then aged 19, a contract that made him British football's first teenage millionaire.

## ❖ THREE UP FOR FORSHAW ❖

Dick Forshaw won League Championship winners' medals with Liverpool in 1922 and 1923. He then moved to Everton, where he won his third League Championship winners' medal in 1928.

## ❖ FIRST IRISH CAP ❖

In February 1912 William "Billy" Lacey crossed Stanley Park and signed for the Reds. Lacey was fast and versatile and could play in any midfield position, although he excelled on the wing. In 1913 he became the first Liverpool player to be capped for Ireland.

## ❖ RESTRAINT OUT OF RESPECT ❖

Following the Reds' 3–2 (Aldridge, Rush 2) extra-time win over Everton in the 1989 FA Cup final, the players did not do the traditional lap of honour around Wembley. This was in memory of the 96 fans that had tragically lost their lives in the Hillsborough Disaster on 15 April 1989.

## ❖ REPEAT OF '77 FINAL ❖

In the semi-finals of the 1977–78 European Cup, Liverpool faced Borussia Moenchengladbach, the team they had beaten in the previous year's final. Despite going down 1–2 (Johnson) in Dusseldorf, Liverpool won 3–0 (R. Kennedy, Dalglish, Case) at Anfield to progress to their second successive European Cup final and a meeting at Wembley with FC Bruges.

## ❖ CROSSING THE PARK ❖

The following players played for both Liverpool and Everton during their careers but never appeared in a Merseyside derby fixture:

Jack Balmer (*amateur at Everton*) ❖ Arthur Berry ❖ Fred Geary
Patrick Gordon ❖ Tom Gracie ❖ Andrew Hannah
Alf Hanson (*trialist with Everton*) ❖ William Harthill
Abraham Hartley ❖ John Heydon (*amateur at Everton*)
Dave Hickson ❖ Alan Irvine ❖ Norman Low (*wartime guest at Everton*) ❖ Neil McBain ❖ Duncan McLean ❖ Anthony McNamara
Frank Mitchell ❖ Johnny Morrissey ❖ David Murray
James Payne ❖ Kevin Sheedy ❖ Donald Sloan

### ❖ WHAT THE REDS SAID (15) ❖

"The Liverpool philosophy is simple, and it is based on total belief. Maybe that has been the key to Liverpool's consistency. We were taught to go out there, play our own game and fear no one."
*Phil Neal*

### ❖ THOSE DAYS ARE GONE ❖

Everton fielded a reserve team against Liverpool in the first ever derby fixture. The Reds won 1–0 (Wyllie) in the Liverpool Senior Cup on 22 April 1893.

### ❖ FIRST LEAGUE DERBY ❖

On 13 October 1894 the first ever League Merseyside derby took place. Everton beat Liverpool 3–0 at Goodison Park in the First Division.

### ❖ SCOTT MOVE STYMIED ❖

In 1934 the Liverpool directors were ready to sign on the dotted line in a transfer that would see the legendary Liverpool goalkeeper Elisha Scott join Everton for £250. However, the proposed move was quickly scrapped when hundreds of Liverpool fans bombarded the *Liverpool Echo* with letters of protest.

### ❖ EUROPEAN CUP LANDMARK GOALS ❖

| No. | Date | Player | Opposition |
| --- | --- | --- | --- |
| 1 | 17 August 1964 | Gordon Wallace | KR Reykjavik |
| 50 | 20 April 1977 | Jimmy Case | FC Zurich |
| 100 | 30 September 1981 | Kenny Dalglish | Oulu Palloseura |
| 150 | 6 March 1985 | Steve Nicol | Austria Vienna |
| 159 | 24 April 1985 | Mark Lawrenson | Panathinaikos |

### ❖ FEWEST PLAYERS ❖

When Liverpool won their seventh Championship in 1965–66, they used only 14 players all season.

### ❖ RED LYON ❖

Gerard Houllier took Lyon to the French championship in 2005–06.

## ❖ UP FOR THE CUP (8) ❖

The second Merseyside derby FA Cup final took place at Wembley on 20 May 1989. And just as three years earlier, Liverpool defeated Everton to claim their fourth FA Cup success. Liverpool began the 1988–89 competition with a comfortable 3–0 away win at Carlisle United in round three. In the next round Liverpool beat Millwall 2–0 at the Den before winning their third successive away tie in the Cup, defeating Hull City 3–2 in the fifth round. The sixth round saw the Reds gain a home tie and they easily disposed of Brentford, winning 4–0. Liverpool's FA Cup semi-final against Nottingham Forest was one of the blackest days in British football: 96 fans lost their lives at Hillsborough. Liverpool beat Nottingham Forest 3–1 at Old Trafford in the replay, the first game having been abandoned after six minutes.

### FA CUP FINAL
*20 MAY 1989, WEMBLEY STADIUM*

**Liverpool** (1) **3**   vs   **Everton** (0) **2**
Aldridge, Rush (2)            McCall (2)
*After extra time*

*Att.* 82,500

*Liverpool:* Grobbelaar; Ablett, Staunton (Venison), Nicol, Hansen; Whelan, Houghton, Barnes, McMahon; Beardsley, Aldridge (Rush)

## ❖ FLOODLIT MASTERS ❖

As a result of the success of the first ever Liverpool v Everton floodlit friendly, the two sides decided to make the two-leg tie an annual event. In many ways it kept the Merseyside derby fixture alive at a time when the Reds languished in Division Two. Between 1957 and 1962, Liverpool won the Floodlit Challenge Cup four times, and when it was discontinued in 1962, the year Liverpool won Division Two, the Reds were allowed to keep the trophy. Today the Floodlit Challenge Cup can be seen in the Liverpool FC Museum at Anfield.

## ❖ WEMBLEY HAT-TRICK ❖

Liverpool have won all three Merseyside derby major competition finals[†]: the 1984 Milk Cup, the 1986 FA Cup and the 1989 FA Cup.

*'The Reds also beat Everton in the final of the Screen Sport Super Cup in 1985–86.*

### ❖ HONOURED BY REDS AND BLUES ❖

In March 1936 Liverpool's first manager, and later club chairman, "Honest John" McKenna, died having served the club for more than 40 years. Like that of Liverpool's founder, John Houlding, before him, McKenna's coffin was carried through the city streets by three Liverpool players and three Everton players. A commemorative plaque dedicated to John McKenna can be seen in the Anfield foyer, while a scroll and casket presented to him after a record 26 years as president of the Football League are in the club museum.

### ❖ SUPERPOWER SUMMIT ❖

When Liverpool met AC Milan in the 2005 UEFA Champions League final in Istanbul, it was the first time the two European giants had met in European competition.

### ❖ THREE IN THE DERBY ❖

The following players have scored a hat-trick for Liverpool in a Merseyside derby fixture[†]:

| Player | Venue | Match Date | Result |
|---|---|---|---|
| Harry Chambers | Home | 7 October 1922 | 5–1 |
| Dick Forshaw | Home | 26 September 1925 | 5–1 |
| Harold Barton | Home | 11 February 1933 | 7–4 |
| Fred Howe (4) | Home | 7 September 1935 | 6–0 |
| Ian Rush (4) | Away | 6 November 1982 | 5–0 |

### ❖ THE *ONZE D'OR* ❖

The *Onze d'Or* (also referred to as *"Onze Mondial* European Footballer of the Year") is a football award presented at the end of every season since 1976 by the French sports magazine *Onze Mondial*. The winner is chosen by a poll of the magazine's readers, who nominate their ideal team of the season, the top three players of which receive the *Onze d'Or, Onze d'Argent* and *Onze de Bronze* respectively. Only players playing in Europe are eligible for nomination. In 1977 Kevin Keegan became the first, and to date only, Liverpool player to win the *Onze d'Or*. He also won it in 1979 when he was at SV Hamburg. In 1991 a Coach of the Year award was introduced, which was won by Gerard Houllier in 2001.

[†]*The legendary Dixie Dean scored two derby hat-tricks during his career, in 1928 and 1931.*

## ❖ WE ARE THE CHAMPIONS (18) ❖

In 1989–90 Liverpool won their 18th Division One Championship – their last top-flight League championship title to date. By that point the League campaign had been reduced to 38 games. The Reds won 13 matches, drew five and lost just once at home in the League while on the road they notched up ten wins, five draws and four defeats. Former European Cup winners Aston Villa pushed the Reds hard all season, with both games between the two main title challengers ending 1–1, with Barnes the scorer at Villa Park and Beardsley netting at Anfield. In the event both sides won 13 times at home, and it was Liverpool's away form that swung the title in their favour as the Birmingham side could only manage eight wins, five draws and four defeats away from Villa Park.

### Barclays League Division 1
#### 1989–90

| | P | W | D | L | F | A | W | D | L | F | A | Pts |
|---|---|---|---|---|---|---|---|---|---|---|---|---|
| 1. Liverpool | 38 | 13 | 5 | 1 | 38 | 15 | 10 | 5 | 4 | 40 | 22 | 79 |
| 2. Aston Villa | 38 | 13 | 3 | 3 | 36 | 20 | 8 | 4 | 7 | 21 | 18 | 70 |
| 3. Tottenham Hotspur | 38 | 12 | 1 | 6 | 35 | 24 | 7 | 5 | 7 | 24 | 23 | 63 |
| 4. Arsenal | 38 | 14 | 3 | 2 | 38 | 11 | 4 | 5 | 10 | 16 | 27 | 62 |
| 5. Chelsea | 38 | 8 | 7 | 4 | 31 | 24 | 8 | 5 | 6 | 27 | 26 | 60 |
| 6. Everton | 38 | 14 | 3 | 2 | 40 | 16 | 3 | 5 | 11 | 17 | 30 | 59 |
| 7. Southampton | 38 | 10 | 5 | 4 | 40 | 27 | 5 | 5 | 9 | 31 | 36 | 55 |
| 8. Wimbledon | 38 | 5 | 8 | 6 | 22 | 23 | 8 | 8 | 3 | 25 | 17 | 55 |
| 9. Nottingham Forest | 38 | 9 | 4 | 6 | 31 | 21 | 6 | 5 | 8 | 24 | 26 | 54 |
| 10. Norwich City | 38 | 7 | 10 | 2 | 24 | 14 | 6 | 4 | 9 | 20 | 28 | 53 |
| 11. Queens Park Rangers | 38 | 9 | 4 | 6 | 27 | 22 | 4 | 7 | 8 | 18 | 22 | 50 |
| 12. Coventry City | 38 | 11 | 2 | 6 | 24 | 25 | 3 | 5 | 11 | 15 | 34 | 49 |
| 13. Manchester United | 38 | 8 | 6 | 5 | 26 | 14 | 5 | 3 | 11 | 20 | 33 | 48 |
| 14. Manchester City | 38 | 9 | 4 | 6 | 26 | 21 | 3 | 8 | 8 | 17 | 31 | 48 |
| 15. Crystal Palace | 38 | 8 | 7 | 4 | 27 | 23 | 5 | 2 | 12 | 15 | 43 | 48 |
| 16. Derby County | 38 | 9 | 1 | 9 | 29 | 21 | 4 | 6 | 9 | 14 | 19 | 46 |
| 17. Luton Town | 38 | 8 | 8 | 3 | 24 | 18 | 2 | 5 | 12 | 19 | 39 | 43 |
| 18. Sheffield Wednesday | 38 | 8 | 6 | 5 | 21 | 17 | 3 | 4 | 12 | 14 | 34 | 43 |
| 19. Charlton Athletic | 38 | 4 | 6 | 9 | 18 | 25 | 3 | 3 | 13 | 13 | 32 | 30 |
| 20. Millwall | 38 | 4 | 6 | 9 | 23 | 25 | 1 | 5 | 13 | 16 | 40 | 26 |

## ❖ LES BLEUS AND THEN THE REDS ❖

Gerard Houllier was French national team coach from 1992 to 1993.

## ❖ PHIL NEAL ❖

Phil Neal was born on 20 February 1951 in Irchester, England. His football career began with Northampton Town, for whom he signed in December 1968. He made his debut for the Cobblers later that season, at the end of which they were relegated to the Fourth division. During his days with Northampton he was normally played in midfield but was versatile enough to fill other positions when needed. Neal was Bob Paisley's first signing, arriving at Anfield for £66,000 in October 1974. On the 9th, he made his debut for the Reds in the Merseyside derby at Goodison Park, starting in place of injured left-back Alec Lindsay. He played well in a 0–0 draw in which Terry McDermott also made his Liverpool debut.

Between November 1976 and September 1983 Neal made a record 417 consecutive appearances for the Reds in all competitions before being forced to sit out a European Cup tie against Odense. He occupied the right-back position for the vast majority of these games. During his time at the club, Neal won just about everything there was to win at club level except the FA Cup. His first trophies came in 1975–76 when he won his first League Championship winners' medal and a UEFA Cup winners' medal, and honours gained during the course of his Anfield career include six First Division Championships, four European Cups (the most won by any Liverpool player), one European Super Cup, one UEFA Cup, four League Cups and five FA Charity Shields. Phil's impressive medal collection makes him the most decorated Liverpool player in the club's history.

On 24 March 1976 Don Revie awarded Phil his first England cap in the 2–1 win over Wales in Wrexham. His Liverpool team-mates, Clemence, Keegan, Ray Kennedy and Thompson also played. Neal went on to win 50 caps for his country, making his final appearance against Denmark on 21 September 1983, and is the second most capped England right-back of all time.

Phil Neal scored 59 goals for Liverpool in 650 appearances, most of them coming from the penalty spot. He converted a penalty in the 1977 European Cup final against Borussia Moenchengladbach and was on the mark again against AS Roma in 1984. Phil left Anfield in December 1985 to take up the position of player/manager at Third Division Bolton Wanderers. He was in charge when the club was relegated to Division Four for the first time in its history but managed to achieve promotion back into Division Three at the first attempt. Phil also managed Coventry City, Cardiff City and Manchester City and was Graham Taylor's assistant during the latter's spell as England manager.

# ❖ THE REDS IN EUROPE, 1964–2006 ❖

Liverpool have a fine European record, having participated in all the major European competitions. Since Liverpool first qualified for Europe, in 1964–65, they have played in 34 tournaments (and, in 2002–03, they played in both the Champions League and UEFA Cup).

| Year | Competition | Home | | | | | | Away | | | | |
|------|-------------|---|---|---|---|---|---|---|---|---|---|---|
| | | P | W | D | L | F | A | W | D | L | F | A |
| 1964–65 | European Cup | 9 | 3 | 1 | 0 | 12 | 2 | 2 | 2 | 1 | 8 | 5 |
| 1965–66 | Cup Winners' Cup | 9 | 4 | 0 | 0 | 9 | 1 | 1 | 1 | 3 | 3 | 5 |
| 1966–67 | European Cup | 5 | 1 | 1 | 0 | 4 | 2 | 1 | 0 | 2 | 4 | 8 |
| 1967–68 | Fairs Cup | 6 | 2 | 0 | 1 | 10 | 2 | 1 | 0 | 2 | 3 | 3 |
| 1968–69 | Fairs Cup | 2 | 1 | 0 | 0 | 2 | 1 | 0 | 0 | 1 | 1 | 2 |
| 1969–70 | Fairs Cup | 4 | 2 | 0 | 0 | 13 | 2 | 1 | 0 | 1 | 2 | 1 |
| 1970–71 | Fairs Cup | 10 | 4 | 0 | 1 | 9 | 1 | 1 | 4 | 0 | 4 | 3 |
| 1971–72 | Cup Winners' Cup | 4 | 1 | 1 | 0 | 2 | 0 | 0 | 0 | 2 | 2 | 5 |
| 1972–73 | UEFA Cup | 12 | 6 | 0 | 0 | 14 | 1 | 2 | 2 | 2 | 5 | 5 |
| 1973–74 | European Cup | 4 | 1 | 0 | 1 | 3 | 2 | 0 | 1 | 1 | 2 | 3 |
| 1974–75 | Cup Winners' Cup | 4 | 1 | 1 | 0 | 12 | 1 | 1 | 1 | 0 | 1 | 0 |
| 1975–76 | UEFA Cup | 12 | 5 | 1 | 0 | 18 | 5 | 3 | 2 | 1 | 7 | 4 |
| 1976–77 | European Cup | 9 | 4 | 0 | 0 | 11 | 1 | 3 | 0 | 2 | 11 | 4 |
| 1977–78 | European Cup | 7 | 3 | 0 | 0 | 12 | 2 | 2 | 0 | 2 | 5 | 5 |
| 1978–79 | European Cup | 2 | 0 | 1 | 0 | 0 | 0 | 0 | 0 | 1 | 0 | 2 |
| 1979–80 | European Cup | 2 | 1 | 0 | 0 | 2 | 1 | 0 | 0 | 1 | 0 | 3 |
| 1980–81 | European Cup | 9 | 3 | 0 | 1 | 19 | 2 | 3 | 2 | 0 | 5 | 2 |
| 1981–82 | European Cup | 6 | 3 | 0 | 0 | 11 | 2 | 1 | 1 | 1 | 3 | 4 |
| 1982–83 | European Cup | 6 | 3 | 0 | 0 | 9 | 2 | 1 | 0 | 2 | 4 | 4 |
| 1983–84 | European Cup | 9 | 3 | 1 | 0 | 7 | 0 | 4 | 1 | 0 | 9 | 3 |
| 1984–85 | European Cup | 9 | 4 | 0 | 0 | 15 | 0 | 2 | 1 | 2 | 3 | 3 |
| 1991–92 | UEFA Cup | 8 | 3 | 0 | 1 | 14 | 3 | 1 | 0 | 3 | 2 | 5 |
| 1992–93 | Cup Winners' Cup | 4 | 1 | 0 | 1 | 6 | 3 | 1 | 0 | 1 | 4 | 5 |
| 1995–96 | UEFA Cup | 4 | 0 | 1 | 1 | 0 | 1 | 1 | 1 | 0 | 2 | 1 |
| 1996–97 | Cup Winners' Cup | 8 | 4 | 0 | 0 | 14 | 4 | 2 | 1 | 1 | 4 | 5 |
| 1997–98 | UEFA Cup | 4 | 1 | 1 | 0 | 2 | 0 | 0 | 1 | 1 | 2 | 5 |
| 1998–99 | UEFA Cup | 6 | 1 | 1 | 1 | 5 | 1 | 1 | 1 | 1 | 6 | 5 |
| 2000–01 | UEFA Cup | 13 | 4 | 1 | 1 | 6 | 1 | 4 | 3 | 0 | 13 | 8 |
| 2001–02 | Champions League | 16 | 5 | 2 | 1 | 12 | 5 | 1 | 5 | 1 | 11 | 7 |
| 2002–03 | Champions League | 6 | 1 | 1 | 1 | 6 | 2 | 1 | 1 | 1 | 6 | 6 |
| 2002–03 | UEFA Cup | 6 | 2 | 0 | 1 | 3 | 2 | 2 | 1 | 0 | 3 | 1 |
| 2003–04 | UEFA Cup | 8 | 3 | 1 | 0 | 7 | 1 | 1 | 2 | 1 | 7 | 6 |
| 2004–05 | Champions League | 15 | 5 | 1 | 1 | 11 | 4 | 3 | 3 | 2 | 9 | 6 |
| 2005–06 | Champions League | 14 | 3 | 2 | 2 | 8 | 3 | 5 | 1 | 1 | 12 | 4 |

## ❖ UP FOR THE CUP (9) ❖

Ian Rush starred in, and scored the second goal in, Liverpool's 2–0 win over Sunderland in the 1992 FA Cup final at Wembley. In the third round of the 1991–92 competition, Liverpool beat Crewe Alexandra 4–0 away. Round four saw Liverpool draw 1–1 away at Bristol Rovers before beating them 2–1 at Anfield in the replay. In the fifth round Liverpool earned a hard-fought scoreless draw at Ipswich Town before beating the Tractor Boys 3–2 at Anfield in another replay. A 1–0 win over Aston Villa in the sixth round earned the Reds a place in the semi-finals. Portsmouth stood between Liverpool and a trip to Wembley, and it took two games to see off the south coast side. Following a 1–1 draw at Arsenal Stadium and a 0–0 draw at Villa Park, Liverpool won the penalty shoot-out 3–1 in the replay and went on to claim the Cup for the fifth time.

### FA CUP FINAL
*9 MAY 1992, WEMBLEY*
**Liverpool** (0) 2     vs     **Sunderland** (0) 0
Thomas, Rush
*Att.* 79,544
*Liverpool:* Grobbelaar; Jones, Burrows, Nicol, Wright; Houghton, Molby, McManaman, Thomas; Rush, Saunders

## ❖ LAST EUROPEAN CUP GOAL ❖

On 24 April 1985 Mark Lawrenson scored Liverpool's 159th and last ever goal in the European Cup as Liverpool beat Greek champions Panathinaikos 1–0 in Athens in the second leg of their 1984–85 semi-final tie. Liverpool lost 1–0 to Juventus in the final, which will be remembered more for the 39 football fans who died when a wall collapsed at the Heysel Stadium than for the football played that night. By the time Liverpool returned to the senior European club competition, it had become the Champions League.

## ❖ REDS LIGHT UP STADIUM ❖

On 21 March 1984 Liverpool met Benfica in their famous Estadio da Luz (Stadium of Light) in Lisbon, having narrowly beaten the Portuguese champions 1–0 (Rush) at Anfield a fortnight earlier. The Reds put on a majestic display of attacking football against the two-times champions of Europe, winning the second leg of their quarter-final 4–1, with goals from Whelan (2), Johnston and Rush.

## ❖ MERSEYSIDE DERBY REDS AND BLUES ❖

The following players played for both Liverpool and Everton in the Merseyside derby during their careers:

Gary Ablett ❖ Nick Barmby ❖ Peter Beardsley
David Burrows ❖ Edgar Chadwick ❖ Dick Forshaw
Don Hutchison ❖ David Johnson ❖ Tosh Johnson
Billy Lacey ❖ Steve McMahon ❖ Abel Xavier

## ❖ WHAT THE REDS SAID (16) ❖

"He was like a fox in that area, the way he hunted for those goals."
*Gerard Houllier, describing Robbie Fowler's hat-trick against Aston Villa in 1998*

## ❖ FIRST DERBY VICTORY ❖

On 25 September 1897, Liverpool recorded their first ever League Merseyside derby win over Everton. Liverpool won the First Division encounter 3–1 (Cunliffe, McQue, Becton) at Anfield.

## ❖ EUROPEAN CUP WINNERS' CUP ❖

Liverpool participated in the European Cup Winners' Cup five times. Although the Reds never won the cup – it was the one European trophy that eluded them – they did reach the final at the first attempt in 1965–66, despite losing two games (away to Juventus and Celtic). The Reds went down 2–1 (Hunt) after extra time to Germany's Borussia Dortmund in front of a crowd of 41,657 at Hampden Park on 5 May 1966.

### Overall ECWC Record

| P | W | D | L | F | A |
|---|---|---|---|---|---|
| 29 | 16 | 5 | 8 | 54 | 29 |

| Season | Round Reached | Home | | | | | | Away | | | | |
|--------|---------------|------|---|---|---|---|---|------|---|---|---|---|
| | | P | W | D | L | F | A | W | D | L | F | A |
| 1965–66 | Final | 9 | 4 | 0 | 0 | 9 | 1 | 1 | 1 | 3 | 3 | 5 |
| 1971–72 | R2 | 4 | 1 | 1 | 0 | 2 | 0 | 0 | 0 | 2 | 2 | 5 |
| 1974–75 | R2 | 4 | 1 | 1 | 0 | 12 | 1 | 1 | 1 | 0 | 1 | 0 |
| 1992–93 | R2 | 4 | 1 | 0 | 1 | 6 | 3 | 1 | 0 | 1 | 4 | 5 |
| 1996–97 | SF | 8 | 4 | 0 | 0 | 14 | 4 | 2 | 1 | 1 | 4 | 5 |

## ❖ PREMIER LEAGUE HAT-TRICKS ❖

Since the FA Premier League began in 1992–93, only six Reds have
scored a hat-trick in the competition. To date, Robbie Fowler leads
the way with eight hat-tricks, closely followed by Michael Owen
on seven:

| Date | Player | Opposition | Venue |
|---|---|---|---|
| 17.4.93 | Mark Walters | Coventry City | Anfield |
| 30.10.93 | Robbie Fowler | Southampton | Anfield |
| 28.8.94 | Robbie Fowler | Arsenal | Anfield |
| 23.9.95 | Robbie Fowler (4) | Bolton Wanderers | Anfield |
| 23.12.95 | Robbie Fowler | Arsenal | Anfield |
| 14.12.96 | Robbie Fowler (4) | Middlesbrough | Anfield |
| 5.10.97 | Patrik Berger | Chelsea | Anfield |
| 14.2.98 | Michael Owen | Sheffield Wednesday | Hillsborough |
| 30.8.98 | Michael Owen | Newcastle United | St James' Park |
| 24.10.98 | Michael Owen (4) | Nottingham Forest | Anfield |
| 21.11.98 | Robbie Fowler | Aston Villa | Villa Park |
| 16.1.99 | Robbie Fowler | Southampton | Anfield |
| 6.9.00 | Michael Owen | Aston Villa | Anfield |
| 15.10.00 | Emile Heskey | Derby County | Pride Park |
| 5.5.01 | Michael Owen | Newcastle United | Anfield |
| 20.10.01 | Robbie Fowler | Leicester City | Filbert Street |
| 28.9.02 | Michael Owen | Manchester City | Maine Road |
| 26.4.03 | Michael Owen (4) | WBA | The Hawthorns |
| 13.11.04 | Milan Baros | Crystal Palace | Anfield |

## ❖ "THE MEAT" DEFEAT THE REDS ❖

On 4 November 1992 Spartak Moscow became the only team to
win at Anfield in the European Cup Winners' Cup. After beating
Liverpool 4–2 (Wright, McManaman) in Moscow, the Russian side
won 2–0 at Anfield. Spartak are nicknamed "The Meat" in reference
to sponsorship from a Moscow-based meat company in the club's
early years.

## ❖ RAFA'S MEN RULE ANFIELD ❖

On 30 October 2002 Rafa Benitez brought his Valencia side
to Anfield for a UEFA Champions League Group B game. The
Spaniards came away with valuable 1–0 win, having already beaten
Liverpool 2–0 in the Mestalla.

## ❖ UP FOR THE CUP (10) ❖

In 1995 Liverpool won the League Cup (at the time the Coca-Cola Cup) with a 2–1 win over Bolton Wanderers in the final at Wembley. On their way to their fifth success in the competition, Liverpool started with a 2–0 home win and a 4–1 away win over Burnley in round two. In the third round the Reds saw off Stoke City 2–1 at Anfield and followed this up with a 3–1 away victory over Blackburn Rovers, a team that would go on to clinch the 1994–95 FA Premier League at Anfield. Arsenal proved difficult opponents in the fifth round until an Ian Rush goal at Anfield settled the tie. Robbie Fowler was the semi-final hero, scoring each time in 1–0 home and away wins over Crystal Palace.

### COCA COLA CUP FINAL
*2 APRIL 1995, WEMBLEY*
**Liverpool** (1) 2     vs     **Bolton Wanderers** (0) 1
McManaman 2                    Thompson
*Att.* 75,595
*Liverpool:* James; Jones, Bjornebye, Scales, Ruddock, Babb; McManaman, Redknapp, Barnes; Rush, Fowler


## ❖ BARCA HUMBLED ❖

Liverpool saw off Spanish giants FC Barcelona in the semi-finals of the 1975–76 UEFA Cup thanks to a solo strike from John Toshack in the famous Nou Camp Stadium in their first-leg match. Two weeks later Liverpool and Barcelona drew 1–1 (Thompson) at Anfield.


## ❖ EUROPEAN JOURNEYS ❖

Up to 31 December 2005 Liverpool had played a European tie in 37 different countries (country names are as at the time the game was played):

Austria ❖ Belgium ❖ Bulgaria ❖ Cyprus ❖ Czech Republic
Denmark ❖ East Germany ❖ England ❖ Finland
France ❖ Germany ❖ Greece ❖ Holland ❖ Hungary ❖ Iceland
Italy ❖ Lithuania ❖ Luxumbourg ❖ Northern Ireland
Norway ❖ Poland ❖ Portugal ❖ Republic of Ireland ❖ Romania
Russia ❖ Scotland ❖ Slovakia ❖ Slovenia ❖ Soviet Union ❖ Spain
Sweden ❖ Switzerland ❖ Turkey ❖ Ukraine ❖ Wales
West Germany ❖ Yugoslavia

## ❖ SHANKLY HONOURED BY FIFA ❖

In 1999 Bill Shankly was awarded a place in the FIFA International Football Hall of Fame.

## ❖ FIRST EUROPEAN ADVENTURE ❖

On 17 August 1964 Liverpool played their first match in a European competition. As League champions, Liverpool entered the European Cup and met the Icelandic side Knattspyrnufelag Reykjavikur (Reykjavik Football Club) away in a preliminary round. Liverpool won 5–0 with goals from Wallace (2), Hunt (2) and Chisnall.

## ❖ DALGLISH HITS NO. 100 ❖

Going into the second leg of their first round European Cup tie against Oulu Palloseura at Anfield on 30 September 1981, Liverpool had notched up 99 goals home and away in the competition. In the 26th minute of the game Kenny Dalglish scored the landmark 100th goal for Liverpool in the European Cup, the Reds going on to win the game 7–0, with further goals from Ray Kennedy, Johnson, McDermott (2), Lawrenson and Rush.

## ❖ LIVERPOOL 19 OULU PALLOSEURA 2 ❖

Liverpool met Finnish champions Oulu Palloseura in the first round of the European Cup in consecutive seasons 1980–81 and 1981–82. The aggregate score of the four games was a mammoth 19–2 in Liverpool's favour.

## ❖ KOP YOUR SHIRTS ❖

When the Finnish side Kuusysi Lahti visited Anfield on 18 September 1991, ending Liverpool's six-year exile from European competition, the word "KOP" was emblazoned across the front of their shirts – it was their sponsor's name. Liverpool won the game 6–1 (Saunders 4, Houghton 2) and the tie 6–2 on aggregate.

## ❖ FIRST OF MANY ❖

Liverpool won their first senior honour in 1893–94, when they lifted the Second Division Championship. Remarkably, it came just two years after the club's formation.

## ❖ 77 SEASONS ❖

Liverpool spent 77 seasons in Football League Division One before the advent of the FA Premier League. Here is their record:

### Overall

| P | W | D | L | F | A | PTS | Win% |
|---|---|---|---|---|---|-----|------|
| 3096 | 1407 | 769 | 920 | 5094 3956 | | 3836 | 45.45 |

| Home | | | | | Away | | | | |
|---|---|---|---|---|---|---|---|---|---|
| W | D | L | F | A | W | D | L | F | A |
| 924 | 354 | 270 | 3164 | 1570 | 483 | 415 | 650 | 1930 | 2386 |

## ❖ MOST LEAGUE POINTS ❖

Liverpool achieved their highest points tally in a single season in 1987–88 when they gained 90 in winning the First Division Championship. However, when Liverpool won the Championship in 1978–79, they registered 68 points under the old system of two points for a win and one for a draw[†]. If those points were converted to today's system of three for a win and one for a draw, then the Reds would have amassed 98 points – i.e. W30, D8, L4.

## ❖ FORTRESS ANFIELD ❖

Liverpool have gone an entire League season unbeaten at Anfield on nine occasions:

1893–94; 1895–96; 1904–05; 1961–62; 1970–71;
1976–77; 1978–79; 1979–80; 1987–88.

## ❖ EURO BABY BOOM ❖

On 2 March 2006 Liverpool Women's Maternity Hospital announced that births in the city were up 30 per cent on that time the previous year. A hospital spokesperson put the baby boom down to Liverpool's UEFA Champions League win over AC Milan in Istanbul the previous May. A number of the girls born were named May.

*Did you know that?*
A similar baby boom followed England cricket's Ashes win in 2005.

[†]*The 30 wins achieved in 1978–79 is a club record.*

## ❖ UP FOR THE CUP (11) ❖

In 2001 Liverpool won the first League Cup (at the time Worthington Cup) final to be held at the Millennium Stadium, Cardiff. Liverpool began their 2000–01 League Cup campaign with a 2–1 win over Chelsea after extra time at Anfield in the third round. Stoke City were then hammered 8–0 on their own ground, then in round five Liverpool squeezed past Fulham 3–0 after extra time at Anfield. Another London team, Crystal Palace, were Liverpool's semi-final opponents. Liverpool lost the first leg 2–1 at Selhurst Park but brought the Eagles down to earth with a 5–0 thumping at Anfield in the second leg. In the final Liverpool met a tenacious Birmingham City side. The match ended 1–1, after extra time, so a penalty shoot-out was held to decide the winner. Liverpool held their nerve and lifted their sixth League Cup, winning 5–4 in the shoot-out. It was a great cup year for the Reds, who claimed both the FA Cup and the UEFA Cup in May 2001 and the UEFA Super Cup in August 2001.

### WORTHINGTON CUP FINAL
*25 FEBRUARY 2001, MILLENNIUM STADIUM, CARDIFF*
**Liverpool** (1) 1    vs    **Birmingham City** (0) 1
Fowler                Purse (pen)
*After extra time*
*Liverpool won 5–4 on penalties*
*Att.* 73,500
*Liverpool:* Westerveld; Carragher, Hyppia, Henchoz, Babbel; Hamman, Smicer (Barmby), Gerrard (McAllister), Biscan (Ziege); Heskey, Fowler

## ❖ A UNIQUE DOUBLE ❖

Mark Walters was the first player to score for the Reds in the FA Premier League, on 19 August 1992 v Sheffield United at Anfield. He was also the first to score a hat-trick for Liverpool in the FA Premier League, on 17 April 1993 against Coventry City at Anfield.

## ❖ FIRST LEAGUE HAT-TRICK SCORER ❖

James Stott became the first Red to score a hat-trick in League football when he scored three times in Liverpool's 6–0 Division Two win over Middlesbrough Ironopolis at Anfield on 7 October 1893. McLean, Henderson and McQueen provided the other goals.

## ❖ RECORD LEAGUE WINS ❖

Liverpool's record home League win is the 10–1 thrashing of Rotherham United on 18 February 1896, with goals from Allan (4), McVean (3), Ross (2) and Becton. The club's record away League win is 7–0 – on 29 February 1896 against Burton Swifts (McCartney, Ross 3, Becton 3) and four weeks later on 28 March 1896 against Crewe Alexandra (Allan 3, McVean 2, McQue, Becton).

## ❖ TIGHT AT THE BACK ❖

The fewest League goals conceded by Liverpool in a season at Anfield is four, during the 1978–79 Championship winning season, while the fewest away League goals conceded in a season is ten, during Liverpool's 1975–76 Championship winning season.

## ❖ PROLIFIC FINISHING ❖

The most League goals scored by Liverpool at Anfield in a season is 68 in 1961–62, while the most away League goals scored by Liverpool in a season is 42 in 1946–47. Both were League title winning years.

## ❖ RECORD LEAGUE DEFEATS ❖

Liverpool's record League defeats have both been by an eight-goal margin – an 8–0 reversal at Huddersfield Town on 10 November 1934 and a 9–1 (Liddell) loss at Birmingham City on 11 December 1954; both games were in League Division Two.

## ❖ FOOTBALL LEAGUE DEBUT ❖

Liverpool made their Football League debut on 2 September 1893, beating Middlesbrough Ironopolis 2–0 (McQue, McVean) at Paradise Field, Middlesbrough, in Division Two.

## ❖ SCOTTISH DEBUTANTS ❖

When Liverpool's Billy Liddell won his first official cap for Scotland on 19 October 1946, his 10 team-mates were also winning their first official caps for their country. It was Scotland's first official international match after the Second World War, although Liddell played for Scotland in unofficial internationals during the hostilities.

## ❖ WHAT THE REDS SAID (17) ❖

"He was never the most gifted player, but I've never known anyone work so hard at his game. He made himself great."
*John Toshack, on his strike partner Kevin Keegan*

## ❖ GERRARD HELPS TSUNAMI VICTIMS ❖

On 15 February 2005 Liverpool's Steven Gerrard played for Andriy Shevchenko's European XI against Ronaldinho's World XI in a benefit match organized for the victims of the 2004 tsunami tragedy in Asia[†]. All proceeds from the match, played at FC Barcelona's Nou Camp stadium, were donated to the FIFA/Asian Football Confederation Tsunami Solidarity Fund. Ronaldinho's side won 6–3 in front of 40,000 fans.

## ❖ EUROPE UNITED IN GRIEF ❖

On 22 April 1989, a week after the Hillsborough Disaster, Anfield was packed for a memorial service while clubs across Europe were united in their grief for the 96 Liverpool fans who lost their lives. Bayern Munich and Napoli, who were playing in the UEFA Cup the week after the disaster, each donated £17,000 to the victims' families. Borussia Dortmund offered the gate receipts from their exhibition match against Dynamo Moscow. In Italy, meanwhile, when AC Milan met Real Madrid in the second leg of their European Cup semi-final, more than 70,000 fans inside the San Siro sang "You'll Never Walk Alone" in a moving tribute to the 96 fans.

## ❖ HARD AS STEEL ❖

In September 1985 Liverpool signed Steve McMahon from Aston Villa for £350,000. He was the first player Kenny Dalglish bought for Liverpool and had originally begun his career at Everton. For the first time since Graeme Souness, the Reds had a player who would add a bit of steel to their midfield, and McMahon more than lived up to his hard-man tag. During his Anfield career he won three Championships, one FA Cup, one FA Charity Shield and the Screen Sports Super Cup. Ironically when Graeme Souness was appointed Liverpool manager in 1991, he sold McMahon to Manchester City for £900,000.

---

*[†]Gerrard's former Anfield team-mate Jari Litmanen (then of Hansa Rostock) also played for Shevchenko's side.*

## ❖ UP FOR THE CUP (12) ❖

In 2001 Liverpool won the first FA Cup final hosted by the Millennium Stadium, Cardiff, with a 2–1 victory over Arsenal courtesy of two Michael Owen goals. In the third round Liverpool beat Rotherham United 3–0 at Anfield and then disposed of Leeds United with a 2–0 win at Elland Road. Liverpool's fifth-round opponents were Manchester City, and Liverpool won a highly entertaining game 4–2. When the sixth round drew Liverpool away from home, they did not have far to travel, making the short journey to Birkenhead to face Tranmere Rovers. Liverpool beat Rovers 4–2 at Prenton Park. In the semi-finals Liverpool overcame Wycombe Wanderers with a 2–1 victory at Villa Park before seeing off Arsenal to claim the FA Cup for the sixth time.

### FA CUP FINAL
*12 MAY 2001, MILLENNIUM STADIUM, CARDIFF*
**Liverpool** (0) 2    vs    **Arsenal** (0) 1
Owen (2)            Ljungberg
*Att.* 74,200
*Liverpool:* Westerveld; Babbel, Hyypia, Henchoz, Carragher; Hamann (McAllister), Murphy (Berger), Smicer (Fowler), Gerrard; Owen, Heskey

## ❖ CUP WINNERS' CUP GOALS ❖

Liverpool scored 57 goals in their five European Cup Winners' Cup campaigns, with the following notable strikes:

| Goal | Player | Date | Opposition (venue) |
|---|---|---|---|
| 1 | Chris Lawler | 13 October 1965 | Juventus (h) |
| 50 | Robbie Fowler | 20 March 1997 | SK Brann Bergen (h) |
| Last | Mark Wright | 24 April 1997 | Paris St Germain (h) |

## ❖ WALES'S FIRST RED ❖

In 1901 Maurice Parry became the first Liverpool player to be capped by Wales. Liverpool signed half-back Parry in August 1900 from Brighton United. He made 221 appearances for the Reds, scoring four goals. He won a Second Division Championship winners' medal with Liverpool in 1904–05 and a First Division Championship winners' medal in 1905–06. After retiring as a player, Parry coached some of Europe's biggest club sides, including Barcelona, Cologne and Frankfurt.

## ❖ EUROPEAN GLORY NIGHTS (7) ❖

On 17 May 2001, Liverpool ended a barren 17 years without European success when they beat the unfancied Spanish side, Alavés, 5–4 in an enthralling UEFA Cup Final. The match got off to a flyer as the Reds cruised into a 2–0 lead thanks to goals from Marcus Babbel and Steven Gerrard inside the first 16 minutes. Esnal, the coach of Alavés, brought on striker Alonso who immediately pulled a goal back for the Spaniards. However, the Reds then scored their third goal against the run of play when Gary McAllister converted a penalty after Michael Owen had been brought down. In the second half the Spanish side threw everything at the Reds and two quick goals from Jaime Moreno levelled the match at 3–3. Gerard Houllier then brought on Vladimir Smicer, Robbie Fowler and Patrik Berger and it was Fowler who restored the Reds' lead with a superb goal in the 73rd minute. Two minutes from time Jordi Cruyff scored to send the game into extra time, a period that saw the Spanish side reduced to nine men. Liverpool won the game on the golden goal rule when Geli scored an own goal in the 116th minute.

### UEFA CUP FINAL
*17 MAY 2001, WESTFALENSTADION, DORTMUND, GERMANY*

**Liverpool (3) 5** vs Alavés (1) 4
Babbel, Gerrard, Alonso, Moreno (2), Cruyff
McAllister (pen), Fowler,
Geli (o.g.)
*After extra time*

Att. 65,000
*Liverpool:* Westerveld, Babbel, Henchoz (Smicer), Hyypia, Carragher, Gerrard, Hamann, McAllister, Murphy, Owen (Berger), Heskey (Fowler)

## ❖ FIRST DERBY WIN AT GOODISON ❖

On 24 September 1898 Liverpool recorded their first ever League Merseyside derby win at Goodison Park. Liverpool beat Everton 2–1 (McCowie 2) in a First Division game.

## ❖ FIRST EIGHT-FIGURE-PLUS RED ❖

Emile Heskey was the first player to cost Liverpool £10 million or more when he arrived from Leicester City in March 2000 in a deal that cost the Reds £11 million.

# ❖ LIVERPOOL'S CHRISTMAS DAY RECORD ❖

| Year | Competition | Opponents | Home/Away | Result |
|------|-------------|-----------|-----------|--------|
| 1894 | Division 1 | Bolton Wanderers | A | 0–1 *(l)* |
| 1896 | Division 1 | Aston Villa | H | 3–3 *(d)* |
| 1897 | Division 1 | Bolton Wanderers | A | 2–0 *(w)* |
| 1899 | Division 1 | Derby County | A | 2–3 *(l)* |
| 1900 | Division 1 | Derby County | H | 0–0 *(d)* |
| 1902 | Division 1 | Bolton Wanderers | H | 5–1 *(w)* |
| 1903 | Division 1 | Derby County | A | 0–2 *(l)* |
| 1905 | Division 1 | Bolton Wanderers | H | 2–2 *(d)* |
| 1906 | Division 1 | Man Utd | A | 0–0 *(d)* |
| 1907 | Division 1 | Chelsea | H | 1–4 *(l)* |
| 1908 | Division 1 | Aston Villa | A | 1–1 *(d)* |
| 1909 | Division 1 | Bolton Wanderers | H | 3–0 *(w)* |
| 1911 | Division 1 | Bolton Wanderers | H | 1–0 *(w)* |
| 1913 | Division 1 | Manchester City | H | 4–2 *(w)* |
| 1914 | Division 1 | Bolton Wanderers | A | 1–0 *(w)* |
| 1919 | Division 1 | Sunderland | H | 3–2 *(w)* |
| 1920 | Division 1 | Chelsea | A | 1–1 *(d)* |
| 1922 | Division 1 | Oldham Athletic | A | 2–0 *(w)* |
| 1923 | Division 1 | Newcastle United | H | 0–1 *(l)* |
| 1924 | Division 1 | Notts County | A | 2–1 *(w)* |
| 1925 | Division 1 | Newcastle United | H | 6–3 *(w)* |
| 1926 | Division 1 | Burnley | A | 0–4 *(l)* |
| 1928 | Division 1 | Burnley | A | 2–3 *(l)* |
| 1929 | Division 1 | Sheffield United | A | 0–4 *(l)* |
| 1930 | Division 1 | Grimsby Town | A | 0–0 *(d)* |
| 1931 | Division 1 | Sheffield Wednesday | H | 3–1 *(w)* |
| 1933 | Division 1 | Portsmouth | H | 2–2 *(d)* |
| 1935 | Division 1 | Arsenal | H | 0–1 *(l)* |
| 1936 | Division 1 | West Bromwich Albion | A | 1–3 *(l)* |
| 1946 | Division 1 | Stoke City | A | 1–2 *(l)* |
| 1947 | Division 1 | Arsenal | H | 1–3 *(l)* |
| 1948 | Division 1 | Manchester United | A | 0–0 *(d)* |
| 1950 | Division 1 | Blackpool | A | 0–3 *(l)* |
| 1951 | Division 1 | Blackpool | H | 1–1 *(d)* |
| 1952 | Division 1 | Burnley | A | 0–2 *(l)* |
| 1953 | Division 1 | West Bromwich Albion | A | 2–5 *(l)* |
| 1954 | Division 2 | Ipswich Town | H | 6–2 *(w)* |
| 1956 | Division 2 | Leyton Orient | H | 1–0 *(w)* |
| 1957 | Division 2 | Grimsby Town | A | 1–3 *(l)* |

Complete record: P39, W13, D10, L16, F60, A66, Pts36.

## ❖ POOR SCOUSER TOMMY ❖

Let me tell you the story of a poor boy,
Who was sent far away from his home,
To fight for his king and his country,
And also the old folks back home.

So they put him in a highland division,
Sent him off to a far foreign land,
Where the flies swarm around in their thousands,
And there's nothing to see but the sand.

As the battle was starting next morning,
Under the radiant sun,
I remember that poor Scouser Tommy,
Who was shot by an old Nazi gun.

As he lay on the battlefield dyin-dyin-dying,
With the blood gushing out of his head (out of his head)
As he lay on the battlefield dyin-dyin-dying,
These were the last words he said:
Oooh, I am a Liverpudlian,
I come from the Spion Kop,
I like to sing, I like to chant,
I go there quite a lot.

Support a team, that plays in red,
A team that we all know,
A team that we call Liverpool,
To glory we will go.

We won the league, we won the cup,
We've been to Europe too,
We played the Toffees for a laugh,
And left them feeling blue 5–0.

1–2, 1–2–3, 1–2–3–4, 5–0!

Rush scored one,
Rush scored two,
Rush scored three,
And Rush scored four ...

## ❖ TV STARS ❖

A number of Liverpool players have appeared on television shows, including:

**Alan Hansen**
Sky TV (pundit), *Football Focus* (BBC; studio guest),
*Match of the Day* (BBC; studio guest),
*US Masters Golf* (BBC), *A Brush With Fame*

**Mark Lawrenson**
*Football Focus* (BBC; studio guest),
*Match of the Day* (BBC; studio guest)

**Phil Thompson**
*Sky Sports Special* (studio guest)

**Ronnie Whelan**
*You're On Sky Sports* (studio guest)

**Paul Walsh**
*Sky Sports Special* (match reporter and studio guest)

**Ian Rush**
*Sky Sports Special* (match reporter)

**Jamie Redknapp**
*Sky Sports Super Sunday/Monday Night Football* (studio guest)

**Kenny Dalglish**
*Sky Sports Super Sunday/Monday Night Football* (studio guest)

**John Barnes**
*ITV Sport* (studio guest), *Channel Five Football* (host)

**David James**
*Beyond the NFL* (Sky Sports)

**Michael Robinson**
*El Dia Despues* (Spanish TV)

**Emlyn Hughes**
*A Question of Sport* (BBC), *Sporting Triangles* (ITV)

**John Aldridge**
*Spanish Football on Sky Sports*

**Jim Beglin**
*ITV Sport* (match reporter)

**Michael Owen**
*A Question of Sport*

## ❖ THE VOICE OF ANFIELD ❖

George Sephton began his public address announcing duties at Anfield in 1971–72 and he is still there today.

## ❖ IAN RUSH MBE ❖

Ian Rush was born on 20 October 1961 in St Asaph, Wales. In April 1980 Bob Paisley paid Chester £300,000 for the lean, wiry but unbelievably quick Welsh teenager. On 13 December 1980 Rush made his debut for the Reds in a 1–1 (Case) draw away to Ipswich Town in Division One but struggled to make any impact and claim a regular starting place in the 1980–81 season. Growing restless with his lack of first-team opportunities, Rush approached Paisley and asked why he was not in the team on a regular basis. Paisley replied: "You don't score enough goals so you're not worth your place", a brutal but honest response. Upon hearing this, Rush contemplated leaving Anfield but then decided to stay and fight for his place.

In 1981–82, Rush's new selfishness in front of goal reaped dividends for him as he scored 30 goals in all competitions that season. Over the course of his Anfield career, spanning two spells with the Reds, club goalscoring records tumbled at his feet. During his first stint with the club, Rush was quite simply the most lethal marksman in British football. He was a goal machine who combined pace with aerial power; he could shoot with both feet with unerring accuracy and power, and he was instinctively in the right place at the right time. Rush kept his best scoring achievements for Everton. He found the net four times in a 5–0 thrashing of the Blues at Goodison Park on 6 November 1982 (Mark Lawrenson netted the other) and scored twice in Liverpool's 1986 Merseyside FA Cup final win. In June 1987 Rush joined Juventus in a £3.2 million deal but could not settle in Italy and returned to Anfield in 1988 for £2.8 million.

During his double spell with the Reds, Rush scored 346 goals in 660 appearances. Among his achievements are the twentieth-century career-record of 44 FA Cup goals (39 of them for Liverpool) and a share, along with Geoff Hurst, in the League Cup career scoring record of 49 goals. With Liverpool, Ian won five First Division Championships, three FA Cups, five League Cups (he was the first to achieve this feat), one European Cup, four Charity Shields and one Screen Sport Super Cup. Rush also won Europe's Golden Boot Award, was a double Footballer of the Year and received an MBE for services to football.

## ❖ FIRST ANFIELD DERBY ❖

On 17 November 1894 Anfield hosted its first League Mersey derby. The First Division encounter ended 2–2 (Ross, Hannah).

## ❖ WHAT THE REDS SAID (18) ❖

"Kenny Dalglish was the reason I signed for Liverpool. It was his reputation and his stature in the game that persuaded me, and the fact that he gave me a particularly smart pair of boots. It is the only 'bung' I have ever received. They were two sizes too big for me, but I didn't half look good in them."
*Steve McManaman*

## ❖ MAXWELL IS ODD ONE OUT ❖

Since 1970, 13 different players have scored on their senior Liverpool debut and 12 of them have been full internationals. The odd one out is Welshman Leyton Maxwell, who scored the second goal in a 4–2 victory against Hull City at Anfield in the Worthington Cup on 21 September 1999. Not only was it Maxwell's debut for the Reds, it proved to be his only appearance.

## ❖ WORLD SOCCER MAGAZINE AWARDS ❖

Since 1982 the magazine *World Soccer* has held a poll among its readers to select the winners of awards in three categories: "*World Soccer* Player of the Year", "*World Soccer* Manager of the Year" and "*World Soccer* Team of the Year". Liverpool have featured in the awards on four occasions:

*Player of the Year*
2001 – Michael Owen

*Manager of the Year*
2001 – Gerard Houllier

*Team of the Year*
2001 – Liverpool
2005 – Liverpool

## ❖ GERRARD'S CUP-FINAL "HAT-TRICK" ❖

On 13 May 2006, Steven Gerrard became the first player to score three goals in an FA Cup Finals since Stan Mortensen did so for Blackpool in their famous 4–3 victory over Bolton Wanderers in 1953. However, as Gerrard's third goal came in the penalty shoot-out, officially, it does not count towards a hat-trick.

## ❖ EUROPEAN REDS ❖

The following table shows those Liverpool players who have made at least 50 appearances for the club in European competition (up to the end of the 2005–06 season):

| | Player | Apps | Starts |
|---|---|---|---|
| 1. | Ian Callaghan | 89 | 88 |
| 2. | Tommy Smith | 85 | 84 |
| 3. | Ray Clemence | 80 | 80 |
| 4. | Emlyn Hughes | 79 | 79 |
| 5. | Jamie Carragher | 78 | 78 |
| 6. | Sami Hyypia | 76 | 76 |
| 7. | Phil Neal | 74 | 74 |
| 8. | Steve Heighway | 67 | 62 |
| 9. | Chris Lawler | 66 | 66 |
| 10. | Steven Gerrard | 66 | 60 |
| 11. | Dietmar Hamann | 61 | 54 |
| 12. | John Arne Riise | 57 | 54 |
| 13. | Kenny Dalglish | 51 | 50 |
| 14. | Ray Kennedy | 50 | 50 |
| 15. | Phil Thompson | 50 | 47 |
| 16. | Michael Owen | 50 | 46 |

## ❖ LIVERPOOL WIN THE LOTTERY ❖

In the 1964–65 European Cup competition, Liverpool met FC Cologne in the quarter-finals. The first leg in Germany ended 0–0 as did the second leg at Anfield. On 24 March the two teams met for a third game at neutral Feyenoord stadium in Rotterdam. This game ended 2–2 (St John, Hunt) and UEFA decided that passage through to the semi-finals would be determined by the toss of a coin. In place of a coin, however, the referee used a wooden chip, one side red and one side white. Liverpool captain Ron Yeats called for the red side. After the first toss the chip landed and stuck vertically in the muddy grass. Just as it appeared to be falling sideways to show the white side, Yeats picked it up and suggested that the referee should toss it again. When the referee flipped the chip a second time, it landed with the red side facing up, and Liverpool went through to the semi-finals where they lost to the eventual winners, Inter Milan.

*Did You Know That?*
Cologne, or FC Koln, are nicknamed "The Billy Goats".

## ❖ LIVERPOOL SCOUSERS XI ❖

**1**
Frank
*LANE*

**2**
Tommy
*SMITH*

**3**
Phil
*THOMPSON*
*(captain)*

**4**
Tom
*BROMILOW*

**5**
Jamie
*CARRAGHER*

**6**
Phil
*BOERSMA*

**7**
Steve
*McMANAMAN*

**8**
John
*ALDRIDGE*

**9**
Robbie
*FOWLER*

**10**
Jack
*BALMER*

**11**
Gerry
*BYRNE*

*Substitutes*
Tony *WARNER* • Don *CAMPBELL* • Mike *MARSH*
Jimmy *CASE* • Tom *BRADSHAW*
*Player-Manager*
John *ALDRIDGE*

### *Did You Know That?*
When Graeme Souness was appointed Liverpool manager in 1990, he brought his close friend and former Red, Phil Boersma, back to the club as a physio and a first-team coach.

## ❖ RSSSF AWARD ❖

The Rec.Sport.Soccer Statistics Foundation (RSSSF) is an organization dedicated to collecting association football statistics of clubs and countries around the world with the aim of building an exhaustive archive of football-related information. In January 1992 RSSSF awarded its inaugural RSS World Player of the Year award. Readers of the Rec.Sport.Soccer Statistics Foundation Newsgroup vote for their player of the previous 12 months. Each voter chooses five players, with a maximum of two being of the same nationality, placing them in order by awarding each player one to five points, five being the highest. To date Michael Owen (2001) is the only Red to have scooped the award, which is awarded annually in January.

## ❖ UP FOR THE CUP (13) ❖

Liverpool won the League Cup for the seventh time with a 2–0 victory over Manchester United in the 2003 Worthington Cup final at the Millennium Stadium, Cardiff. In Round Three Liverpool beat Southampton 3–0 at Anfield. Ipswich Town were a tough nut to crack in the fourth round at Anfield before Liverpool finally went through to the next round with a 5–4 penalty shoot-out win after the game had ended 1–1 after extra time. Seven goals were scored in Liverpool's fifth-round tie, with the Reds edging past Aston Villa 4–3 at Villa Park. They then went on to beat Sheffield United 3–2 over two legs in the semi-finals. Liverpool's victory over United in Cardiff was their second against the club in a League Cup final, following their success in 1983.

### WORTHINGTON CUP FINAL
*2 MARCH 2003, MILLENNIUM STADIUM, CARDIFF*
**Liverpool (1) 2      vs      Manchester United (0) 0**
Gerrard, Owen
*Att.* 74,500
*Liverpool:* Dudek; Carragher, Henchoz, Hyypia, Riise;
Diouf (Biscan), Hamann, Gerrard, Murphy;
Owen, Heskey (Baros [Smicer])

## ❖ LAST TEN ENGLAND CAPS ❖

The following table shows the last ten Liverpool players to earn England caps. The years refer only to international appearances while Liverpool players.

| Player | Years |
| --- | --- |
| Jamie Redknapp | 1995–99 |
| Robbie Fowler | 1996–2001 |
| David James | 1997 |
| Paul Ince | 1997–99 |
| Michael Owen | 1998–2004 |
| Jamie Carragher | 1999–2005 |
| Nick Barmby | 2000–01 |
| Steven Gerrard | 2000–05 |
| Emile Heskey | 2000–04 |
| Danny Murphy | 2001–03 |
| Peter Crouch | 2005 |

*A total of 55 Liverpool players have been capped by England.*

## ❖ LIVERPOOL CHARTBUSTERS ❖

In keeping with the splendid musical heritage of their Merseyside home, Liverpool FC have made several notable forays into the UK's pop music charts. These are the songs that got the Kop rocking:

**Liverpool Football Club**
*UK, male football team vocalists (21 WEEKS)*                                    *pos/wks*

| | | | |
|---|---|---|---|
| 28 May 77 | **We Can Do It (EP)** *State STAT 50* | 15 | 4 |
| 23 Apr 83 | **Liverpool (We're Never Gonna...)/**<br>**Liverpool Anthem** *Mean MEAN 102* | 54 | 4 |
| 17 May 86 | **Sitting on Top of the World**<br>*Columbia DB 9116* | 50 | 2 |
| 14 May 88 | **Anfield Rap (Red Machine in Full Effect)**<br>*Virgin LFC 1* | 3 | 6 |
| 18 May 96 | **Pass and Move (It's the Liverpool Groove)**<br>*Telstar LFCCD 96* [1] | 4 | 5 |

[1] Liverpool FC and The Boot Room Boyz

*© Courtesy of* The Book of UK Hit Singles & Albums, *published by Guinness World Records and the UK Charts Company.*

## ❖ WHAT THE REDS SAID (19) ❖

"Kevin is like the Mona Lisa – beyond price."
**Tommy Smith**, *on Kevin Keegan*

## ❖ BRITAIN'S MOST EXPENSIVE TEENAGER ❖

Ian Rush became Britain's then most expensive teenager when Bob Paisley paid Chester £300,000 for his services in March 1980.

## ❖ POPE SUPPORTS LIVERPOOL ❖

In 2004 Pope John Paul II[†] met players from the Polish national football team. During their visit to the Vatican, the pontiff informed Liverpool goalkeeper Jerzy Dudek that he was a keen supporter of Liverpool and listened out for their results whenever they were playing.

*[†] Pope John Paul II used to play football during his early years in Krakow. Like Dudek, he was a goalkeeper.*

## ❖ GRAEME SOUNESS ❖

Graeme Souness was born in Edinburgh on 6 May 1953. He started his career as an apprentice at Tottenham Hotspur under the legendary Bill Nicholson, but the young Scot became impatient at his lack of first-team opportunities. After making a solitary appearance for the London club, Souness moved to Middlesbrough in 1973. From his early days Souness was a much-feared midfielder who never shirked a challenge or confrontation and thought he could win the ball even if it was 60–40 in his opponent's favour. Souness spent five seasons at Ayresome Park, in 1974 winning the first of 54 international caps for Scotland in a 3–0 win over East Germany.

In January 1978 Bob Paisley tempted Souness to leave the northeast and move to Anfield. He cost the club £352,000 and only five months after his arrival set úp a goal for Kenny Dalglish in the European Cup final win over FC Bruges. Souness was a powerhouse of a player in a combative Liverpool midfield. In 1981 he replaced Phil Thompson as club captain, leading the Reds to three consecutive League Championships during his tenure.

Graeme Souness played 359 times for the Reds, scoring 55 goals. In his time as a player with the club, he amassed a huge collection of trophies, including five First Division Championship winners' medals, four League Cup winners' medals and three European Cup winners' medals. At the end of the 1983–84 season, Graeme Souness left Anfield and joined Sampdoria in Italy. He stayed in Italian football for two seasons before being invited to take up the player/ managership of Rangers in the summer of 1986. Souness was sent off on his debut for the club, but went on to guide Rangers to four Scottish Premier League titles and four Scottish League Cups.

In April 1991, however, Graeme left Glasgow to return to Liverpool as manager after the shock resignation of Kenny Dalglish. Souness underwent major heart surgery in 1992, not long before leading Liverpool out at Wembley in that year's Cup final, which they won 2–0 (Thomas, Rush) against Sunderland. Nevertheless, prior to the win had come a major turning point in Souness's career. He had given an exclusive interview to the *Sun* newspaper on the anniversary of the Hillsborough Disaster. Liverpool fans had boycotted the paper after it printed unsubstantiated stories about what Liverpool fans did on that fateful day in 1989. Many fans turned against Souness, and in January 1994, after a humiliating FA Cup exit to Bristol City, Souness and Liverpool parted company. He went on to manage Benfica, Galatasaray, Southampton, Blackburn Rovers and Newcastle United.

## ❖ A SECOND HOME ❖

It is no wonder that Liverpool considered Wembley to be their second home. They playing there 29 times in 25 years from 1971 to 1996. The Reds' Wembley record in that time was P29, W15, D6, L8.

| Year | Competition | Match | | Result |
|------|-------------|-------|---|--------|
| 1996 | FA Cup Final | Man Utd v. Liverpool | 1–0 | (l) |
| 1995 | League Cup Final | Liverpool v. Bolton Wanderers | 2–1* | (w) |
| 1992 | FA Charity Shield | Leeds United v. Liverpool | 4–3 | (l) |
| 1992 | FA Cup Final | Liverpool v. Sunderland | 2–0 | (w) |
| 1990 | FA Charity Shield | Liverpool v. Man Utd | 1–1* | (d) |
| 1989 | FA Charity Shield | Liverpool v. Arsenal | 1–0 | (w) |
| 1989 | FA Cup Final | Liverpool v. Everton | 3–2* | (w) |
| 1988 | FA Charity Shield | Liverpool v. Wimbledon | 2–1 | (w) |
| 1988 | FA Cup Final | Wimbledon v. Liverpool | 1–0 | (l) |
| 1987 | League Cup Final | Arsenal v. Liverpool | 2–1* | (l) |
| 1986 | FA Cup Final | Liverpool v. Everton | 3–1 | (w) |
| 1986 | FA Charity Shield | Everton v. Liverpool | 1–1* | (d) |
| 1984 | League Cup Final | Liverpool v. Everton | 0–0* | (d) |
| 1984 | FA Charity Shield | Everton v. Liverpool | 1–0 | (l) |
| 1983 | League Cup Final | Liverpool v. Man Utd | 2–1* | (w) |
| 1983 | FA Charity Shield | Man Utd v. Liverpool | 2–0 | (l) |
| 1982 | League Cup Final | Liverpool v. Tottenham H | 3–1* | (w) |
| 1982 | FA Charity Shield | Liverpool v. Tottenham H | 1–0 | (w) |
| 1981 | League Cup Final | Liverpool v. West Ham Utd | 1–1* | (d) |
| 1980 | FA Charity Shield | Liverpool v. West Ham Utd | 1–0 | (w) |
| 1979 | FA Charity Shield | Liverpool v. Arsenal | 3–1 | (w) |
| 1978 | European Cup Final | Liverpool v. FC Bruges | 1–0 | (w) |
| 1978 | League Cup Final | Nottingham F v. Liverpool | 0–0* | (d) |
| 1977 | FA Charity Shield | Liverpool v. Man Utd | 0–0* | (d) |
| 1977 | FA Cup Final | Man Utd v. Liverpool | 2–1 | (l) |
| 1976 | FA Charity Shield | Liverpool v. Southampton | 1–0 | (w) |
| 1974 | FA Charity Shield | Liverpool v. Leeds Utd | 1–1** | (w) |
| 1974 | FA Cup Final | Liverpool v. Newcastle Utd | 3–0 | (w) |
| 1971 | FA Cup Final | Arsenal v. Liverpool | 2–1* | (l) |

\* = After extra time; \*\* = Won on penalties after extra time.

## ❖ LAST OF THE LONG TIES ❖

On 27 February 1991 Liverpool and Everton played in the last ever second replay in an FA Cup tie. Everton won the fifth-round match 1–0.

### ❖ EUROPEAN GLORY NIGHTS (8) ❖

Liverpool's triumph in a penalty shoot-out over AC Milan in the 2005 UEFA Champions League final represents one of the greatest comebacks the competition has ever seen. Liverpool looked down and out at half-time in Istanbul, trailing 3–0 to the Italians. However, three goals in five minutes from Gerrard, Smicer and Alonso breathed life back into the side and visibly shook the Italians. The game ended 3–3 and remained that way after extra time, resulting in a penalty shoot-out which Liverpool won 3–2. Liverpool's march to the final began in Austria on 10 August 2004 with a 2–0 third qualifying round win over AK Graz. On the way to Turkey Liverpool also met AS Monaco, Olympiakos, Deportivo La Coruna, Bayer Leverkusen, Juventus and finally Chelsea in the semi-finals.

**UEFA CHAMPIONS LEAGUE FINAL**
*25 MAY 2005, ATATURK STADIUM, ISTANBUL*
**Liverpool (0) 3**    vs    Milan (3) 3
Gerrard, Smicer, Alonso     Maldini, Crespo (2)
*After extra time*
*Liverpool won 3–2 on penalties*
*Att.* 60,000
*Liverpool:* Dudek; Finnan (Hamann), Hyypia, Carragher, Traore; Kewell (Smicer 23), Alonso, Gerrard, Riise; Garcia, Baros (Cisse 85)

### ❖ NEW ANFIELD GIVEN GREEN LIGHT ❖

On 11 April 2006, Liverpool's plans for a new 60,000-seater stadium in nearby Stanley Park were approved by the local council without any alterations being made to the original plans submitted by the club in 2004.

### ❖ FORGETTABLE ANFIELD DEBUT ❖

Tony Warner was nothing if not loyal. The goalkeeper made 120 appearances on the Liverpool team-sheet between 1994 and 1999 but not once did he play, and it remains the club record for a substitute never used. On 15 March 2006, after spells at Cardiff City and Millwall, plus an international appearance for Trinidad and Tobago, Warner finally made his Anfield debut, with Fulham. Liverpool, however, showed little mercy, winning 5–1 (Fowler, Brown, (o.g.), Morientes, Crouch and Warnock).

## ❖ UP FOR THE CUP (14) ❖

On 13 May 2006, just as they had done 12 months earlier in Istanbul, Liverpool won a Cup final after a nail-biting penalty shoot-out finale. To reach the final, the Reds disposed of Luton Town, 5–3, away in the third round and Portsmouth, 2–1, away in the fourth round. Manchester United were seen off 1–0 at Anfield in round five, while an emphatic 7–0 drubbing over Birmingham City at St Andrews in the quarter-final set up a semi-final clash against Chelsea at Old Trafford. The Reds' 2–1 win left the Blues chasing only the Premier League title.

As far as FA Cup Finals went this one had it all: lots of goals, a few twists and turns and a finish that some Reds could not bear to watch whilst others peeked through tiny gaps between their fingers. West Ham United, in their first FA Cup Final in 26 years, took a 2–0 lead inside the first 30 minutes, thanks to a Jamie Carragher own goal and a goal from Dean Ashton. However, the Reds pulled a goal back through Djibril Cisse on 32 minutes.

In the second half the Reds equalized when captain Steven Gerrard scored after 54 minutes from 10 yards out. When Paul Konchesky's cross-cum-shot looped over Pepe Reina to give the Hammers a 3–2 lead midway through the half, it was the voices of the London fans singing "I'm Forever Blowing Bubbles" that pierced the sun-filled stadium. Then, with the game just into stoppage time, Gerrard, despite suffering from cramp, somehow managed to lash a 30-yard powerful drive past Shaka Hislop to force extra time.

The additional 30 minutes produced no more goals, although Reina produced a brilliant save in the last minute, so it was down penalty kicks. Reina, a man who arrived at Anfield from Spanish club Villareal with an impressive record of penalty kick saves, produced three in the shoot-out to give Liverpool their seventh FA Cup.

### FA CUP FINAL
*13 MAY 2006, MILLENNIUM STADIUM, CARDIFF*

**Liverpool** (1) **3**     vs     **West Ham United** (2) **3**
Cisse, Gerrard 2                   Carragher (o.g.), Ashton,
                                   Konchesky

*After extra time*
*Liverpool won 3–1 on penalties*
Att. 71,140

*Liverpool:* Reina; Finnan, Hyypia, Carragher, Riise; Kewell (Morientes), Gerrard, Sissoko, Alonso (Kromkamp), Cisse, Crouch (Hamman)

## ❖ ALL-TIME PREMIER LEAGUE TABLE ❖

Liverpool lie third in the all-time Premier League table. This is what the full table looks like at the end of the 2005–06 season.

| Team | P | W | D | L | W | D | L | Pts |
|------|---|---|---|---|---|---|---|-----|
| Manchester United | 544 | 192 | 57 | 23 | 147 | 69 | 56 | 1143 |
| Arsenal | 544 | 171 | 66 | 35 | 118 | 80 | 74 | 1013 |
| Liverpool | 544 | 167 | 62 | 43 | 98 | 74 | 100 | 931 |
| Chelsea | 544 | 160 | 69 | 43 | 101 | 78 | 93 | 930 |
| Newcastle United | 502 | 149 | 56 | 46 | 69 | 76 | 106 | 786 |
| Aston Villa | 544 | 126 | 78 | 68 | 77 | 80 | 115 | 767 |
| Tottenham Hotspur | 544 | 126 | 73 | 73 | 69 | 70 | 133 | 728 |
| Blackburn Rovers | 468 | 123 | 54 | 57 | 67 | 71 | 96 | 695 |
| Leeds United | 468 | 118 | 60 | 56 | 71 | 65 | 98 | 692 |
| Everton | 544 | 113 | 78 | 81 | 64 | 68 | 140 | 677 |
| Southampton | 506 | 107 | 70 | 76 | 43 | 67 | 143 | 587 |
| West Ham United | 426 | 98 | 56 | 59 | 50 | 55 | 108 | 555 |
| Middlesbrough | 422 | 84 | 61 | 66 | 47 | 62 | 102 | 516 |
| Manchester City | 354 | 63 | 54 | 60 | 40 | 47 | 90 | 410 |
| Coventry City | 354 | 65 | 56 | 56 | 34 | 56 | 87 | 409 |
| Sheffield Wednesday | 316 | 63 | 50 | 45 | 38 | 39 | 81 | 392 |
| Wimbledon | 316 | 62 | 46 | 50 | 37 | 48 | 73 | 391 |
| Leicester City | 308 | 51 | 51 | 52 | 33 | 39 | 82 | 342 |
| Charlton Athletic | 266 | 51 | 35 | 47 | 34 | 37 | 62 | 327 |
| Bolton Wanderers | 266 | 50 | 45 | 38 | 31 | 32 | 70 | 320 |
| Derby County | 228 | 47 | 30 | 37 | 20 | 32 | 62 | 263 |
| Nottingham Forest | 198 | 35 | 32 | 32 | 25 | 27 | 47 | 239 |
| Fulham | 190 | 48 | 20 | 27 | 15 | 27 | 53 | 236 |
| Sunderland | 228 | 37 | 32 | 45 | 21 | 23 | 70 | 229 |
| Ipswich Town | 202 | 35 | 29 | 37 | 22 | 24 | 55 | 224 |
| Queens Park Rangers | 164 | 36 | 20 | 26 | 23 | 19 | 40 | 216 |
| Norwich City | 164 | 32 | 28 | 22 | 18 | 23 | 41 | 201 |
| Birmingham City | 152 | 30 | 21 | 25 | 14 | 24 | 38 | 177 |
| Crystal Palace | 160 | 20 | 25 | 35 | 17 | 24 | 39 | 160 |
| Portsmouth | 114 | 23 | 15 | 19 | 9 | 11 | 37 | 122 |
| Sheffield United | 84 | 16 | 16 | 10 | 6 | 12 | 24 | 94 |
| West Bromwich Albion | 114 | 14 | 15 | 28 | 5 | 18 | 34 | 90 |
| Oldham Athletic | 84 | 15 | 14 | 13 | 7 | 9 | 26 | 89 |
| Bradford City | 76 | 10 | 15 | 13 | 4 | 5 | 29 | 62 |
| Wigan Athletic | 38 | 7 | 3 | 9 | 8 | 3 | 8 | 51 |
| Barnsley | 38 | 7 | 4 | 8 | 3 | 1 | 15 | 35 |
| Wolverhampton W. | 38 | 7 | 5 | 7 | 0 | 7 | 12 | 33 |
| Swindon Town | 42 | 4 | 7 | 10 | 1 | 8 | 12 | 30 |
| Watford | 38 | 5 | 4 | 10 | 1 | 2 | 16 | 24 |

## ❖ WEBSITES ❖

www.news.bbc.co.uk
news.bbc.co.uk/sport1/hi/football/eng_prem
beehive.thisisderbyshire.co.uk ❖ www.designmuseum.org
www.englandfanzine.co.uk ❖ www.englandfc.com
www.englandfootballonline.com
finance-almanac.blogspot.com
football.guardian.co.uk ❖ www.goalkeepersaredifferent.com
icliverpool.icnetwork.co.uk ❖ www.ifhof.com
www.lfcbootroom.net ❖ www.lfc4life.com
www.lfchistory.net ❖ www.lfconline.com
liverpool.rivals.net ❖ www.liverpoolfc.tv
www.liverweb.org.uk ❖ www.napit.co.uk
www.nationalfootballmuseum.com ❖ www.rsssf.com
www.shankly.com ❖ www.shanklygates.co.uk
www.sheffieldforum.co.uk ❖ www.skysports.com
soccernet.espn.go.com ❖ www.the-english-football-archive.com
www.thefa.com ❖ www.toffeeweb.com
www.wembleystadium.com ❖ en.wikipedia.org

## ❖ BOOKS ❖

❖ *A Football Compendium: An Expert Guide to the Books, Films & Music of Association Football* (Second Edition), compiled by Peter J Seddon, Redwood Books, 1999.

❖ *The Little Book of Liverpool*, edited by Geoff Tibballs, Carlton Publishing Group, 2005.

❖ *Liverpool In Europe*, by Ivan Ponting & Steve Hall with Steve Small & Alex Murphy, Carlton Publishing Group, 2005.

❖ *Liverpool FC The Historic Treble*, Carlton Publishing Group, 2001.

❖ *The Official Liverpool Illustrated Encyclopedia*, by Jeff Anderson with Stephen Done, Carlton Publishing Group, 2003.

❖ *The Official Liverpool Illustrated History* (Second Edition), by Jeff Anderson with Stephen Done, Carlton Publishing Group, 2003.

❖ *Record Collector: Rare Record Price Guide 2002*, by Sean O'Mahony, Parker Mead Ltd, 2000.

# 🐝 INDEX 🐝